IMPROVE YOUR FAMILY'S DIET <u>AND</u> YOUR FAMILY'S HEALTH AND HAPPINESS

- The step-by-step gradual change to more nutritious foods
- How and where to find protein, vitamins, and minerals essential for every stage of growth
- Tips for pregnancy, breast feeding and infant foods
- How to make wholesome eating delicious fun for kids of all ages
- How to deal with holidays, candy-toting relatives, and school lunches
- Mouth-watering recipes for meals and treats
  ...and much, much more!

"REFRESHING...PROMOTES THE CONCEPT OF NUTRITION FOR CHILDREN WITH BALANCE AND OBJECTIVITY."
Gary Null, host of "Natural Living"

THE COMPLETE GUIDE AND COOKBOOK FOR RAISING YOUR CHILD AS A VEGETARIAN

Michael and Nina Shandler

BALLANTINE BOOKS • NEW YORK

The questionnaire on pages 184–185 is from Millard J. Bie-
venue's "Why They Can't Talk to Us," from the *New York Times
Magazine*, September 14, 1969. © 1969 by The New York Times
Company. Reprinted by permission.
The recipe for "Mineral-Rich Water" on pages 205–206 is from
Better Foods for Better Babies by Gena Larson, Copyright ©
1972 by Gena Larson, published by Keats Publishing, Inc., 36
Grove Street, New Canaan, CT.

Library of Congress Catalog Card Number: 80-26173

ISBN 0-345-34188-0

This edition published by arrangement with Schocken Books

Printed in Canada

First Ballantine Books Edition: December 1982
Fourth Printing: March 1989

CONTENTS

FOREWORD

by Barry D. Elson, M.D.

ALTHOUGH vegetarianism has been widely practiced in many different cultures around the world for thousands of years, it is only since the early 1960s that people in large numbers in industrialized countries have begun to eliminate meat from their diets. It is amazing how quickly this approach has caught on. No longer perceived as a curious "fad" indigenous to a fanatical subculture, it has become firmly entrenched in the eating habits of many people of all ages and backgrounds—and rightly so!

Scientific studies have demonstrated a close relationship between meat consumption and the onset of heart disease and cancer of the colon. Pesticides and radioactivity have appeared in meat products in alarming concentrations over the past few years. It has been shown that the amount of land required to raise vegetarian foods is a small fraction of that required for the purpose of raising animals for slaughter.

In my mind, the real question today is not "Why become a vegetarian?" but "Why eat meat?" Heart disease, cancer, environmental toxins, and food scarcity have been and will continue to be on the rise. Our children are sure to be at risk for exposure to these modern ills. If we love our children, we need to take a long, hard look at the nutritional habits they will practice for the rest of their lives.

It has been amply documented that children thrive on a well-rounded, judiciously planned vegetarian diet. All of the nutrients your child needs are present in vegetarian foods in ample supply. However, planning a healthful vegetarian menu is an acquired skill. It is not enough to simply avoid the use of meat products. The nutrients in nonmeat foods are scattered over a wide variety of different food types; they need to be carefully combined, often in proper proportions. But don't let this need for planning put you off. Take a look at the dietary patterns of various non-Western cultures; there you will see completely healthful "planning" practiced in a subconscious way. The peoples of these cultures do not need to think in terms of the traditional Western nutritional categories, such as protein and vitamins. They have developed their own categories through the years that seem to bring about the same results: healthy people. I am reminded of my recent trip to the Himalayas in northern Nepal. There I encountered the simplest of village people, who ate meat products only on rare occasions, if at all. I still marvel at the way they would scamper effortlessly past us, on the steep mountain trails, often carrying more than a hundred pounds on their backs! Their diets were often models of "good" vegetarian planning, even by Western standards. For example, they almost always combined beans with grains in such a way as to provide a nutritionally complete protein in each meal. Without knowing what protein is, the Nepali cook was able to instinctively provide it in proper proportions for her family. And so can you.

The Complete Guide and Cookbook for Raising Your Child as a Vegetarian includes a basic primer in good nutrition for every parent, vegetarian or not. It will provide everything you need to know to be sure that your children will thrive on the food you provide them. It will help you develop your own "instinct" for healthful menu planning. But it is much more than just a cookbook or a set of prescriptive rules. The book begins with a clear and easily understood introduction to basic nutritional theory. It then provides sensitive guidance in meeting the special needs your children will have at various stages of life.

What follows are the recipes themselves, which will give new ideas to even the most experienced vegetarian cook, I am sure.

In the first part of the book, each of the important categories of vital nutrients are explained in detail. The opening chapter explores many and varied reasons for choosing a vegetarian diet, including analyses from the medical, economic, and ethical points of view. There is an important discussion on how to involve your children in this transformation. In the ensuing chapters protein, carbohydrates, vitamins, minerals, and fats are thoroughly and accurately discussed. You will learn what these terms describe, what role they play in healthful living, and how to ensure their provision in your menu at home. There is a careful discussion of which types of foods are best avoided (and why) as well as a guide to special foods that will easily provide high quantities of important nutrients for your child.

In the second part, you will find a description of children's specific nutritional needs through every phase of growth. Michael and Nina Shandler, who are the parents of two happy, healthy vegetarian children, rightly begin with the very beginning, the period of pregnancy, when every cell of the fetus's body is derived from what the mother takes at mealtime. At no other time is a mother's nutritional program so critical for the future health and development of her child. Here, a well-rounded and safe vegetarian program is outlined for the mother-to-be.

The authors then discuss breast-feeding and offer useful how-to tips for the first-time nursing woman and for special situations that may arise. Discussed in detail here are recent studies conducted by the U.S. Environmental Protection Agency (EPA) and the Environmental Defense Fund (EDF), which found that nursing mothers who ate meat products had unsafe levels of pesticides in their milk; vegetarian mother's milk contains two or three times *lower* levels of pesticides.

The following chapters provide wise and accurate advice about first foods for your infant (always a tricky issue), deal with the impetuous whims of the toddler, ensure balance in the diet of the school-age child on-the-run, and help teenagers satisfy their own unique nutritional and social needs.

The third part is the "cookbook." Here, the preceding ideas are put into practice. These recipes are designed to fulfill nutritional needs and appeal to your child's sense of what tastes good. It is a gold mine of ingenious food combinations and useful tips on gaining your child's acceptance of your kitchen labors.

What we have here is a comprehensive and practical guide in nutrition for the concerned parent. For at least ten years, I have been aware of the need for just such a book. It belongs on the shelf of every parent who is concerned about his or her child's nutrition, vegetarian or not.

ACKNOWLEDGMENTS

OUR primary gratitude goes to our children, Manju and Sara, without whom this book would be a dry, impersonal study. Our wish for their well-being is the spirit that motivated the research and writing of these pages.

We are indebted to Patricia Woodruff, our editor at Schocken Books, who suggested we undertake this project, patiently encouraged us throughout the long research process, and kindly forgave our impatience during frustrating periods.

As in the past, Kendra Crossen has painstakingly smoothed the rough edges of our original manuscript. We are, again, thankful for her precision, clarity, and thoroughness.

We are grateful to Howard Fuchs, who worked as a research assistant during the final months of this project.

Finally, we are indebted to Barry Elson, M.D., who acted as medical editor and consultant as we did the research for this book.

MICHAEL AND NINA SHANDLER

INTRODUCTION

ALL parents want the best for their children, and when our first child was born in 1973, we were certainly no exception. Faced with the responsibilities of parenthood for the first time, we wanted to be absolutely sure that the natural-food, vegetarian diet we had been following for a number of years would provide our newborn daughter with a health-giving legacy.

Throughout Nina's pregnancy, well-intentioned relatives, friends, and even our doctor attacked our dietary preferences with everything from emotional laments of "You're too thin" to scientific criticism of "How can you be sure about your protein intake?" Somehow we remained aloof from these doubts, confident that our diet was more healthful than the refined-food, meat-centered diet that characterizes the fare in most homes. Indeed, Nina was in excellent health throughout her pregnancy, the birth itself was natural without the slightest complication, and our daughter was a delightfully healthy infant. Yet, as Nina nursed her and the responsibility of parenthood was driven home by every cry, gurgle, and sigh, the voices of our concerned friends and relatives began to echo in our ears. What if our diet was not adequate after all? We realized that our daughter's health and happiness were, to a large extent, in our hands, and the more we adjusted to parenthood, the more determined we became not to take risks for the sake of our beliefs and personal preferences.

At first through discussions with knowledgeable friends, and then through study that took us into medical and research libraries, we began an extensive reevaluation of our diet. We were concerned, of course, not only about the adequacy of our own eating patterns but, more specifically, about the special dietary needs of pregnancy, lactation, and child development. We read extensively for several months and made some adjustments in our diet as a result. However, we did conclude that a diet of natural vegetarian foods, chosen in proper proportions from the various food categories, is the most healthful possible legacy that parents can pass on to their child, whether he is in the womb, nursing at the breast, or eating at the family table.

As we discovered, the greatest hazards to our children's health are posed by a diet of foods high in refined flour, refined sugar, fat, animal protein, and canned and processed foods loaded with all sorts of stabilizers, chemicals, and preservatives—the main ingredients of the average American diet. In fact, the average American derives 45 percent of the calories he consumes from fat and 30 percent from refined carbohydrates, leaving the rest of the nutrients necessary to health to be assimilated from the remaining 25 percent. Our doubts were certainly dispelled quickly by learning these facts, and now, after seven further years of research and dietary experimentation, we agree wholeheartedly with informed nutritionists and doctors that such poor eating habits acquired in childhood mark the beginning of the road toward a number of serious illnesses, such as heart disease, diabetes, arteriosclerosis, and cancer, to name only a few.

As a result of our research, we were able to confidently discard the cynicism and, as it turned out, the ignorance that had characterized our early critics' complaints. All went well for the first few years as Nina breast-fed our daughter and she grew from a strong, alert baby into a radiantly energetic and healthy child. But around the time she reached the age of three, influences that we had not anticipated began to enter our home. It became obvious to us that in a society where a three-year-old is indoctrinated by enticing television idols like "Tony the Tiger," old-fashioned oatmeal is going to seem rather dull in comparison. And we had not taken into account Grandma and Grandpa, trick-or-treat, Christmas stockings, the inevitable birthday parties, or the Easter bunny. Nor had we anticipated the temptations a child encounters in the world of day care and school. Bringing up our child on natural foods and as a vegetarian, completely avoiding the food-stuffs that most children consider normal, we at times felt that we were depriving her culturally.

These problems, for all their seeming triviality, are real and of concern to all conscientious parents. We realized that our child's life should be enriched with traditional celebrations of holidays and with the unself-conscious company of her peers. And we recognized that we would have to make adjustments in our lives and diets to fill these needs without compromising our nutritional standards.

Intense though our nutritional research had been in the beginning, we now launched into a phase of kitchen experimentation designed to provide our daughter with healthful natural vegetarian food alternatives to the hundreds of enticing junk foods and snacks that are designed to hook youthful consumers at a very early age. We came up with a number of "all-American" alternatives that looked and tasted good but contained only healthful vegetarian ingredients. We devised, for example, several ways to make holiday sweets without sugar and to generally satisfy our daughter's growing need for "regular stuff." And her friends, who regularly visit our house, have been enthusiastic guinea pigs. We even learned how to successfully make meat taste-alikes, the subject of our book *How to Make All the Meat You Eat Out of Wheat* (Rawson, Wade, 1980).

We are satisfied that despite the obvious differences between our children's eating habits and those of the majority of their peers, our children are well adjusted, well accepted, and healthy. Acutely aware of the special problems that raising a child as a vegetarian poses, we wrote this book as a help to other parents who want to give their children a healthful dietary legacy. The diet we recommend in this book is nutritionally balanced and includes dairy products and eggs, although we also offer suggestions for families who cannot or do not wish to eat these foods. We hope we have succeeded in providing practical answers to the many questions that are raised in a home where health is held in high regard.

Authors' Note

We have used the pronoun "he" when referring to a child, whether male or female, for the sake of stylistic simplicity and ease of reading. It is not our intention to imply, nor is it our feeling, that male children are in any way preferable to female children.

A NUTRITIONAL GUIDE FOR VEGETARIAN PARENTS

1.

BECOMING A VEGETARIAN FAMILY

WHETHER you are a vegetarian couple expecting your first child or a family with one or more children contemplating becoming vegetarian, you are entering a largely unknown and relatively uncharted dimension of family life. When your family joins the millions of other vegetarians in North America, they become part of a minority group that has unique social problems. The 1970s, along with many other sociopolitical changes they ushered in, also gave birth to a completely new phase of North American history—the first time that large numbers of vegetarian children had been brought up in an overwhelmingly meat-centered society. For example, if your toddler has been brought up as a vegetarian, he will eventually notice the difference between his diet and his grandparents'. During his preschool years, he will become increasingly aware that the neighbors eat differently. When he attends public school, he may be the only vegetarian in his class. As a teenager, when meeting at hamburger joints becomes a social event, he will be distinctly different from his peers.

To you who grew up on the average American diet, the

minority status you acquire by choosing to become a vegetarian and, perhaps, simultaneously rejecting chemical additives, processed foods, sugar, and refined foods, is a welcome position, a choice made after careful and mature thought. But for your children this difference between themselves and their peers is a mixed blessing. Your first child may be born vegetarian or he may follow you in that direction later in life. He may believe in not killing animals for food. He may accept on faith your disdain for refined, processed foods. He is, however, growing up in a society where a largely profit-motivated food-processing industry regularly uses the media to indoctrinate the public into believing that meat-eating and sugar-consuming are not only healthful but also a boon to happiness. In short, your child has acquired a life style he did not choose, and the differences between his dietary patterns and those of his peers cannot but pose dilemmas for him. The earlier he becomes vegetarian, the fewer problems he will face, but as he grows up, or if he becomes vegetarian later in life, the temptations and contradictions will become greater in number and more complex.

Let's look at the situation from the child's point of view for a moment. A recurring problem is likely to be posed in his mind, as he comes increasingly in contact with elders other than his parents who shape his thinking and attitude: Can he trust his teacher, who defines one-quarter of a balanced diet as "the meat group"? Should he believe Grandpa, who says that meat is the best possible protein food, or you, who claim that it is saturated with disease-causing substances? It would be easy for a vegetarian child to develop prematurely into a cynic who doubts everything he is told. Or he might acquire feelings of superiority by virtue of his special status and insight. Indeed, it would be logical for a vegetarian child to reject his peers and his culture, leaving him feeling intensely isolated. Or the very opposite might happen—he might rebel against his parents' values and life style in order to conform to the customs of his peers.

Of course, most of us would prefer that our children take none of these extreme postures, but develop into well-adjusted, enthusiastic people who are able to enjoy the beneficial influences of society and to choose healthful alternatives to its harmful aspects. We also want our children to have a tolerant attitude toward people, not judging meat-eaters to be bad, unkind, or ignorant simply because of their eating habits. And no doubt most of us want our children to remain open to the lessons that many kind, intelligent, and wise people who happen to eat meat can teach them. Moreover, we would probably want them to be realistic enough to recognize the inconsistencies or dogmatic attitudes of some vegetarians.

Balancing your children's attitudes toward society with a wholesome example is part and parcel of being a conscientious parent, and this is underlined even more emphatically when the task at hand is raising healthy vegetarian children.

Actually the atmosphere in your home is as important to the health of your child as is his diet. An impeccably healthful diet imposed with an iron hand by tyrannical parents can lead to undesirable repercussions in the form of stress-related ills: headaches, indigestion, and allergies, to name only a few. Moreover, when dietary changes are imposed in an atmosphere of repression, the emotional strain can have a devastating effect on home life as a whole. However, if your family encourages open communication of both ideas and feelings, your choice of vegetarianism can be an opportunity for increased family harmony as well as health. Then, becoming a vegetarian family can be an exciting adventure into the ethics, ecology, and economics of food consumption. If your children are of school age or older, your family's dietary preferences can become a forum for discussion of individual choices, values and life styles. The transition to vegetarianism, if approached thoughtfully and creatively, can mean much more to a family than simply eliminating meat from the diet. It can become a vehicle of transformation of family life that encourages mutual respect, regardless of family members' various ages, needs, and roles. In addition a family can regain an understanding of the natural connection between the earth and food, health, and happiness, which is often lost in this fast-paced, fast-food society, where children often believe that all food is made in a factory.

WHY BE A VEGETARIAN?

Whatever your reasons for choosing vegetarianism, it will be profitable to be able to articulate a variety of justifications for your choice. As your child grows older he will inevitably begin to question the validity of his diet. He will wonder why his food is vastly different from that of his grandparents, neighbors, and peers. If you yourself feel clear about why you decided to take your family the vegetarian route, you will welcome these questions as opportunities for explaining your child's dietary legacy with clarity and compassion.

Family Economics

The basic economic consideration for vegetarianism is the family food budget. Most children understand early in life that cost plays a major role in all family decisions; they know that their desires are limited by the dollars available. A vegetarian diet can stretch the food dollar, providing far greater nutritional value for less money.

In 1979 both the *East-West Journal* and *Prevention* magazine compared the average shopping list for a natural-foods diet with the average American supermarket shopping list. The *East-West Journal* estimated that a family of four, eating a natural vegan diet (one containing no meat, eggs, or dairy products), could eat well for $44.88 a week, while the same family would require $84.14 a week to feed themselves from the supermarket. The total family weekly saving would be $39.26. *Prevention* analyzed the weekly cost of food for one person. It concluded that a supermarket diet costs approximately $20.21 per person a week, while a natural-foods diet costs $13.98. The weekly individual saving would be $6.23. According to *Prevention*, the family of four would save $24.92 a week on a natural-foods diet. Although these figures obviously fluctuate according to specific dietary habits as well as inflation, any child will readily understand that being vegetarian is a more economical way to live.

Ethical and Moral Considerations

At some point your child's consciousness and concern will reach beyond his own home into the wider economical-political arena. When he reaches this stage he will be interested to know that the economics of diet reach beyond the family food budget and into the coffers of big business. The majority of groceries bought in North America are manufactured by large corporations whose main interest is in producing a profitable product. Logically speaking, if profit is a primary motivation, the ideal will be to produce a commodity with the cheapest possible ingredients that can be sold for the highest possible price. For example, the food industry has long used sugar and heavy starches to increase bulk and decrease manufacturers' costs. Nutritionally empty foods are concocted with the aid of chemical preservatives and other additives in the name of "convenience." Grains are refined and stripped of their nutrients—and then "fortified" with artificial vitamins, which become a further selling point. Enough people eat such foods daily to fill the coffers of the food manufacturers, as well as to add billions of dollars to the health care bills of the nation, thanks to the ill health resulting from such poor eating habits. Being conscious of the economics of food processing translates into not making a contribution to the profits of unscrupulous businesses by buying nutritionally deficient foods.

In no place is the morality of the food producers more questionable than in the beef industry. Most cattle are treated cruelly from the moment of birth until they are slaughtered. They begin life on a diet of chemicals and feed; they graze for a short time and are moved to feed lots for the final four months of their lives. During this period each animal is force-fed more than a ton of grain, legumes, and protein supplements, as well as drugs to stupefy and sterilize it. It is confined to a cubicle too small to allow even minimal exercise. As a result of this treatment, the animal gains 700 pounds during its incarceration, to reach a weight of 1,200 pounds before slaughter. Similar examples of inhumane practices are found in the raising of other meat animals and poultry and even in the production of eggs.

The obvious cruelty of raising animals in this fashion (not to mention killing them) is only one aspect of the immorality of meat-eating. According to Frances Lappé, author of *Diet for a Small Planet*, the grain used to feed cattle is enough to feed every person in the world a bowl of grain each day of the year. It is impossible not to wonder why starvation is necessary in a world that can feed cattle so abundantly.

The use of chemicals in cattle feed is questionable not only because they stupefy the animals, but because they are potentially dangerous to humans. One hundred and forty-two chemicals are used solely to produce greater quantities of meat at less cost to the producers. The fact that many of these additives are proven mutagens and carcinogens is of little concern to profit-motivated industry. The most indefensible of these chemicals is DES, a hormone that has been banned as a drug for humans by the Federal Drug Administration (FDA) because it causes cancer. However, regular doses of DES very effectively contribute to fast weight gain in cattle, and recent investigation shows that its use is extremely widespread despite the possible danger to people who eat meat. (See chapter 6 for further comments on DES.)

The Ecology of Meat-Eating

Grazing occurs on 42 percent of the land available in this country. Where overgrazing occurs, the land suffers from depletion and ruination. A mere 17 percent of this country's land is used to produce crops. Of these crops, 97 percent of the legumes and 90 percent of the grain are fed to livestock rather than to people. Land depletion is becoming a growing problem. Some people estimate that in less than ten years not enough farmland will be preserved to feed this nation's population. Considering this decline in productive land, the vegetarian child might well question the wisdom of using and misusing much arable land for the production of meat.

The need to conserve fossil fuel also casts doubt on the wisdom of meat production and consumption. To produce one calorie of food energy in the form of beef requires 100 calories of fossil fuel energy. To produce one calorie of food energy as grain requires only one calorie of oil-based energy. According to research by Mary Rawitscher and Jean Meyer, president of Tufts University (reported in *East-West Journal,* June 1979), if everyone in this country were to substitute a pound of bread just once a month for a pound of meat, the fossil fuel saved would be 121 million barrels of oil per year. Following this line of thought through to its logical conclusion: If everyone became vegetarian, we would save approximately 1.2 billion barrels of oil per year, or about 40 percent of the oil imported from OPEC nations.

Water is a precious commodity your child will come to respect as a basic food for the plants he eats. Water is consumed in enormous quantities as well as polluted by livestock producers. Growing cattle require eighty times as much water as growing tubers, and it is estimated that half of the water pollution in the United States is caused by feed lots, broiler installations, and hog facilities. In these times when water shortages are severe, particularly in the West and Southwest, and when small-town populations all over the country are being told that their drinking water is unsafe, your child may well wonder why a meat-centered diet is held to be so desirable. Even to an elementary school age child the wisdom of meat-based protein production will seem foolish in light of these facts.

The Health Benefits of Growing Up Vegetarian

When your child takes on the distinction of being vegetarian, he will undoubtedly encounter the skeptical comments of grandparents, neighbors, and teachers who believe that his diet is unhealthful. Any insecurity provoked by these comments from central figures in a child's life can be prevented by teaching him the facts about the health benefits of vegetarianism.

One way to approach building your child's confidence in his vegetarian diet is by using the examples of successful vegetarian cultures in faraway places. Children enjoy hearing about the lives of people in Africa, for example, and other exotic lands. If your child is of elementary school age or younger, stories can be embellished with all your imagination. If he has reached adolescence, a simple relating of the facts will meet more receptive ears.

Details of the diets of the Masai, an East African tribe, and that of the Hunzas, a tribal people of northern India, provide a fascinating study in contrasts. The Masai are a meat-eating people who live almost entirely on freshly killed game. The Hunzas eat almost no meat, relying instead primarily on fresh, locally grown produce and milk products. Although there are obvious climatic and cultural differences that account for the differences in diet, the effects of each diet are revealing. The Masai, contrary to what most meat-loving Americans might expect, are an extremely short-lived people. While the consumption of meat is, of course, not the only factor affecting the longevity of the Masai, it is nevertheless interesting to note that by the time they reach twenty years of age they begin to age dramatically, often dying of "old age" by the time they reach thirty or forty. The Hunzas fare extraordinarily well in comparison. They are famous for their robust health, and they live to be ninety to one hundred years old. This pattern is followed in other cultures as well. Eskimos, Greenlanders, Lapplanders, and Russian Kurgis eat a predominantly meat-centered diet and have a life expectancy of about thirty to forty years. On the other hand the Bulgarians, Russian Caucasians, Yucatán Indians and East Indian Todas eat a predominantly vegetarian diet and live to be very old.

Another example that gives credence to the value of a vegetarian diet is drawn from history. During World War I the Allied blockade of Germany also cut off supplies to Denmark. Both countries found themselves short of food. In Germany, people continued to eat as normally as they could under the circumstances; but in Denmark, the government consulted Dr. Milkel Hindehede of the Laboratory of Nutrition Research in Copenhagen, who suggested drastic changes in the Danish meat-centered diet. Dr. Hindehede recommended curtailing all livestock production and feeding the people with whole grains formerly used to nourish cattle. His suggestions were accepted, and the entire Danish population was forced onto a vegetarian diet consisting mainly of barley, porridge, potatoes, green vegetables, milk, small amounts of butter, and whole grain rye bread with bran added. Thus, Denmark became a massive controlled experiment in vegetarianism. Analysis of the effects of the German and Danish diets showed that while the disease-based death rate in Germany rose, the death rate by noncommunicable disease in Denmark decreased by 34 percent. A joke of the time observed that in Germany the cows were healthy but the people were dying, whereas in Denmark the people were healthy but the cows were dying. After the war, when diets returned to normal, the Danish disease-related death rate returned to its prewar level.

You can assure your child that if he avoids meat and eats a well-balanced vegetarian diet, studies show that he is more likely to be free of heart disease, cancer, diabetes, and obesity. Of course, you must be conscious of his basic nutritional needs and his specific dietary requirements at every stage of growth. The ominous predictions of concerned grandparents or unsympathetic pediatricians *can* come true if you fail to supply these needs.

VEGETARIANISM IS MORE THAN NOT EATING MEAT

Health is not achieved by the mere elimination of meat from the diet. A vegetarian diet should be well balanced and free from refined, processed, and chemicalized foods, and sugar. These foods must be replaced by whole grains, natural foods, fresh produce, and nutritious sweeteners. A child needs all of these foods in wide variety in order to satisfy his growth demands.

The adoption of any diet in which variety is severely limited or that follows prescribed rules without taking into account the specific needs of individual children can have dangerous long-term effects. For example, a fruitarian diet (consisting mainly of fruits and nuts) can be severely lacking in protein and can result in kwashiorkor, a disease that stunts mental and physical growth. A fanatically strict "mucusless" diet has been known to cause severe, irreparable damage to the digestive system. A raw food diet can be lacking in carbohydrates, making a child listless and dangerously thin. An "advanced" macrobiotic diet imposed inappropriately can lead to vitamin B_{12} and protein deficiencies, ultimately causing nervous-system degeneration. Therefore, unless you are versed in the basic nutritional content of every food available on a restricted diet, and take enormous pains to supplement the diet with foods that compensate for the deficiencies, such diets are dangerous for children.

A vegetarian diet that includes milk and eggs (lacto-ovo-vegetarianism) or milk but not eggs (lacto-vegetarianism) will give your child adequate amounts of Vitamin B_{12} and calcium, two of the most essential nutrients children need. If balanced with grains, other protein sources (legumes and nuts), cooked vegetables, and raw fruit, these two forms of vegetarianism provide an optimum diet for health.

Parents who choose a vegan diet, using no meat, eggs, or milk products, will need to take special care that children receive B_{12}, calcium, zinc, and riboflavin, even if they eat a diet of balanced proteins, grain, and cooked and raw produce.

There are, however, reasons for choosing a nondairy, eggless diet. Aside from the desire not to exploit animal life in any way, the primary reason is lactose intolerance or allergy. Many children, especially those of African or Jewish descent, are unable to digest milk. They have severe allergic reactions, including gastrointestinal problems, blocked sinuses, and coughing, whenever dairy products are eaten. Even when lactose can be tolerated in its sugar form, some children experience severe congestion from homogenized and pasteurized milk. Many such children experience no ill effects from unprocessed raw milk, either goat's or cow's, both of which can be extremely valuable foods in the vegetarian child's diet.

If your child has a reaction to processed milk, you might try to find a reputable source of raw milk before eliminating milk from his diet entirely. If you object to eating any foods of animal origin, you can use soy products, including soy milk fortified with nutritional yeast, which are excellent ways to ensure that your child receives the essential nutrition supplied by goat's or cow's milk.

INTRODUCING VEGETARIANISM
TO YOUR FAMILY

Changing from a "normal" diet to a balanced vegetarian diet requires a transformation of the diet as a whole. If the change is approached in a blitzkrieg fashion, it can be traumatic for children two years of age or older. The result of heavy-handed hastiness could easily be rebellion and failure to accomplish the goal of a healthy attitude toward vegetarianism. A gradual change, in which you systematically substitute wholesome foods for the old undesirable ones, while simultaneously learning to use new foods with creativity, has the best possibility of success. Your transition to vegetarianism should include the following changes:

1. Gradually eliminate meat from the diet while substituting a variety of wholesome protein-complementary vegetarian dishes in their place. (For suggestions on how to accomplish this step, see chapter 2, "Can the Vegetarian Child Get Enough Protein?")
2. Gradually replace refined grains and breads with whole grains and breads. (For suggestions, see chapter 3, "Carbohydrates: Food for Fuel.")
3. Eliminate refined sugar and learn to use malt, blackstrap molasses, dried fruit, fresh fruit and fruit juices, honey, and maple syrup as sweeteners. (For details, see chapter 3.)
4. Replace refined, bleached vegetable oils and margarine with high-quality cold-pressed vegetable oils, butter, or a homemade "butter" substitute. (For details, see chapter 5, "Fats: Overused and Underrated.")
5. Replace highly processed, sugar- and chemical-laden "convenience" foods with fresh, natural, whole foods. (Suggestions for achieving this step are found throughout the book as well as in the recipe section.)
6. Replace canned, processed, and frozen produce with fresh vegetables and fruits in season.

In making the switch to vegetarianism, especially if it is a "midterm" switch, you should exercise patience and tolerance for your children's foibles. As the chapters in the second section of the book indicate in detail, children at different ages differ widely in development as well as temperament, and parents will inevitably be tested when changes in eating patterns are introduced. The golden rule in this situation is to go slowly—remember, slow and steady wins the race. At least until the teenage years, parents exert the major influence on their children. However, this influence is best exerted not by laying down laws, but by simply teaching by example.

2.

CAN THE VEGETARIAN CHILD
GET ENOUGH PROTEIN?

WE well remember Nina's mother's face when she found out that her granddaughter was being brought up without meat. "How could she possibly get enough protein?" was her alarmed response. "The poor child." Bless her heart, Grandma couldn't help feeling that we were committing a crime, at best depriving our daughter of a time-honored cultural and familial heirloom, and at worst failing to provide her with the nutrition that was her birthright. And even though our daughter had enjoyed radiant health since she was born, Grandma always insisted that she looked "a little pale" and was "too thin." We couldn't blame Grandma for her feelings, for we knew she wanted the best for her granddaughter—but so did we. Our research had convinced us that consumption of commercially produced meat offers not only dubious health benefits, but a long-term legacy conscientious parents would not want to pass on to their children.

The American meat-centered, high-protein diet is, among other things, a relic of outdated protein research fifty to seventy-five years old. Modern research, worldwide, supports conclusively the relatively low-protein, high-carbohydrate diet of most traditional cultures. The high-protein myth in vogue in industrialized countries is encouraged and perpetuated by advertising money from the dairy and beef industries. Food is big business, and unfortunately it seems the industry is more interested in profit than in the real well-being of the people.

Since 1950, when the average American ate sixty pounds of meat a year, his consumption has increased an astonishing 103 percent to 122 pounds a year. This phenomenal increase in meat consumption is, in our opinion, linked at least partially to the massive increase in hospital bills (inflation aside) that this country has also witnessed in the past few decades. Dr. Paavo Airola, the well-known nutritionist, reports in his book *How to Get Well* that there is mounting evidence from independent unbiased sources that overconsumption of protein, which in this country means animal protein, leads to a host of diseases including hyperacidity, nutritional deficiencies, accumulation of uric acid and other purines in the tissues, and intestinal putrefaction, and contributes to arthritis, kidney disease, schizophrenia, pyorrhea, osteoporosis, atherosclerosis, heart disease, and cancer.

If there is any doubt about Dr. Airola's statements, we need only turn to a study reported in the prestigious *Journal of the American Medical Association*. The study was an in-depth examination of the health of the one million American Seventh-Day Adventists, most of whom, for religious reasons, do not eat meat (and do not smoke either). In comparison to the rest of the population, the Seventh-Day Adventists show 40 percent less coronary disease, 400 percent fewer deaths from respiratory disease, 100 percent lower mortality rate from all causes, 1,000 percent lower death rate from lung cancer, and 50 percent less dental cares among their children. It is interesting to note that the Seventh Day Adventists generally lead the same sort of lives as most Americans. They are far from being an obscure and isolated sect.

We have already mentioned some of the cultures outside of the United States that give credence to the case against the overconsumption of meat—such as the Hunzas, who live on a diet high in unrefined carbohydrates and low in protein, particularly animal protein. The life expectancy of these people is more than twenty years longer than that in the United States, where 71 percent of the protein consumption is from animal sources. American per capita consumption of meat is higher than in any other industrialized country, and Americans are in twenty-first place in life expectancy compared with other industrialized countries!

While we could go on almost indefinitely citing both circumstantial and direct evidence that meat consumption is detrimental to health, it is more important now to take a closer look at protein itself. Most people understand that protein is supremely important to health, but few understand clearly what it is and how much we really need. Moreover, most Americans mistakenly believe that their protein must come from meat and other animal sources or else they will become weak and sick.

WHAT IS PROTEIN?

Proteins are food substances made up of chemical compounds called amino acids. About twenty amino acids are known, all of which are needed by human beings to build tissues and repair broken-down cells. Some bacteria and single-celled animals can manufacture all of these amino acids. A human being can manufacture approximately twelve amino acids in his own body, but he must get the other nine amino acids simultaneously and in the right proportions from the food that he eats in order to fulfill his body's need for "complete" protein. These nine amino acids are therefore called the "essential" amino acids.

In only three categories of foods are all of the essential amino acids known to be present in healthful proportions: eggs, dairy products, and flesh. But if these three are the only "complete" proteins, how can we explain the fact that millions of people in the world enjoy good health and yet seldom if ever eat *any* flesh, dairy products or eggs? To understand their secret, let us see what happens to protein foods when they are ingested.

When protein foods are eaten, the digestive system breaks the protein down into its component amino acids. The amino acids in each protein molecule are linked together like beads on a necklace, but in the process of digestion, the "necklace" is unstrung. The body then sets to work to discover whether all the essential amino acids are available and in what proportion. For example, when you eat eggs, which contain all the essential amino acids in abundant proportions, your digestive system disassembles the eggs' amino acids. Then these amino acids are reassembled into the protein pattern that your body needs.

However, if the food you eat is lacking (or weak in) one or more of the essential amino acids, protein synthesis will be poor and may even stop completely. For example, if you ate half an ounce of peanuts, which are weak in certain amino acids, your body would assimilate only *half* the protein compared with the amount it would assimilate if you ate a similar amount of egg (about one-quarter of an egg), a "complete" protein. This shows that the essential amino acids should be present in the proportion the body can fully utilize.

PROTEIN COMPLEMENTATION

The secret of surviving without meat as a source of complete protein can now easily be understood. So long as all the essential amino acids are available in appropriate amounts, the body will successfully assimilate them regardless of their source. In other words, if you combine in a meal protein foods that complement each other's essential amino acid strengths and weaknesses, so as to supply an adequate proportion of all of them, your digestive system will act on the *total* of the essential amino acids in your body.

Let's consider a traditional Latin American peasant meal of brown rice and black beans. If we analyze the content of an average serving of brown rice, we find it consists of about 5 grams of protein, but it is weak in two of the essential amino acids. Therefore, if the rice were eaten alone, a relatively small proportion of complete amino acids would be assimilated. An average portion of black beans contains about 12 grams of protein and is rich in the two essential amino acids that the brown rice lacks. Moreover, the beans are weak in the amino acids that the rice has in abundance. If the beans were eaten alone, only a small proportion of complete protein would be utilized. However, when the beans and rice are mixed together, the *combination* boosts the total available complete protein by 43 percent! This delicious and inexpensive meal provides complete protein and is a good example of a case in which the whole is greater than the sum of its parts.

While it is true that with such a meal, complete protein is abundantly available at a fraction of the cost of meat, eggs, or dairy products, we are not suggesting that eggs and dairy products be ousted from the diet. Dairy products

---

NATURAL PROTEIN FOODS

The following are natural vegetarian foods that, when combined according to the guidelines for protein complementation listed on page 24, supply judicious amounts of complete protein.

Legumes
black beans, broad beans, lima beans, kidney beans, black-eyed peas (cow peas), chickpeas (garbanzos), soybeans, dried peas, mung beans, navy beans, tofu

Whole Grains
barley, millet, brown rice, oats, buckwheat, rye, wheat, bulghur, wheat germ, corn

Seeds
pumpkin or squash seeds, sesame seeds, sunflower seeds

Nuts
almonds, cashews, coconuts, filberts (hazelnuts), peanuts, pine nuts, pistachios, macadamia nuts, walnuts

Dairy Products
milk, yogurt, cheeses, kefir, eggs

Supplementary Foods
brewer's yeast, nutritional yeast

made from raw, unhomogenized milk and fertilized "free-range" eggs provide an extremely good source of complete protein. However, dairy products and eggs tend to produce excess mucus in some adults and children. Although a certain amount of mucus is necessary for health and body lubrication, excess mucus is unhealthful. Milk and eggs have also be related to specific allergies in some individuals.

The box on page 23 lists high-protein foods from natural vegetarian sources. There are literally hundreds of different ways of combining these foods to achieve complete protein complementation, and it is very simple and easy to do. If you use the following five simple guidelines in preparing your family's diet, it is virtually impossible not to get enough complete protein. Recipes based on these principles are provided later in the book.

GUIDELINES FOR PROTEIN COMPLEMENTATION

1. Encourage your children to eat grains and legumes at the same meal.
2. Serve a small quantity of seeds with legume meals.
3. Serve grains and milk together.
4. Serve milk products with plant proteins (beans, nuts, seeds, or grains).
5. Serve eggs with plant proteins.

HOW MUCH PROTEIN DO WE NEED?

Now that we know *how* to complement various foods to achieve complete protein, the question that inevitably comes up is "Just how much protein do we need?"

Protein needs are different in adults and children. As we mentioned earlier, protein is used by the body mainly to build tissues and repair cells. Since an adult has stopped growing, his protein needs are almost exclusively for maintenance, whereas a child requires protein not only for maintenance but for growth. The child therefore must consume more protein relative to his body weight than an adult, and must also take in a higher percentage of complete protein in his daily diet. Only one-fifth of an adult's protein intake needs to be complete protein; the rest can easily come from other, not necessarily protein-complementary sources. But a child has to get between one-third and one-half of his protein intake from complete protein sources; the rest can also come from other, not necessarily complementary-protein sources.

For example, an eight-year-old child weighing about sixty-six pounds will need about 36 grams (about 1¼ ounces) of protein per day. Of this total, a shade over 14 grams (half an ounce) must come from complete protein! Vegetarian parents in Western industrial societies need have no fear that their children will not get either enough complete protein or enough total protein. The complementation techniques discussed in this chapter will ensure both sufficient complete protein and sufficient total protein.

By contrast, an adult weighing 154 pounds needs about 56 grams (about 2 ounces) of total protein daily. Of the total, about 11 grams (well under half an ounce) should come from complete protein. As you can see, for a normally healthy person, it is not at all difficult to get either sufficient complete protein or total protein requirements in the diet.

The following table is included here to give you an idea of total protein requirements. However, it should be emphasized that you need not use a gram scale to calculate your family's needs. Just make sure that you follow the protein complementation rules, and let your children eat as much as they can comfortably digest. Nature, in her inexplicable wisdom, will take care of the rest.

	Age	Weight (lbs.)	Total Range of Daily Needs for Protein (grams)
Infants	0.0–0.5	13	13 (no. of lbs. × 1)
	0.5–1.0	20	18 (no. of lbs. × .9)
Children	1–3	29	23
	4–6	44	30
	7–10	62	34
Boys	11–14	99	45
	15–18	145	56

	Age	Weight (lbs.)	Total Range of Daily Needs for Protein (grams)
Men	19–22	154	56
	23–50	154	56
	51+	154	56
Girls	11–14	101	46
	15–18	120	46
Women	19–22	120	44
	23–50	120	44
	51+	120	44

Pregnant mothers: Add 30 grams to above.
Nursing mothers: Add 20 grams to above.

Source: Recommended Dietary Allowances, National Academy of Sciences, revised 1980.

VEGETABLE PROTEIN/MEAT EQUIVALENCIES

The following tables give an approximation of how much protein is in various natural foods, measured in terms of their meat equivalency. These comparisons vividly illustrate the protein-enhancing effects of protein complementation. All the serving sizes used have been calculated to approximate the amounts a five- to eight-year-old could comfortably eat. This will give you an idea of the protein value in an average serving compared with meat. All measurements are for uncooked food.*

As can be seen from the charts, if children are presented with complementary-protein meals, parents can rest assured that they will get what they need. However, getting and eating, as any mother will affirm, are sometimes very different things. The fussy eater is a challenge not only to Mother Nature's nutritional wisdom but also to the ingeniousness and inventiveness of patient parents. We have found that more harm than good is done by transferring

---

* Equivalents are derived from tables in *Diet for a Small Planet;* Ballantine Books plans to publish a tenth anniversary edition of this classic in 1981.

PEAS OR BEANS AND RICE

If Eaten Separately:

	Usable Protein Equivalent to:
⅛ cup beans or peas =	.52 oz. steak
¼ cup brown rice =	.44 oz. steak
	.96 oz. steak
	(1 oz.)

If Eaten Together:
Add 43% complementation enhancement =
    1.43 oz. steak

PEAS OR BEANS AND WHEAT

If Eaten Separately:

	Usable Protein Equivalent to:
⅛ cup peas or beans =	.52 oz. steak
¼ cup whole wheat flour =	.42 oz. steak
	.94 oz. steak
	(1 oz.)

If Eaten Together:
Add 33% complementation enhancement =
    1.33 oz. steak

PEAS OR BEANS AND CORN

If Eaten Separately:

	Usable Protein Equivalent to:
⅛ cup peas or beans =	.52 oz. steak
¼ cup corn meal =	.19 oz. steak
	.71 oz. steak

If Eaten Together:
Add 50% complementation enhancement =
    1.07 oz. steak

SOYBEANS AND RICE

If Eaten Separately:

	Usable Protein Equivalent to:
⅛ cup soybeans =	1.25 oz. steak
¼ cup brown rice =	.44 oz. steak
	1.69 oz. steak

If Eaten Together:
Add 32% complementation enhancement =
    2.23 oz. steak

RICE AND MILK

	Usable Protein Equivalent to:
If Eaten Separately:	
¼ cup brown rice =	.44 oz. steak
1 cup milk =	1.67 oz. steak
	2.11 oz. steak

If Eaten Together:
Add 29% complementation enhancement =
    2.72 oz. steak

WHEAT AND MILK

	Usable Protein Equivalent to:
If Eaten Separately:	
¼ cup whole wheat cereal =	.42 oz. steak
1 cup milk =	1.67 oz. steak
	2.09 oz. steak

If Eaten Together:
Add 13% complementation enhancement =
    2.36 oz. steak

WHEAT AND MILK AND PEANUTS

	Usable Protein Equivalent to:
If Eaten Separately:	
¼ cup whole wheat flour =	.42 oz. steak
1 cup whole milk =	1.67 oz. steak
4 tablespoons peanut butter =	1.75 oz. steak
	3.84 oz. steak

If Eaten Together:
Add 34% complementation enhancement =
    5.14 oz. steak

RICE AND YEAST

	Usable Protein Equivalent to:
If Eaten Separately:	
¼ cup brown rice =	.44 oz. steak
1 tablespoon brewer's yeast =	.88 oz. steak
	1.32 oz. steak

If Eaten Together:
Add 57% complementation enhancement =
    2.07 oz. steak

our anxiety about protein intake, or any other nutritional concern, to a resistant child. If they are kept relatively unspoiled by junk food, children, like animals, tend to be instinctively in touch with their nutritional needs. Of course, there are exceptions to this generality: Cows will eat apples until their stomachs explode, given the chance; and children will quickly get addicted to candy and eat it until their teeth fall out, given *half* a chance. At times a healthy, reasonably disciplined child will eat voracious quantities of everything set in front of him, and at other times he will eat less than a bird. This is to be expected.

HOW TO ELIMINATE MEAT GRADUALLY

If your child is becoming vegetarian, he fully expects to "give up" meat. If you have discussed the economic, ethical, ecological, and health ramifications of meat-eating with him, his only reservation may be a lingering desire for the taste of meat.

In the beginning, serve meat every other day. Later reduce meat to a weekly meal. Then eliminate red meat, serving chicken, turkey, or fish once a week. Soon the meat can be eliminated without notice. However, even when all the meat has disappeared from your home, your child may occasionally be tempted by meat in a restaurant or at his grandparents'. Until he develops a personal commitment to a vegetarian diet, occasional meat-eating should not be denied him.

As you eliminate meat, be sure to substitute appealing complementary-protein dishes. Also bear in mind that forcing your child into a steady diet of, say, lentils and rice might make his desire for meat grow rather than subside.

Learn the art of "sneak-feeding" to supplement your child's diet. This simply means adding a tasteless nutritional ingredient to a dish so that the child is unaware that he is eating it. This is one way to increase protein intake without causing trauma at the table. Our older daughter, for example, claims that she hates eggs and nutritional yeast, but when they are disguised in her food, she calmly eats them. However, if she suspects even for a moment that she's been duped, she refuses to eat any more of that particular dish.

To help your child understand the importance of protein and other nutrients, teach him about how his body works. Most children, if they are approached gently rather than by an uptight parent trying to shoehorn some food down their throats, are fascinated with food and the magical workings of their bodies. If you take this approach, there is little doubt that your child will get every bit as much protein in his diet as he needs.

3.

CARBOHYDRATES: FOOD FOR FUEL

THE human being's need for fuel has been likened to the automobile's need for gasoline. In their relative need for fuel adults can be likened to conservative family sedans, while children are more like highly tuned racing cars. Without gasoline, automobiles, no matter what kind, cannot function, and similarly without carbohydrates both adults and children grow weak and eventually die. Technology, if pressed hard enough, can always find alternative forms of energy to power automobiles; but unless there is a major biological and ecological metamorphosis in nature, human beings are destined to remain dependent on carbohydrates for their basic fuel supply.

ENERGY FROM THE SUN

The energy to power our bodies originally comes from the sun. The sun's energy is stored in plants through an awesome process called photosynthesis. When we eat the plants, this energy is released and our bodies are given the power to move, think, grow, and function.

From the moment they start growing, plants stretch up

so that their leaves can be exposed to the sun. At the same time, they thrust their roots into the earth in search of water. While they are reaching for sun and water, plants absorb carbon dioxide from the atmosphere. The solar energy soaked up by the leaves facilitates the fusion of the water soaked up by the roots with the carbon dioxide absorbed from the atmosphere. This reaction in the plant is the first stage of photosynthesis, and results in the emission of oxygen into the atmosphere, where man and other animals depend on it for life. In photosynthesis, a series of complex biochemical reactions causes the fusion of water and carbon dioxide in the plant, and the resulting hydrated carbons, or carbohydrates, are eaten by man.

In the process of carbohydrate digestion, the oxygen reacts with the carbohydrates, producing carbon dioxide and water and releasing the original energy derived from the sun, an energy now used to power our bodies. The carbon dioxide is exhaled into the atmosphere and used by plant life, and the water is excreted to fertilize the earth. This miraculous carbohydrate-production cycle of plants is continuous, allowing humans and animals to move from place to place with the ability to replenish their internal need for the sun's energy simply by eating carbohydrates.

SUGAR AND STARCH

The carbohydrate molecule is a relatively simple structure, consisting of carbon, hydrogen, oxygen, and the energy of the sun that was trapped during their fusion in the plant. The smallest carbohydrate molecule produced by the plant is called a "sugar" while a complex chain of these sugars is called "starch."

The blood sugar in our bloodstream is made up of glucose, one of the simple carbohydrate sugars. The level of glucose in the bloodstream denotes, to a large degree, the amount of energy and vitality that a person is feeling at a given moment. When carbohydrates are digested, the body immediately recognizes whether they are simple sugars or the more complex starches. Sugars, especially those with a predominance of glucose, are almost immediately absorbed into the bloodstream, while the more complex starches are *broken into their respective sugar units* and used *one by one, as the blood sugar level drops*. Therefore, whereas the ingestion of sugars generally will cause a rapid increase in blood sugar level, the ingestion of starches allows a steady supply of sugar to be absorbed into the bloodstream.

The human body functions best with about 100 milligrams of glucose per 100 cubic centimeters of blood. This level is so important to normal functioning that the body will go to great lengths to maintain it. For example, when a child (or an adult) eats a food that has table sugar added to it, the sugar is rapidly absorbed into the bloodstream because table sugar is so high in glucose. This rapid absorption causes the blood sugar level to soar almost immediately. This sudden increase of glucose in the bloodstream is followed quickly by feelings of euphoria, energy, and excitement—a sugar "rush." But the body reacts by pumping insulin from the pancreas into the bloodstream in an attempt to neutralize the excessive blood sugar. This neutralization often results in the so-called hypoglycemic cycle, characterized by a feeling of letdown. Children particularly enjoy the sugar "rush" and are thus extremely susceptible to sugar addiction.

Millions of children spend a major portion of their lives involved in this vicious sugar cycle, while their parents have difficulty understanding why they seem to have periods of hyperactivity every day. There is now a growing amount of evidence linking several extremely serious diseases, including arteriosclerosis, heart disease, and diabetes, with poor childhood eating habits, most particularly the addiction to refined sugar and other refined carbohydrate products. The linkage of these diseases to the consumption of refined carbohydrates and sugars is disturbing when you consider that the average American child consumes over 20 pounds of candy, close to 500 bottles of soft drink, and 200 pieces of heavily sugared gum each year.

There are alternatives to refined sugar that parents should learn to use. For example, malt, which is a more complex sugar than refined table sugar, contains B vitamins and many essential minerals; and blackstrap molasses, a cane product from which most of the sugar has been removed, contains more calcium than milk. These sweet alternatives are absorbed into the bloodstream much more slowly than refined sugar and provide nutrients as well as more prolonged energy.

Although honey has become an extremely popular alternative to refined sugar, we use it sparingly. It is almost twice as sweet as sugar and is thought to affect children's teeth more severely than sugar. Moreover, honey is often used in baking, or in hot drinks and foods. Thus heated, honey loses its delicate enzymes. In Ayurvedic medicine small quantities of raw honey have been used for thousands of years in herbal and medicinal remedies. Ayurvedic doctors consider it a valuable medicine, but not a food. In fact, these doctors regard it to be poison when cooked.

A dangerous trend during this century has been the increasing reliance on sugars as a source of carbohydrates in the American diet. Since World War II especially, the consumption of complex carbohydrates or starches, such as grains, has rapidly decreased. Unfortunately, what has taken their place is a multitude of refined convenience foods that are high in calories, particularly from refined sugar and refined flours, which offer, at best, vastly inferior nutrition and, at worst, large numbers of ingredients linked or suspected of being linked to cancer, heart disease, and diabetes. A vegetarian diet that avoids refined sugars and starches and processed foods, and contains unrefined grains, flours, and natural whole foods, is an important step in reversing this trend.

BENEFITS OF CARBOHYDRATES

Carbohydrates are the body's natural first choice for energy requirements. However, the body is a versatile organism, and if carbohydrates are unavailable, it will convert protein to carbohydrates to supply the fuel that it needs. This use of protein for energy diminishes the amount of protein available for growth, increasing the potential for protein deficiency. Providing sufficient carbohydrates ensures that the precious proteins that children especially need are available. Carbohydrates therefore have an important role to play in "saving" protein for its proper work.

Carbohydrates also play an essential role in the utilization of fats. If a child eats dietary fats without taking in sufficient carbohydrates, the effect in his body is similar to what happens if you try to burn wood in a woodstove without enough air—instead of burning, the wood smolders, giving off acrid smoke and providing no warmth at all. If fats are eaten without sufficient carbohydrates, organic compounds called ketones develop that eventually may produce a dangerous condition called ketosis.

Although adequate amounts of carbohydrates in the form of starch are needed for health and energy, the quality of the starches consumed affects the overall nutrition supplied to the body. One gram of carbohydrate, whether refined or unrefined, supplies 4 calories or energy units; but if a child's daily diet is dominated by refined or "stripped" carbohydrates, the result is that although he may get an abundance or even an excess of calories, his diet is very likely to be deficient in essential nutrients such as protein, vitamins, minerals, and fiber. These nutrients occur naturally in unrefined products such as whole grains.

MAKING THE SWITCH TO NATURAL CARBOHYDRATE FOODS

A young child will probably not even notice the slow disappearance of processed foods from the home. A school-age child will be more observant. If your child wonders why packaged foods are slowly disappearing from the kitchen, you can explain that there are forty known nutrients that are essential in supporting vital body functions such as digestion and metabolism and which he needs. Tell him that some researchers now believe that in addition to the known essential nutrients, health depends on the concurrent presence within food of delicate micronutrients. Many nutritionists posit that natural, whole foods contain sizable quantities of these nutrients and micronutrients. But when foods are refined, canned, frozen, or otherwise tampered with, the nutrient value of the food suffers.

Besides the depletion of nutrients, there is the dubious value of added refined starches, chemicals, dyes, and preservatives. You can explain that each of these is "bad" for different reasons. Refined sugars—including sugar concealed in products under such aliases as sucrose, dextrose, corn syrup, and lactose—are added to foods in large quantities to increase taste and weight because it is cheaper than using natural ingredients. Some packaged cereals, for example, are over 50 percent sugar. The sugar in many processed foods is "hidden," so that people do not even realize the quantity that is being consumed.

Salt is often added in such high concentration that the use of processed foods beginning in childhood could hasten any inclination toward high blood pressure.

Refined starches are used, like sugar, to add bulk without adding any more expensive food to a package. This makes it possible to produce a product that appears to be substantial at very little expense to the manufacturer.

Chemicals and dyes are used masterfully to hide the lack of food content in processed "goods." Such foods are created in laboratories by chemists who are paid to produce new products in which convenience rather than nutrition is the priority. Explain to your child that many food additives are untested, making him a guinea pig for the "food chemists." Of those that have been tested, red dye #3 has been shown to have adverse effects on children, contributing greatly to hyperactivity. You can explain that you don't want to buy any product that might make him have difficulty learning and enjoying school.

Once you explain the detrimental nature of processed food to your child, he can be involved in the elimination of these foods. Together you can read labels and decide which foods should be avoided. Foods that he particularly likes can easily be made at home from better ingredients. For example, homemade ketchup and salad dressings can be made to taste as good as—or better than—the commercial varieties, which may contain as much as 30 percent sugar. Foods that pose more difficult challenges can be the source of shared kitchen experimentation. If he is allowed to participate in the search for new nutritious substitutes, he will be much more excited by the successes and tolerant of the failures.

If you do not have much time for cooking, always have an ample supply of natural unpasteurized fruit juices available to quench the thirst that follows vigorous play. (Water, of course, is the true "natural" thirst-quencher, but your children may prefer juice.) Juices can be diluted half and half with water, with little loss of taste and a saving to the family budget. Or blend fruit and milk together to make your own shakes. Your child may feel a good deal of pride at being one of the few kids in the neighborhood to get milkshakes on a regular basis. If your children especially insist on the bubbliness of commercial pop, buy sparkling mineral water and add fruit juice to it for sweetening. Also introduce your family to herb teas sweetened with honey, or try making your own lemonade with real lemons and pure honey. Kids will love it.

White and refined sugars can be avoided in everything from baked goods to beverages. Substituting blackstrap molasses, malt, maple syrup, or rice syrup for sugar, once you have experimented and mastered the simple technique of substitution, actually enhances the flavors of many foods. Another excellent way to sweeten pies, cakes, and cookies is by using fruits such as raisins or apples in baking.

Be sure to avoid bringing into your home any refined grain products; instead, use products made from 100 percent whole grain. Beware of the whole wheat breads sold in supermarkets; nearly all of these products have at least a half-dozen other ingredients in them, including sugar and preservatives. Most health food or natural food stores now carry breads and cookies baked with completely natural, unrefined ingredients. If you can't find good bread in your area, you are better off baking your own.

If your children ask why they may not have squishy white bread, illustrate your reasoning with the following chart. It shows clearly that a diet higher in refined starch is likely to contribute to nutrient debt. It may be helpful to a child eight years or older to see how two commonly used flours shape up against one another. Even at an early age, children are impressed by the discrepancy in these figures.

Whole Wheat Flour (⅔ cup)		Enriched White Flour (⅔ cup)	
1.1	mg	Pantothenic Acid	.465 mg
.34	mg	Vitamin B₆	.06	mg
4.3	mg	Niacin*	3.5	mg
.12	mg	Riboflavin*	.26	mg
.55	mg	Thiamine* (B₁)	.44	mg
113	mg	Magnesium	25	mg
370	mg	Potassium	95	mg
3.3	mg	Iron*	16	mg
41	mg	Calcium*	2.9	mg
2.3	g	Fiber	.3	g
13.3	g	Protein	10.5	g

* These nutrients are added to white flour to enrich it. Calcium is only required to be added to self-rising flour and self-rising corn meal.

Most children will accept brown rice, millet, bulghur, and whole grain pastas as substitutes for refined products. But a child who has become accustomed to squishy white bread may find whole wheat bread heavy and disagreeable. If he still likes white bread after two or three months, avoid the use of bread as much as possible. Instead serve whole grain crackers, tortillas, and whole wheat pita bread. If necessary, use these same alternatives in school lunches.

The most appetizing way to accustom a reluctant child to whole grain bread is to serve it hot with a generous portion of butter or homemade spread. Hot bread can be obtained in two ways. You can bake it fresh and serve it immediately, or you can buy unsliced whole grain loaves, brush them lightly with water, and heat them in the oven. Both will have a smell and flavor that even a fussy preschooler will find irresistible.

Once your child no longer resists the very idea of whole grain breads, you can begin to experiment to find his favorite bread. Some breads are sweeter, some lighter, some more flavorful than others. In time, he will discover his preference.

Freshly baked snacks are an old standby of experienced vegetarian parents. However, baking for children with whole grains and without honey or sugar requires a little unique expertise. Our first daughter, who was "born vegetarian," never liked any home-made cookies or cakes until, after long experimentation, we discovered that cakes baked with some brown rice flour in addition to wheat flour have a light moistness, and cookies made with wheat germ are soft and chewy.

To satisfy a child's occasional craving for candy, malt is invaluable. Originally we bought it because of its taste and resistance to heat as well as its excellent nutritional value, but after experimenting for some time we found that malt, unlike honey, will soldify when heated. It thus can be easily used to make healthful caramel candies, popcorn balls, and even lollipops. (See chapter 17 for recipes.)

Most children love fresh fruits, and they should be used freely to satisfy a sweet tooth, especially on a hot summer day. Watermelon, pineapple, blueberries, raspberries, grapes, cherries, oranges, apples, bananas, and strawberries are mouth-watering possibilities with high vitamin content. Children particularly love berries in milk, and apples or bananas with peanut butter.

When fresh fruit is out of season, canned, frozen, or even dried fruit should be used sparingly. Dried fruit has an extremely high sugar content and thus will have detrimental effects on teeth and energy cycles if used excessively.

When you refuse to buy canned or otherwise processed vegetables and instead always have plenty of fresh vegetables available, children will in all likelihood respond with enthusiasm, since most of them prefer raw carrots and fresh corn to any devitalized canned vegetable. With a little encouragement they will consume fresh vegetables heartily. A good way to ensure that they eat well from this important source of natural sugars and starches is to cut vegetables (carrots, celery, broccoli, zucchini, cauliflower, string beans, and green and red peppers) into small pieces and provide a delicious dip in which to dunk them.

Children are more likely to want canned fruit drenched in heavy sugar syrups than canned vegetables. It can be explained that these fruits are extremely high in sugar content and that they have been cooked so much that they have lost the valuable nutrients available in fresh fruits. Since imported fruit contains many chemicals from pesticides and fertilizers now banned in the United States, and since local fruits are fresher, those grown in your region and in season provide the greatest nutritive value. This reasoning can easily be imparted to children.

Though it is not always easy to find organically grown fruits and vegetables (those produce grown without chemical fertilizers and pesticides), especially out of season, we are convinced that such produce is more healthful and tastier than their commercial counterparts, and well worth the trouble to find. We enjoy growing our own vegetables organically during the summer. It's amazing how much food a small piece of land will produce. We use only natural compost and manure in the soil, and the taste of these vegetables is superb. The money that we save by growing our own is put toward the higher cost of organic food in winter months. To us the quality of these foods is worth the extra cost for the health they provide.

THE VARIETY IN NATURAL CARBOHYDRATE FOODS

Many people who are habituated to a diet high in refined and processed foods, especially carbohydrates, wonder how a natural food diet can possibly contain enough variety to make interesting and varied meals and snacks. A guided tour of a well-supplied natural foods store will reveal the vast variety of carbohydrate-rich goods available that contain abundant nutrients provided by nature.

Begin by inspecting the grain section. There you will find long-grain brown rice, medium-grain brown rice, short-grain brown rice, basmati rice, millet, bulghur, cracked wheat, whole wheat berries, toasted buckwheat groats, raw buckwheat groats, couscous, whole rye, wheat flakes, rice flakes, rolled oats, rye flakes, barley, triticale, and popcorn, along with whole wheat flour, brown rice flour, sweet brown rice flour, corn meal, corn flour, rye flour, buckwheat flour, oat flour, and millet flour. That's nineteen grains and nine whole grain flours. Compare that number to the grains found in an entire large supermarket, including all of the processed foods. The supermarket will certainly be found to be lacking in variety.

If the variety of grains still leaves the participant of this tour unconvinced, then walk a short distance to the pasta section. Here you will find whole wheat spaghetti, buckwheat spaghetti, whole wheat and soy spaghetti, whole wheat elbow macaroni, buckwheat elbow macaroni, tomato elbow macaroni, spinach flat noodles, whole wheat flat noodles, whole wheat alphabet macaroni, spinach lasagna, whole wheat lasagna, whole wheat spirals, whole wheat pasta shells, whole wheat stuffing shells, Japanese udon (whole wheat noodles) and Japanese soba (whole wheat and buckwheat noodles). Seventeen kinds of whole grain pasta are readily available to make all of the favorites kids love—from homemade alphabet soup to macaroni and cheese. Load all of the canned and packaged pasta in a well-supplied grocery store into a shopping cart and you'll find by far less to choose from for lunch and dinner. The same impressive choice is available in every carbohydrate food that is needed for your child's health, including legumes, breads, and natural sweeteners.

Contrary to popular opinion, eating whole foods is an adventure into a well-charted territory. There are a multitude of excellent natural foods cookbooks on the market, and for unrefined carbohydrate foods especially designed to appeal to children, we have included an extensive recipe section in this book.

4.

VITAMINS AND MINERALS

SOON after the Dutch colonized the island of Java in the
seventeenth century, an epidemic of a disease that affects
the brain, nervous system, heart, and digestive tract began
wiping out thousands of Dutch men, women, and children,
as well as local inhabitants who had adopted the Dutch
customs. The disease was called beriberi. Although the
Dutch sent their best doctors to try to find out what had
caused the epidemic, they met with no success. Some
doctors thought it must be a jungle disease peculiar to
Java, while others thought it might be due to the damp
tropical air. Yet others reasoned that the disease was
caused by eating the fish that were abundant around the
island. The epidemic went on for many years.

One of the doctors who came to Java in later years, a
man named Christian Eijkman, gathered a number of
chickens together, which he housed next to his laboratory.
His theory was that beriberi was caused by "germs," which
had recently been discovered. So Dr. Eijkman collected
blood from beriberi victims and began to regularly inject
this blood into his chickens, on the hypothesis that the
germs in the blood would soon infect the chickens. He
spent years in his experiment, but his chickens showed no

signs of getting beriberi. Determined that his theory was right, Dr. Eijkman continued undaunted. And sure enough, one day he woke up to discover that *all* of his chickens were wandering around the yard obviously very ill with beriberi.

But Dr. Eijkman was suspicious. Even though he desperately wanted to claim that he had discovered that beriberi was caused by a type of germ, it concerned him that all of his chickens had become infected. You see, Dr. Eijkman liked to eat eggs, and he didn't want to infect himself by eating eggs from chickens he was trying to infect with beriberi. He had therefore not subjected several of the chickens to this treatment. What puzzled him now was that even these chickens were sick. He asked his houseboy whether any of his own chickens could have inadvertently become mixed up with the others. The houseboy insisted that he had not confused any of the chickens, but he said that he had been feeding the chickens leftovers from the doctor's table because the chicken feed had run out some time before and he hadn't wanted to interrupt the doctor's experiments with such a minor thing.

After further observations, Dr. Eijkman realized that the chickens had become sick, not because of a mysterious "germ," but because of the quality of their food. In those days chicken feed was made from unpolished brown rice, which, so far as the colonists were concerned, was not fit for human consumption. People ate fluffy polished white rice, in the style of conquerors and the wealthy classes all over the colonial world. When the chickens were forced to subsist on polished rice, they, like the Dutch colonists, became prone to beriberi.

Dr. Eijkman published his findings in 1890, but he was ridiculed in medical circles for over twenty years. Medical researchers of the time preferred more sophisticated and scientific theories. But in 1911, Dr. Casimir Funk, a Polish chemist, doing research in England, read about Dr. Eijkman's observations and spent four months refining a ton of brown rice. He took the brown rice polishings and concentrated them until he had six ounces of an almost pure chemical. He called this substance "Vitamine."

Dr. Funk's "discovery" was the first in a long series that isolated and identified intrinsic nutrients in natural foods that are essential to health, growth, and normal physical, emotional, and mental functioning. These substances, of course, we know today as vitamins and minerals. Dr. Funk had actually refined the brown rice polishings into vitamin B_1 or thiamine, the deficiency of which causes beriberi. But Dr. Funk's discovery that vitamin B_1 came from the polishings of brown rice did not change the dietary habits of the times. In fact, the dietary trends of the colonists, established as far back as the 1600s, became more strongly confirmed in the 1900s under the profit-motivated umbrella of a highly sophisticated food refining and packaging industry. These food processors have consistently rationalized refining by reasoning that lost vitamins and minerals can always be put back *after* refining, in the process known as "enrichment." However, the enriched product is hardly the same as the original, for the manufacturers add only some of the lost nutrients; many essential micronutrients are simply discarded.

Despite evidence to the contrary, consumers are told by dozens of television and radio ads every day that refined and processed foods are "good for you." The success of such advertising is disturbing. According to the editors of *Food for People, Not for Profit*, since World War II, the consumption of soft drinks in the United States has increased by 80 percent, consumption of pastry by 70 percent and consumption of potato chips by 85 percent. During this same period the consumption of nutritious foods such as dairy products is down 21 percent, that of vegetables 23 percent, and that of fruits 25 percent.

Vitamins and minerals comprise about 5 percent of a child's bodily constituents. The crucial role these minute substances play in millions of chemical reactions from digestion to walking, talking, and thinking cannot be emphasized enough. Yet many children in industrialized countries, where nutrition is self-righteously proclaimed "superior," in fact suffer from vitamin and mineral deficiencies. This phenomenon is to a large extent due to the massive trend in industrialized cultures toward consumption of refined foods laden with sugar and chemical additives, and the simultaneous decrease in consumption of whole, natural foods.

In its 1977 report, the Senate Select Committee on Nutrition and Human Needs definitely linked this dietary trend to a number of fatal diseases among adults, including cancer and heart disease. In addition to this admission by a respected U.S. government body, there is steadily mounting evidence that a predominantly refined-food diet has repercussions on the health of our children as well. The deficiencies resulting from such dietary habits are now suspected to play a large role not only in many so-called unavoidable childhood ailments, but in other more subtle symptoms such as irritability, fatigue, temper tantrums, inability to concentrate, low blood sugar, restlessness, hyperactivity, shyness, and depression, to name only a few. Only too often children exhibiting these symptoms are dragged off to psychologists or psychiatrists, where they meekly, but in vain, answer questions about what is upsetting them. This is not to say that psychologists and psychiatrists do not have much valid insight, compassion, and understanding to offer both parents and children, but rather to note how amazing it is that so many of the problems that bring children before such authorities in the first place often disappear when these children's nutrition improves. Fortunately, nowadays there is a growing number of nutritionally aware doctors, nutritional counselors, and therapists who respect the work of such researchers as Dr. Ben Feingold whose dietary programs to reverse the effects of junk foods containing sugar and chemical colorings and preservatives have proven extremely effective in cases involving hyperactive children.

Although there is a growing awareness about the consequences of an inadequate or inappropriate diet, the problem of vitamin and mineral deficiency among children in industrialized countries is massive. In 1968–1970, the U.S. government conducted a ten-state survey on the health status of white, black, and Hispanic children ranging from newborns to sixteen-year-olds. Between 41.4 and 53.4 percent of the children studied were shown to have a below-standard intake of vitamin C, and between 39.4 and 94.8 percent were below standard in intake of calcium.

The accompanying table of RDAs is provided for parents who desire a scientific analysis of the recommended daily vitamin and mineral allowances for children and teenagers. These figures are provided only as a guideline. As we stated in chapter 2, the healthiest peoples in the world, usually found in traditional cultures, eat natural, chemical- and preservative-free foods, relying on nature to provide what their bodies need. However, in these times of ecological and environmental imbalance, parents may question the vitamin and mineral content of even natural foods. We discuss vitamin and mineral supplementation later in this chapter. Suffice it to say here that simply feeding children vitamin and mineral tablets *instead* of a wholesome and varied diet devoid of junk food is not the way to sound nutrition. Even conservative nutritionists and researchers will admit that science has many more vitamins and minerals yet to discover and that natural foods contain more invisible life-giving nutrients that cannot as yet be isolated in a test tube.

Foods grown without pesticides and chemicals, as well as eggs and dairy products from animals who are not fed antibiotics and other chemicals to speed up their growth or production, remain the best sources of vitamins and minerals. In the following sections we list the functions of each of the vitamins and minerals, the natural foods that contain them in outstanding quality and quantity, and the possible symptoms of specific vitamin and mineral deficiencies. The information contained in this section is for the general nutritional education of parents. Many of the symptoms listed are common ones that could be due to causes other than a deficiency. Therefore, self-treatment with supplements is not recommended. Instead, if symptoms of vitamin or mineral deficiency are suspected, the guidance of a physician or a competent nutritional therapist should be promptly sought.

It should be noted that certain foods and drugs such as coffee, alcohol, aspirin, birth control pills, refined sugar, tobacco, and sulfa drugs have an "antivitamin" effect. Parents should see to it that their children are protected from these substances, especially in the formative years.

VITAMINS

Vitamin A

Functions. Vitamin A aids in the protection of the mucous membranes in the nose, mouth, throat, and lungs, and

thereby reduces susceptibility to infections and the effects
of air pollution. It aids in the growth and repair of body
tissues and in the maintenance of soft, healthy skin. It is
instrumental in the normal secretion of gastric juices necessary for protein digestion. It also aids in the formation of
strong bones and teeth, in the development of healthy
blood, and in the maintenance of normal eyesight.

Sources. Alfalfa sprouts, avocados, green beans, peas,
corn, squash, tomatoes, beet greens, spinach, broccoli,
carrots, apricots, yellow peaches, milk, and milk products
such as cream and butter.

Symptoms of Deficiency. Allergies, sinus troubles, loss of
smell, and general susceptibility to infections; itching and
burning of the eyes and a tendency toward night-blindness;
rough and dry skin, skin blemishes, dry hair; soft tooth
enamel; general fatigue.

Note: Intake of massive amounts of vitamin A over a
period of 4 months or longer may result in vitamin A
excess. Symptoms are lethargy, malaise, abdominal pain,
headache, increased eating, and brittle nails.

Vitamin B Complex

Functions. "B complex" refers to a series of functionally
related water-soluble substances crucial to health. These
substances include thiamine (B_1), riboflavin (B_2), niacin,
pyridoxine (B_6), cyanocobalamin (B_{12}), biotin, choline,
folacin, inositol, pantothenic acid, and para-aminobenzoic
acid (PABA). We will first discuss these vitamins as a
related "complex" acting together, and then cover each of
them in more detail.

The B-complex vitamins are the most important nutritional substances for the health of the nerves. They are also
crucial in providing the body with energy because one of
their important functions is to catalyze the conversion of
carbohydrates into glucose, which the body burns as fuel
to produce energy. They play a role in the metabolism of
fats and protein, and they are essential to the maintenance
of muscle tone in the gastrointestinal tract. They also aid
in the maintenance of the health of the skin, hair, eyes,
mouth, and liver.

Sources. Whole grain cereals such as wheat, rye, brown
rice, and oats. Brewer's yeast and nutritional yeast are also

RECOMMENDED DAILY DIETARY ALLOWANCES FOR CHILDREN AND TEENAGERS[1]

	Age (years)	Weight kg	lb	Height cm	in	Vitamin A (mcg RE)[2]	Vitamin D (mcg)[3]	Vitamin E (mg α-TE)[4]	Vitamin C (mg)	Thiamine (mg)	Riboflavin (mg)
Infants	0.0–0.5	6	13	60	24	420	10	3	35	0.3	0.4
	0.5–1.0	9	20	71	28	400	10	4	35	0.5	0.6
Children	1–3	13	29	90	35	400	10	5	45	0.7	0.8
	4–6	20	44	112	44	500	10	6	45	0.9	1.0
	7–10	28	62	132	52	700	10	7	45	1.2	1.4
Males	11–14	45	99	157	62	1000	10	8	50	1.4	1.6
	15–18	66	145	176	69	1000	10	10	60	1.4	1.7
	19–22	70	154	177	70	1000	7.5	10	60	1.5	1.7
Females	11–14	46	101	157	62	800	10	8	50	1.1	1.3
	15–18	55	120	163	64	800	10	8	60	1.1	1.3
	19–22	55	120	163	64	800	7.5	8	60	1.1	1.3

1. The allowances are intended to provide for individual variations among most normal persons as they live in the United States under usual environmental stresses. Diets should be based on a variety of common foods in order to provide other nutrients for which human requirements have been less well defined.
2. Micrograms of retinol equivalents. 800 RE =4,000 International Units. 1,000 RE = 5,000 IU.
3. Micrograms of cholecalciferol, or vitamin D_3. 10 mcg cholecalcerol = 400 IU of vitamin D.
4. Alpha-tocopherol equivalents.

	Niacin (mg NE)[5]	Vitamin B6 (mg)	Folacin (mcg)	Vitamin B12 (mcg)	Calcium (mg)	Phosphorus (mg)	Magnesium (mg)	Iron (mg)	Zinc (mg)	Iodine (mcg)
Infants	6	0.3	30	0.5[a]	360	240	50	10	3	40
(continued)	8	0.6	45	1.5	540	360	70	15	5	50
Children	9	0.9	100	2.0	800	800	150	15	10	70
(continued)	11	1.3	200	2.5	800	800	200	10	10	90
	16	1.6	300	3.0	800	800	250	10	10	120
Males	18	1.8	400	3.0	1200	1200	350	18	15	150
(continued)	18	2.0	400	3.0	1200	1200	400	18	15	150
	19	2.2	400	3.0	800	800	350	10	15	150
Females	15	1.8	400	3.0	1200	1200	300	18	15	150
(continued)	14	2.0	400	3.0	1200	1200	300	18	15	150
	14	2.0	400	3.0	800	800	300	18	15	150

5. Niacin equivalents. 1 NE = 1 mg of niacin or 60 mg of dietary tryptophan.

6. The RDA for vitamin B_{12} in infants is based on average concentration of the vitamin in human milk. The allowances after weaning are based on energy intake (as recommended by the American Academy of Pediatrics) and consideration of other factors, such as intestinal absorption.

Source: Food and Nutrition Board, National Academy of Sciences—National Research Council, Recommended Daily Dietary Allowances, revised 1980.

excellent sources of B-complex vitamins. Some children enjoy the taste of these supplemental foods, while for others it is best to hide their taste in other dishes.

Symptoms of Deficiency. Because the American diet contains so many refined grain products and refined foods in general, the evidence of B vitamin deficiency in the United States is widespread. Symptoms may include tiredness, irritability, nervousness and depression, poor appetite, insomnia, neuritis, acne, anemia, and constipation. The problem is further aggravated by massive popular use of sugar and alcohol, which destroy the B vitamin complex. Widespread use of antibiotics in Western countries also contributes to vitamin B deficiency.

Vitamin B₁ (Thiamine)

Functions. Vitamin B_1 is extremely important for children because it is linked to the health of the nervous system, and a deficiency of it can negatively affect mental outlook. It is known to have an influence on improving individual learning capacity, and it is necessary for consistent growth in children. It stabilizes the appetite by improving food assimilation and digestion, especially of starches and sugars.

Sources. Thiamine is lost in all commercial milling processes, which strip away the bran, germ, or husk of grain to make a whiter, lighter product. Since refining is so common a practice, U.S. law requires that isolated thiamine be added to many such refined products. This is a sad nutritional compromise because far more nutrients are taken out in the refining process than can possibly be introduced artificially. Parents should therefore ensure that their children's diet is rich in unrefined grains and flours. Fresh raw wheat germ and bran can also provide useful additional thiamine. Brewer's yeast and blackstrap molasses are also good sources. Other sources include alfalfa sprouts, legumes, bananas, apples, avocados, nuts, milk, and soy milk.

Symptoms of Deficiency. Early signs of thiamine deficiency include numbness and tingling in the extremities, easy fatigue, loss of appetite, irritability, and emotional instability. If these symptoms are not alleviated by a dietary intake of thiamine, confusion and memory loss have been shown to appear. These symptoms are followed closely by gastric distress, abdominal pain, and constipation. Other potential symptoms are shortness of breath and hypersensitivity to noise.

Vitamin B_2 (Riboflavin)

Functions. Riboflavin is instrumental in the sustenance of the skin, nails, and hair and is important in the maintenance of good vision. It is essential for normal growth and development and, in conjunction with other vitamins of the B complex, instrumental in the utilization of food energy. It is also necessary for cell respiration.

Sources. Brewer's yeast is the best natural source of riboflavin. Others include whole grains, milk, alfalfa sprouts, soy sprouts, wheat germ, eggs, citrus fruits, bananas, tomatoes, apricots, legumes, peas, and seeds.

Symptoms of Deficiency. According to the editors of the well-known *Nutritional Almanac*, riboflavin deficiency is the most common vitamin deficiency in the United States. Common symptoms include cracks and sores in the corners of the mouth and a red, painful tongue. Other symptoms include lassitude, trembling, sluggishness, dizziness, vaginal itching, burning of the eyes, eye fatigue, and a feeling of "sand in the eyes." Retarded growth and digestive disturbance may also reflect riboflavin deficiency.

Vitamin B_6 (Pyridoxine)

Functions. Pyridoxine must be present for the production of red blood cells and antibodies, and it facilitates the release of glycogen from the liver for energy. It is essential in the process of vitamin B_{12} absorption, as well as for the production of hydrochloric acid and assimilation of magnesium, two vital bodily constituents. It aids in the regulation of body fluids and the normal functioning of the nervous system by balancing sodium and potassium in the body.

Sources. Whole grains and brewer's yeast. About half of the pyridoxine contained in whole grains is lost in the process of milling. This vitamin is not replaced by "enrichment," and since pyridoxine is relatively difficult to find in the diet, children can easily develop a pyridoxine "debt" if they eat mainly refined foods. Other sources are blackstrap molasses, brown rice, nuts and seeds, and wheat germ.

Symptoms of Deficiency. Symptoms of pyridoxine deficiency may be similar to those involved in riboflavin and niacin deficiencies: muscular weakness, nervousness, irritability, depression, and arthritis. Pyridoxine deficiency may be indicated in hypoglycemia (low blood sugar) or in diabetes. Learning disabilities and visual disturbances are also possible symptoms of pyridoxine deficiency. In infants, pyridoxine deficiency can cause convulsions, increased irritability, and anemia.

Vitamin B$_{12}$ (Cyanocobalamin)

Functions. Vitamin B$_{12}$ is essential to longevity, and it is necessary to protein, fat, and carbohydrate metabolism. It also contributes to a healthy nervous system and a normal appetite.

Sources. Dairy products, eggs, miso, seaweed, tempeh, comfrey, spirulina plant plankton.

Symptoms of Deficiency. Symptoms may take as long as five or six years to appear. Deficiency is often characterized by nervous disorders, pernicious anemia, general weakness, and walking and speaking difficulties. Vegans (whose diet contains no animal products of any kind, including dairy products) should take brewer's yeast that has vitamin B$_{12}$ added or spirulina plant plankton to ensure that their daily requirements for this important vitamin are met.

Biotin

Functions. Biotin functions actively in the oxidation of fatty acids and carbohydrates and in the manufacture of fatty acids. It also helps in the metabolism of carbohydrates, fat, and protein, and facilitates cell respiration.

Sources. Biotin is found in trace amounts in many natural foods such as legumes, whole grains, egg yolks, brewer's yeast, soybeans, and mung bean sprouts.

Symptoms of Deficiency. Deficiencies of biotin are only evident in people whose diet includes large amounts of raw egg whites. Symptoms include muscular pain, poor, appetite, insomnia, gray skin color, depression, and fatigue.

Choline

Functions. Choline is active in the utilization of fats and cholesterol in the body. It prevents the accumulation of fats in the liver and aids in the movement of fats into the cells. It plays a vital role in the health of the liver and the gall bladder and in the health of the myelin sheaths surrounding the nerves, where it also helps in the transmission of nerve impulses. It facilitates the formation of lecithin.

Sources. Egg yolks, legumes, soybeans, wheat germ, lecithin, and brewer's yeast.

Symptoms of Deficiency. Choline deficiency results in the depositing of fat in the liver and can contribute to bleeding stomach ulcers, blockage of the kidney tubes, and heart trouble. If deficiency persists, high blood pressure, impaired liver and kidney function, and an intolerance to fats may occur.

Folacin (Folic Acid)

Functions. Folacin helps maintain the appetite and facilitates hydrochloric acid production. It helps the liver to carry out its functions. It is useful in the breakdown and utilization of proteins. It also helps in red blood cell formation, and it generally helps to facilitate body growth and reproduction.

Sources. Green leafy vegetables, brewer's yeast, milk products, whole grains, dates, fenugreek seeds.

Symptoms of Deficiency. Digestive disturbances, poor absorption, and metabolic disorders can result from a deficiency. Another possible symptom is anemia, which may not be corrected by iron supplementation alone. Prematurely graying hair in adults and growth problems in children may also be symptoms of deficiency.

Inositol

Functions. Inositol is very important to the process of lecithin production and consequently to the metabolism of fat and cholesterol, and it is helpful in retarding hardening of the arteries. It is vital to the processes involved in hair growth.

Sources. Milk, brewer's yeast, blackstrap molasses, nuts,

vegetables, whole grains, lecithin, and oranges and other citrus fruits.

Symptoms of Deficiency. Constipation, eczema, and abnormalities of the eyes can be symptoms of deficiency. High cholesterol and loss of hair may also be indications that inositol is inadequate in the diet.

Niacin

Functions. Niacin aids in the metabolism of proteins, fats, and carbohydrates. It improves circulation and reduces the cholesterol levels in the blood. It aids in the production of hydrochloric acid, and it is essential in maintaining the health of the nervous system, skin, tongue, and digestive system.

Sources. Brewer's yeast, milk products, cooked rhubarb, peanuts, wheat germ.

Symptoms of Deficiency. Early signs of niacin deficiency include loss of appetite, muscular weakness, canker sores, indigestion, general fatigue, mild depression, bad breath, irritability. Intermediate signs of deficiency include nausea, recurring headaches, vomiting, tender gums, stress, tension, nervousness. Advanced deficiency results in pellagra, a disease characterized by dermatitis, diarrhea, tremors, nervous disorder, and inflamed skin.

Para-aminobenzoic Acid (PABA)

Functions. PABA is active in protein metabolism and in the formation of red blood cells. It is also important to the health of the skin and the intestines and to the pigmentation of the hair. (The current nutrition "establishment" has cast doubt on the need for PABA in humans. However, other sources that we respect do consider it an important nutrient.)

Sources. Brewer's yeast, wheat germ, molasses.

Symptoms of Deficiency. Fatigue, constipation, digestive disorders, depression, nervousness, headaches, prematurely gray hair.

Pantothenic Acid

Functions. Pantothenic acid is essential in the process of cellular metabolism, and it takes part in the conversion of carbohydrates, fats, and proteins into energy. Maintenance of a healthy digestive tract is another of its functions. It is instrumental in improving the body's ability to withstand stress and in retarding premature aging. It is also very important to the functioning of the adrenal glands and to healthy skin.

Sources. Brewer's yeast, egg yolks, whole grain cereals, wheat germ. It is also produced by bacteria in the intestines.

Symptoms of Deficiency. Since pantothenic acid is abundant in many foods, deficiency is rare. Hypoglycemia (low blood sugar) may indicate pantothenic acid deficiency. Other symptoms are abdominal pain, nausea, and numbness and tingling of hands and feet.

Vitamin C (Ascorbic Acid)

Functions. Vitamin C is instrumental in fighting bacterial infections and is an affective anti-allergen. It is also often used in preventing and treating viral infections such as the common cold. However, the efficacy of vitamin C against the common cold has not been proved. It plays a part in healing wounds and burns because it helps to build connective tissue, and it also aids in red blood cell formation and the prevention of hemorrhaging. It is helpful in the formation of healthy teeth and bones, and it enables other essential vitamins and minerals to perform their functions.

Sources. Green peppers, citrus fruits, broccoli, papaya, strawberries, rose hips, acerola cherries.

Symptoms of Deficiency. Hay fever and lowered resistance to respiratory infections may indicate a vitamin C deficiency. Other symptoms may include easy bruising, slow healing of cuts, wounds, and fractures, nosebleeds, dental cavities, bleeding gums, anemia, and poor digestion. Severe deficiency may cause scurvy.

Vitamin D

Functions. Vitamin D is extremely important for normal growth in children. It also aids in the processes involved in normal blood clotting and in the maintenance of the nervous system and the heart.

Sources. Sufficient exposure to sunlight converts a cholesterol-related compound in the skin into vitamin D.

However, since air pollution, clouds, windows, and clothing all inhibit this transformation, vitamin D sources should also be included in the diet. Dietary sources include egg yolks. (Fortified milk contains added vitamin D, but we prefer the use of raw milk. See the discussion under "Magnesium" in the minerals section.)

Symptoms of Deficiency. Severe cases of vitamin D deficiency lead to a bone disorder called rickets in children and osteomalacia in adults. Symptoms include softening of the skull, softening of the bones, bowing of the legs, spinal curvature, poorly developed muscles, and nervous irritability. Early symptoms may include burning sensations in the mouth and throat, diarrhea, poor metabolism, near-sightedness, insomnia, and nervousness.

Note: Excess vitamin D is toxic; symptoms are loss of appetite, vomiting, and increased urination.

Vitamin E

Functions. Vitamin E facilitates blood flow to the heart by dilating blood vessels, and it acts as an anticoagulant, preventing blood clots. It aids in supplying nourishment to cells and protects red blood cells from destruction by poisons in the bloodstream. It also protects the body from environmental poisons in air, water, and food. It has an extremely important role to play in both male and female reproductive processes, and in premature infants prevents anemia and protects against blindness.

Sources. Cold-pressed vegetable oils, raw nuts and seeds, soybeans, wheat germ oil.

Symptoms of Deficiency. Dr. Wilfred Shute, a prominent physician and researcher, has found that the typical American diet, with its emphasis on refined-flour products from which the vitamin E–rich germ has been removed, results in large-scale deficiencies of this important nutrient in the U.S. population. Symptoms of deficiency (in animal studies) include gastrointestinal disease, dry, dull, or falling hair, heart disease, heart defects in newborns, muscular wasting, sterility, impotence, and varicose veins.

Unsaturated Fatty Acids (Vitamin F)

Functions. "Vitamin F" aids in the lubrication of all cells and helps to maintain their resilience. Its presence is necessary in the regulation of blood coagulation and in removing cholesterol deposits from the arteries. It is essential for glandular activity and therefore plays an important role in normal growth. It is also essential for mucous membrane and nerve health and it nourishes the skin. It is important to respiration.

Sources. Cold-pressed vegetable oils, wheat germ, and seeds, especially sunflower seeds.

Symptoms of Deficiency. "Vitamin F" is extremely important in a child's diet, for without it growth and teeth formation can be retarded. Symptoms of deficiency include brittle and lusterless hair, dandruff, dry skin, brittle nails, allergies, and inability to gain weight.

Vitamin K

Functions. Vitamin K is essential for the process of normal blood clotting. It is important for longevity and vitality and for normal functioning of the liver.

Sources. Kelp, alfalfa, green leafy vegetables, milk, yogurt, egg yolks, blackstrap molasses, oatmeal, safflower oil. Vitamin K is also synthesized by intestinal bacteria.

Symptoms of Deficiency. According to the National Research Council, vitamin K is abundantly available in most diets. Symptoms of deficiency, however, include diarrhea, a tendency toward hemorrhaging, miscarriage, and nosebleed.

Bioflavonoids

Functions. Bioflavonoids are essential in increasing the strength of the capillaries, and their presence is essential for the proper absorption of vitamin C. They also help to prevent hemorrhages and ruptures in the blood vessel walls. They protect against colds and influenza and minimize bruising.

Sources. Lemons, grapes, plums, grapefruit, apricots, strawberries, black currants, prunes, blackberries, rose hips, cherries, buckwheat, green peppers.

Symptoms of Deficiency. Deficiency of bioflavonoids creates symptoms very similar to those of vitamin C deficiency. The tendency to bleed, bruise, or hemorrhage easily is particularly evident, and purple or blue spots may appear on the skin.

MINERALS

Calcium

Functions. Calcium is extremely important for children because, in cooperation with phosphorus, it helps build and maintain bones and teeth and facilitates normal growth. It is important to the process of blood clotting and speeds up all healing processes. It is essential for normal heart action and all other muscle movements. It is vitally needed by pregnant and lactating women. Calcium aids in the proper utilization of iron, and it helps to provide a balance between magnesium, sodium, and potassium.

Sources. Milk and dairy products, endive, lettuce, kale, cabbage, watercress, Brussels sprouts, dandelion greens, broccoli, navy beans, almonds, sunflower seeds, walnuts, sesame seeds, and millet. (See table.)

Symptoms of Deficiency. Early signs of calcium deficiency include nervousness, muscle cramps, and numbness and tingling in the arms or legs. Moderate symptoms of deficiency include cramps, joint pains, tooth decay, insomnia, irritability, and impaired growth.

Chromium

Functions. Chromium is essential to the metabolism of glucose for energy as well as the synthesis of fatty acids and cholesterol.

Sources. Hard water, corn oil, whole grain cereals. Brewer's yeast provides a dependable source for this important mineral and should be included in a child's diet if there is any doubt about chromium intake.

Symptoms of Deficiency. Chromium deficiency is common in the United States because the soil generally tends to be deficient in it. It is therefore found only in low quantities in crops and in the water supply. Also contributing to this problem is the widespread refining of grains, which effectively removes any chromium. Symptoms of deficiency include high or low blood sugar, hardening of the arteries, and heart disease.

Copper

Functions. Copper is essential for the absorption of iron and is involved in protein metabolism and in healing processes. It is necessary for proper formation of bones, brain, nerves, and connective tissues, and it helps to maintain natural hair color. It is also necessary for the production of RNA, which is an important factor in synthesizing proteins.

Sources. Whole grains, beans, peas, green leafy vegetables, almonds, prunes, pomegranates, and raisins.

Symptoms of Deficiency. Copper deficiencies are relatively unknown. Children who have iron-deficiency anemia and kwashiorkor (a disease brought on by protein deficiency) may also have copper deficiency.

Iodine

Functions. Iodine regulates the body's production of energy, promotes its growth and normal development, and stimulates metabolism. It aids in proper development and functioning of the thyroid gland, which is responsible for a healthy disposition, normal speech, and healthy hair, nails, skin, and teeth.

Sources. Iodized sea salt, seaweeds (kelp, dulse, Irish moss), mushrooms, Swiss chard, turnip greens, garlic, watercress, artichokes, egg yolks, pineapples, pears, and citrus fruits.

Symptoms of Deficiency. Pregnant women who take in low amounts of iodine run the risk of giving birth to children suffering from cretinism, a disease characterized by mental and physical retardation. Other severe deficiencies may cause enlargement of the thyroid gland, or another medical condition called hyperthyroidism. This disease is common in countries where iodine is found only in small quantities in the soil and water. Other symptoms include anemia, lethargy, fatigue, lack of interest in sex, low blood pressure, and a tendency toward obesity.

Iron

Functions. Iron is vital in the formation of hemoglobin, the cornerstone matter of red blood cells. Hemoglobin transports oxygen from the lungs to the tissues. The tissues depend on this supply of oxygen to maintain all life functions. This process aids greatly in increasing resistance to disease and stress. Vitamin C enhances absorption of iron.

Sources. Leafy green vegetables, blackstrap molasses, peaches, apricots, bananas, raisins, prunes, whole grain cereals, brewer's yeast, alfalfa, walnuts, sesame seeds, dry beans, lentils, kelp, dulse, egg yolks, whole rye. (See table.)

Symptoms of Deficiency. Deficiencies of iron may lead to iron-deficiency anemia, abnormal fatigue, lowered resistance, general run-down feeling, pale skin, headaches, constipation, brittle nails, and difficulty in breathing.

Women of menstruating age and especially pregnant women are prone to iron deficiency, and great care should be exercised in providing optimum amounts of iron in their diets.

Magnesium

Functions. Magnesium aids the process of bone growth and is important in the healthy functioning of nerves and muscles. It is an important catalyst in the enzyme reactions associated with the conversion of blood sugar into energy. It aids in maintaining muscle tone and in the metabolism of carbohydrates and proteins. It is instrumental in the efficient utilization of B-complex vitamins, vitamin E, fats, calcium, and other minerals.

Sources. Whole grains, brown rice, unmilled raw wheat germ, soybeans, figs, corn, apples, raw and cooked green leafy vegetables, alfalfa, lemons, peaches, almonds, and other nuts and seeds.

Symptoms of Deficiency. Deficiencies of magnesium will contribute to the loss of calcium and potassium from the body, so that these minerals will eventually also become deficient. Symptoms of deficiency may include feelings of apprehensiveness, muscle twitch, tremors, confusion, and disorientation. If a child exhibits symptoms of magnesium deficiency, the first thing to do is to take him off commercial pasteurized milk, which has high amounts of synthetic vitamin D_2 (calciferol) added to it. Vitamin D_2, like fluorine, has the tendency to bind with magnesium and carry it out of the body, creating a magnesium deficiency. This is one of the main reasons we recommend that parents give their children milk that does not contain added vitamin D. Severe deficiencies of magnesium can lead to kidney damage, kidney stones, atherosclerosis, heart

SOURCES OF CALCIUM

	Amount	Calcium (mg)		Amount	Calcium (mg)
Milk Products			**Grains and Beans**		
nonfat, noninstant milk powder	1 cup	1,508	soy flour	1 cup	366
ricotta cheese (part skim)	1 cup	669	black beans (dry)	1 cup	270
skim milk powder	¾ cup	400	soybeans (dry)	1 cup	226
low-fat milk	1 cup	350	chickpeas (dry)	1 cup	300
skim milk	1 cup	302	tofu	1 cake	260
buttermilk	1 cup	300	pinto beans (dry)	1 cup	257
whole milk (cow's)	1 cup	291	miso	1 cup	131
whole milk (goat's)	1 cup	320	navy beans (dry)	1 oz.	144
Swiss cheese	1 oz.	270	carob flour	¼ cup	120
Edam cheese	1 oz.	225			
Cheddar cheese	1 oz.	211	**Seeds and Nuts**		
cottage cheese (2% fat)	1 cup	155	almonds (raw)	1 cup	332
yogurt (low-fat)	1 cup	415	hazelnuts (raw)	1 cup	282
			Brazil nuts (raw)	1 cup	260
Vegetables			sunflower seeds (raw)	1 cup	174
collard leaves (cooked)	1 cup	360	sesame seeds (raw)	1 cup	165
bok choy (cooked)	1 cup	250	peanuts (roasted)	1 cup	104
kale (cooked)	1 cup	206			
mustard greens (cooked)	1 cup	284	**Seaweeds**		
mustard greens (raw)	1 cup	180	agar	1 oz.	112
broccoli (raw)	1 stalk	160	hiziki	1 oz.	392
broccoli (cooked)	1 cup	155	wakame	1 oz.	362
okra (cooked)	1 cup	150	dulse	1 oz.	159
dandelion greens (cooked)	1 cup	150	kelp powder	1 tbsp.	156
parsley (raw)	1 cup	122	**Supplemental Foods**		
beet green (raw)	1 cup	119	nutritional yeast	1 tbsp.	375
			blackstrap molasses	1 tbsp.	137

Herbs rich in calcium (recommended for pregnant women): arrowroot, camomile, cleavers, chives, coltsfoot, dandelion root, flaxseed, horsetail grass, nettle, plantain, shepherd's purse, sorrel.

Calcium tea for pregnant women: 6 parts horsetail grass, 4 parts oat straw, 4 parts comfrey root, 2 to 3 cups per day.

Source: Courtesy of Barry D. Elson, M.D.

attacks, impaired protein metabolism, chronic nervous irritability, and chronic depression. If symptoms of deficiency appear, the entire diet of the child should be reevaluated, and the sources of magnesium listed above should be included.

Manganese

Functions. Manganese plays an important role, as a component of enzymes, in the metabolism of carbohydrates, fats, and proteins. It helps to nourish the nerves and the brain and plays an important role in the coordination between the brain, nerves, and muscles. It also affects skeletal development and reproductive and mammary gland functions.

Sources. Green leafy vegetables, spinach, beets, Brussels sprouts, oranges, grapefruit, apricots, blueberries, whole grains, bran, raw nuts, kelp, raw egg yolks, raw wheat germ, peas.

Symptoms of Deficiency. Deficiencies of manganese, which usually appear in the context of general malnutrition, may lead to retarded growth, abnormal bone development and deformities, digestive disturbances, and muscular-coordination failure. Deficiency in infants may lead to paralysis, convulsion, blindness, and deafness. It also may affect glucose tolerance and be a factor in diabetes.

Phosphorus

Functions. Phosphorus functions in the body as a partner to calcium. In a healthy body the balance between calcium and phosphorus is 2.5:1. Phosphorus is very important in the formation of healthy bones and teeth, and it is needed to maintain healthy nerves and efficient mental activity. It also plays an important role in the metabolism of carbohydrates, fats, and proteins, and is therefore essential for the growth, maintenance, and repair of cells and the production of energy.

Sources. Whole grains, seeds, nuts, legumes, egg yolks, dairy products.

Symptoms of Deficiency. Though not common in the United States, phosphorus deficiency may result in retarded growth, poor bone and tooth quality, tooth decay, nervous

		Amount	Iron (mg)			Amount	Iron (mg)
Fruits	prune juice	1 cup	10.5	Vegetables	asparagus (raw)	1 spear	1.6
	prunes (dried and softened)	1 cup	6.3		beet greens (raw)	3.5 oz.	3.3
	prunes (cooked)	1 cup	4.8		beet greens (cooked)	1 cup	2.8
	elderberries (raw)	1 cup	7.3		broccoli (cooked)	1 cup	1.2
	apricots (dried)	1 cup	7.2		Brussels sprouts (cooked)	1 cup	1.7
	raisins	1 cup	5.8		Swiss chard (raw)	3.5 oz.	3.2
	dates	1 cup	5.3		dandelion greens (steamed)	1 cup.	3.3
	dried figs	4	2.5		Jerusalem artichoke (raw)	4 small	3.4
					kale (raw)	3.5 oz.	2.2
Beans	black beans (dry)	½ cup	7.8		parsley (raw)	1 cup	3.7
	chickpeas (cooked)	1 cup	6.9		spinach (raw)	1 cup	1.7
	split peas (cooked)	1 cup	10.2		New Zealand spinach (raw)	1 cup	2.6
	pinto beans (cooked)	1 cup	6.1		tomato juice	1 cup	2.2
	lima beans (cooked)	1 cup	6.0		tomato paste	1 cup	9.2
	lima beans (green)	1 cup	4.3		tomato puree	1 cup	4.2
	soybeans (cooked)	1 cup	5.4		potato flour	1 cup	19.0
	tofu	4 oz.	2.3				
	soy milk	1 cup	9.9	Grains	rice bran	1 cup	16.9
	navy beans (cooked)	1 cup	5.1		wheat germ (raw)	1 cup	9.4
	lentils (cooked)	1 cup	4.2		wheat germ (toasted)	1 cup	8.0
					wheat bran (raw)	1 cup	4.5
Nuts and Seeds	pumpkin and squash seeds	1 cup	16.0		millet (dry)	1 cup	15.5
	sunflower seeds	1 cup	10.3		barley (dry)	1 cup	5.4
	sesame seeds	1 cup	9.6		rice (dry)	1 cup	3.3
	almonds	1 cup	6.6		bulghur (dry)	1 cup	6.3
	black walnuts	1 cup	6.1		soy flour	1 cup	9.9
	peanuts (roasted)	1 cup	5.3		whole wheat flour	1 cup	4.0
				Supplemental Foods	blackstrap molasses	1 tbsp.	3.2
					nutritional yeast	1 tbsp.	1.7

Herbs rich in iron (recommended for pregnant women): burdock root, mullein leaves, parsley, nettle, strawberry leaves, watercress, yellow dock.

Source: Courtesy of Barry D. Elson, M.D.

disorders, brain malfunction, general weakness, and possibly rickets. Loss of appetite and weight loss or gain may also occur.

Potassium

Functions. Potassium is essential for normal growth, muscle contraction and nourishment, and proper heart functioning, and it facilitates normal nerve impulse conduction. It serves as an alkalizing agent in acid-alkaline balance in the blood and tissues. It keeps the skin healthy, and it aids in converting glucose to glycogen for energy. It also helps the kidneys to detoxify the blood, and it promotes the secretion of necessary hormones.

Sources. Vegetables, especially green leafy vegetables, oranges, whole grains, sunflower seeds, nuts and milk, potatoes, bananas, and mint leaves.

Symptoms of Deficiency. Young infants who suffer from chronic diarrhea may develop potassium deficiencies. Early symptoms of potassium deficiency may include general weakness and fatigue, poor reflexes, and soft, weak muscles. Adolescents deficient in potassium may develop acne.

Sodium

Functions. Sodium helps to maintain normal fluid levels in the cells. It helps keep other minerals in the blood soluble so that they do not build us as deposits in the bloodstream. Sodium also plays an important role in digestion and in many glandular secretions and other bodily functions.

Sources. Kelp, celery, watermelon, asparagus, sea salt, and virtually all foods.

Symptoms of Deficiency. Most people ingest sodium far in *excess* of the amount needed for optimum health. Over-consumption may contribute to the development of high blood pressure, which may lead to other complications. The best way to reduce sodium is by eliminating the use of table salt.

In the rare cases of sodium deficiency, symptoms may include intestinal gas, weight loss, vomiting, muscle shrinkage, mental apathy, and respiratory failure. Some causes of sodium deficiency may be excessive sweating and chronic diarrhea.

Sulfur

Functions. Sulfur is known as the "beauty mineral" because it maintains glossy hair, a clear and youthful complexion, and healthy nails. It is also involved in oxidation-reduction reactions, in tissue respiration and tissue formation, and in collagen synthesis.

Sources. Legumes, nuts, seeds, eggs, cabbage, dried beans, Brussels sprouts, radishes, turnips, celery, onions, string beans, horseradish, watercress, soybeans, and kale.

Symptoms of Deficiency. Skin disorders such as eczema, blemishes, and rashes, and brittle nails and hair may result from sulfur deficiency.

Zinc

Functions. Zinc is vital in the formation of DNA, the principal constituent of chromosomes, which transmit genetic traits. Zinc is essential to the normal development of the reproductive organs, particularly to the normal functioning of the prostate gland. It plays a part in the absorption and action of vitamins, particularly the B complex. It is helpful to other enzymes in the processes of digestion and metabolism. It is a vital constituent of insulin and is involved in carbohydrate metabolism. It speeds up the healing of wounds and burns and is essential in normal bone formation.

Sources. Wheat germ, wheat bran, pumpkin seeds, sunflower seeds, brewer's yeast, milk, eggs, onions, nuts, and green leafy vegetables. Sour-dough whole grain bread makes zinc available and easily assimilable. Sprouted grains have the same effect.

DO CHILDREN NEED VITAMIN AND MINERAL SUPPLEMENTS?

As can readily be seen from the preceding sections, vitamins and minerals play an essential role in every aspect of normal physical, emotional, and mental development. In order that a child's diet supply all the necessary vitamins and minerals, he will need to eat consistently from high-quality natural food sources. Since junk foods, sugar, and refined foods in general contribute "empty" calories and often act as "antivitamins" and "antiminerals," we recommend that they be eliminated from the diet. It is not only possible but quite easy to feed children nutritious meals made from natural foods that they really enjoy. The recipe section of this book is specifically designed with their health as well as their tendency to fussiness in mind. To provide an additional measure of safety, we also suggest using a *natural* multivitamin and mineral supplement formulated for children.

Some readers may take exception to using supplements, especially in pill form, because they feel these are unnatural, even though they may be made from natural sources. We ask such readers to carefully consider our four main reasons for recommending multivitamin and mineral supplementation:

1. Parents tend to develop a more or less fixed repertoire of meals they provide for their children, usually based on about a one-week cycle. It is quite possible that this repertoire of meals may inadvertently fail to provide all the vitamins and minerals that growing children need every day.

2. In spite of parents' best intentions, children at different times vary widely in their food intake. Daily supplementation is like health insurance against those times when they are not eating well. Few children will object to swallowing a tablespoon of a pleasant-tasting vitamin-mineral tonic or chewing a sweet-tasting tablet—or, if they are older, swallowing a tasteless pill with a little water.

3. The soil in many parts of the United States is now known to be deficient in important minerals. Food grown in such soil is therefore also deficient in those minerals. Supplementation can help to provide those few nutrients that even natural foods may lack.

4. In most communities in the United States today, to a greater or lesser extent depending on where they are situated, people routinely breathe toxins in the air and drink chemical pollutants in the water. Radiation and pollution are growing worse all the time, to the point where people in several communities now are terribly concerned about their own lives, the health of their offspring, and the possible damage to future generations. This is a present-day

reality that can rightly be called a plague on our children. Vitamins and minerals have been shown to provide a degree of protection against these invisible forces, and the use of supplements as a protective buffer against environmental poisons may be extremely helpful while this danger threatens us. Certainly the addition of a multivitamin-mineral supplement to a child's diet will do no harm in this regard. Parents living in places that are particularly threatened may wish to consult a physician trained in prophylactic vitamin therapy, who may recommend larger doses of certain vitamins or minerals.

In cases where an inadequate or refined-food diet over a sustained period of time has created symptoms of nutritional deficiency, parents are well advised to seek the guidance of a nutritional therapist, who may or may not use massive vitamin and mineral supplementation to reestablish nutritional balance. "Megavitamin" or "orthomolecular" therapy should only be recommended on an individual basis by a trained nutritionist or physician, as each person's needs vary according to age, weight, and physical, emotional, and mental characteristics.

Remember that children should not be encouraged to think that popping vitamin pills is all the nutrition they need be concerned about. Children need nutritional education and, perhaps even more importantly, a consistently good dietary example provided by their parents.

SUPPLEMENTARY NATURAL FOODS

In addition to the use of a natural multivitamin-mineral supplement formulated for children, we also recommend the liberal use of the following natural supplementary foods. Some of these foods are excellent healthful alternatives to undesirable products. For example, carob powder is a delicious, nutritious, and naturally sweet substitute for cocoa, which contains caffeine, a proven antivitamin. Others of these foods can be used to "beef up" a recipe, without the child's ever realizing he is eating it. For example, a tasteless brewer's yeast or nutritional yeast added to a bean dish improves its nutritional quality immensely.

Alfalfa

The sprouts of this leguminous plant are now sold in many supermarkets in the United States and Canada and in most natural food stores. It is easy to sprout alfalfa seed at home. Alfalfa sprouts contain high quantities of many vitamins and minerals, especially vitamin K and calcium. They have the advantage of providing a delicious fresh vegetable in the wintertime, when many fresh vegetables are out of season.

Blackstrap Molasses

Blackstrap molasses contains more calcium than milk, more iron than eggs, and the most potassium of any food. It is rich in copper, magnesium, phosphorus, pantothenic acid, inositol, vitamin B complex, and vitamin E. Try blending a tablespoon of it with a glass of milk for a nutritious milkshake that children really enjoy.

Brewer's Yeast and Nutritional Yeast

Because of their rather bitter taste, children usually do not like these yeasts. However, there are now brewer's yeasts and nutritional yeasts available that are quite palatable and suitable for children. Brewer's yeast and nutritional yeast contain the highest amount of B vitamins compared to any other food. They contain sixteen amino acids, fourteen minerals, and seventeen vitamins, and are one of the best sources of RNA, a nucleic acid that helps prevent premature bodily degeneration. They also help to prevent constipation and for this reason alone can be very valuable in a child's diet.

Carob

Carob, or St. John's bread, is ground into a fine flour that makes an excellent sweet substitute for cocoa. It is a bowel conditioner and is high in calcium, potassium, phosphorus, magnesium, and iron. It also contains vitamin A, niacin, and traces of B_1 and B_2. It contains 2 percent fat, compared with 52 percent fat in cocoa. It is even a safe food for babies.

Dulse

Dulse is a dried red seaweed popular in Scotland, Ireland, and Iceland. It makes an excellent substitute for salt. It contains 23.5 percent protein, 44.3 percent carbohydrates, 26.7 percent mineral salts, and 3.8 percent fats. It is very high in iodine, is a good source of vitamin B_{12}, and is rich in all the needed minerals because, unlike land plants, its minerals are constantly replenished by its saltwater environment. Dulse is very good added to salads, although it should first be washed in fresh water. Children often enjoy munching on a small piece of dulse as a snack. It can be bought at many natural food stores.

Kelp

Like dulse, kelp is a seaweed extremely rich in essential minerals. It makes an excellent salt substitute. It is available in dried, powdered, and tablet forms.

Malt

Malt is a delicious and nutritious substitute for sugar and honey. It is made from germinated barley that has been cooked into a sweet syrup. Malt is high in enzymes. B-complex vitamins, and minerals and is used as a tonic in wasting diseases. It is about 40 percent as sweet as sucrose (sugar) and can be used to make healthful candies for children (see chapter 17). It is also excellent in baking.

Sesame Tahini

Because children tend not to chew sesame seeds well, the seeds often pass out in the stool completely undigested. Since sesame seeds are an excellent source of calcium and vitamin E, tahini, an oily paste made from sesame seeds, is an extremely easy-to-digest supplementary food. It is also high in lecithin, a natural demulcent found in every cell in the body. Tahini can be bought at most natural food stores and Middle Eastern food stores. It can be used in salad dressings or mixed with malt to form a delicious and healthful "candy." We use it extensively in the recipe section of this book.

Wheat Germ

Wheat germ is the heart of the wheat kernel, and is usually milled away in the refining process. It is high in protein, B-complex vitamins, vitamin E, iron, copper, magnesium, calcium, and phosphorous. It is extremely healthful served with milk as a cereal. Children like it, and a little goes a long way.

5.

FATS: OVERUSED
AND UNDERRATED

FAT is an ugly word in weight-conscious America, and well it ought to be. Forty-five percent of the calorie intake of the average American is in the form of fat. This represents so much more fat than is actually needed by the average person that the Senate Select Committee on Nutrition has made the substantial reduction of dietary fat consumption a *national dietary goal*. Certainly such habitual overconsumption of fat, which is extremely high in calories, routinely displaces the nutritional contribution of many essential nutrients needed by adults and, more pertinently, by growing children.

Fortunately, the average vegetarian diet is substantially lower in fat than the average conventional American diet. Nevertheless the facts about fat need to be clearly understood so that parents can discriminate among the various types of oil on the market as well as other foods whose fat content is invisible.

THE ROLE OF FATS IN THE DIET

Fats supply concentrated energy and carry fat-soluble vitamins. In addition they are a valuable source of essential fatty acids, which are necessary for normal growth and healthy blood, arteries, and nerves. Fats also work as lubrication for the body much as oil lubricates the pistons of a car.

Fat, then, is an essential nutrient. But just as a car's engine will cease to function properly if too much oil is poured into it, so too will the human body suffer from an oversupply of fat. Fats are "hidden" in a variety of foods, including eggs, beans, nuts, avocados, and cheese. Therefore, care should be taken to regulate fat intake.

The average American consumes about twice as much total dietary fat as he needs, about a 100 pounds per year. Since a gram of fat generates 9 calories, or two and a quarter times more calories than a gram of carbohydrates, it is easy to see that even small quantities of fat contribute relatively large amounts of calories. Although individual differences in metabolism and activity will exert some control over how quickly calories are burned, generally when more calories are consumed than used, the excess is converted into body fat.

If too many calories are consumed over a period of time, obesity results. Obesity has been definitively linked to diabetes, hypertension, arteriosclerosis, heart disease, gall bladder disease, and liver disease. It can be postulated, therefore, that the earlier a child gets started on a high-fat, high-calorie diet, the greater his chances will be of developing one of these dreaded diseases at some time in his life.

Of course, not all body fat is useless blubber that bodes only danger to health and growth. Fatty tissue is needed by the body to provide insulation from the cold, to conserve internal body heat, and to protect vital organs by acting as a shock absorber. The amount of fatty tissue needed depends on locality, season, and climate. In most of North America children obviously need more fat for warmth in winter than in summer. Similarly, Eskimo children need to be chubbier than Mexican children to maintain healthy activity.

SATURATED VERSUS UNSATURATED FAT

In addition to the question of the quantity of fat in the diet, there is a raging debate over the *kinds* of fat that are healthful. Central to this debate are the terms "saturated," "unsaturated," "polyunsaturated," and "cholesterol." As with many popularized concepts, these terms have been exploited by advertisers for the sake of corporate profits. But despite the widespread publicity, these terms remain largely misunderstood. What do they really mean?

All fats are made up of two substances: fatty acids and glycerin. Fatty acids consist basically of carbon atoms and hydrogen atoms. The following illustration shows the molecular structure of one unit of fatty acid.

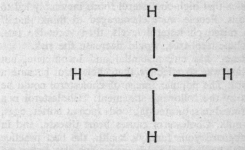

When the carbon atom at the center is attached to the maximum four hydrogens it can take, as illustrated, it is considered hydrogen-"saturated." But when the carbon atom at the center is surrounded by fewer than four hydrogen atoms, it is called "unsaturated" because it has the ability to take on more hydrogen atoms. When a particular fat contains several unsaturated fatty acids, it is referred to as "polyunsaturated," *poly* meaning "many." Animal fats are saturated, and most vegetable fats are polyunsaturated.

The difference between saturated and polyunsaturated, then, is simply one of hydrogen saturation. However, saturated fats contain cholesterol, a substance that has gained a very poor reputation in the past twenty years.

The Cholesterol Controversy

The cholesterol controversy reached its peak in the 1950s when medical researchers felt tremendous frustration about their inability to deal with the rapidly increasing rate of arterioscelerosis. Earlier in the century it had been found that severe arteriosclerosis is often accompanied by high levels of cholesterol in the blood. The cholesterol formed plaques in the arteries of arteriosclerosis victims, eventually strangling the blood supply to the heart. From this observation medical researchers assumed that cholesterol caused arteriosclerosis and that reduced cholesterol consumption would help to prevent the disease. Therefore high-cholesterol foods, such as eggs, dairy products, and animal fats, began to come under increasing fire. By the 1950s a massive advertising campaign was launched that first promoted the idea that high-cholesterol foods inevitably led to arteriosclerosis. People were encouraged to think that if animal fats raised cholesterol levels, then vegetable fats, which are cholesterol-free, would decrease the risk.

The evidence was circumstantial and incomplete, but the advertising was so effective that cholesterol became a dreaded word. The popular image of cholesterol could be summarized by the following statement: "Cholesterol is a kind of fat found in saturated-fat foods such as butter, eggs, and whole milk. Cholesterol causes heart disease, and in order to safeguard your family's health, the best practice is to omit high-cholesterol foods from your diet. Saturated fats should be replaced by polyunsaturated fats, which contain no cholesterol. A healthful diet is as low as possible in cholesterol." Is this statement true or false? Let us look closely at the actual nature of cholesterol as evidenced by extensive and recent research.

Most people think that cholesterol is a kind of fat. It is really an alcohol in solid form that is present in saturated fats in such food as egg yolks and dairy products. It is true that polyunsaturated fats, such as vegetable oils, are cholesterol-free. But contrary to the notion that cholesterol is "bad for you," it is absolutely essential in human metabolism; without its presence in all body tissues, especially in the brain, the spinal cord, nerves, liver, and blood, we would die. In fact, it is so important to human life that even if you were to eat a cholesterol-free diet, your body would manufacture its own supply to suit its needs. Every day the body manufactures three to four times as much cholesterol as could possibly be consumed in the diet. If you reduce your dietary cholesterol intake, your body produces more of it, and if you increase your cholesterol intake, your body produces less of it. No matter what you do, cholesterol will always be present in the body.

In his book *Food Is Your Best Medicine*, Dr. Henry G. Bieler underscores the role of cholesterol in the bloodstream by comparing the flow of blood through the blood vessels to the flow of a mighty river. The flow of blood is so powerful, he says, that unless the vessels through which it flows contains an excellent lubricant, it would, like a mighty river, quickly erode the natural channels—the blood vessels, veins, and arteries. The result would be a flood inside the body that would literally cause us to drown in our own blood. However, nature prevents that from happening by providing us with an ideal lubricant. We now know that this lubricant is cholesterol.

However, there are finer and coarser grades of cholesterol, just as there are varying grades of automotive oil. A poor grade of oil provides inferior lubrication for the pistons of a car, and they can be expected to break down much sooner than if a better quality oil had been used. Some respected nutritionists now think that the use of refined, bleached, or otherwise processed fats and oils, so commonly used in Western countries, is a substantial factor in causing an inferior cholesterol to be developed in the human body. It is this inferior cholesterol which breaks down easily and contributes to the formation of plaques in the blood vessels, the first sign of arterial disease.

Between 1949 and 1973, 65 percent of American families gave up butter because of its high cholesterol content and replaced it with margarine, a highly processed fat that advertisements often proclaim is "cholesterol-free." Very few people, even today, realize that although margarines are indeed made from cholesterol-free polyunsaturated vegetable oils, the margarines themselves are actually saturated fats and contain artificial cholesterol. During hydrogenation, the process used to make the oils solid at room temperature, a saturated fat similar to beef fat is actually created by the chemical reaction that takes place. Thus, people who switched from butter to margarine because they wanted to reduce or eliminate cholesterol defeated their own purpose. In 1949, at the beginning of the mass conversion to margarine, 400,000 people died of heart disease, and by 1973 this figure had doubled to 800,000. Indeed the facts support the views of researchers like Dr. Henry Bieler and Dr. Roger Williams, who made the point that fats, whether saturated or unsaturated, should be as little processed as possible if health is a genuine priority.

In addition to the overconsumption of fats, there is mounting evidence that a number of other factors, both dietary and nondietary, may contribute to high cholesterol levels. Lack of exercise, stress, smoking, overeating, and the consumption of refined sugars and carbohydrates have all been shown to increase cholesterol levels. These factors, in conjunction with a diet high in processed fats such as margarine, undoubtedly prove to be a deadly combination. A less stressful, less sedentary life style and the strict use of only natural fats, contributing a reasonable quantity to the total caloric intake, will go a long way toward preventing obesity and high cholesterol levels.

Should Eggs Be Cut Out of the Diet?

The same sort of anticholesterol campaign that was aimed at butter has also affected the consumption of eggs in the last twenty years. We consider eggs to be a highly nutritious food source, and unless you or your children suffer from egg-related allergies, we highly recommend the use of free-range fertilized eggs. Although eggs do have high levels of cholesterol, they also contain large quantities of lecithin, a natural emulsifier that has been shown to be effective in dissolving cholesterol deposits. In fact, eggs contain no more than enough lecithin to emulsify their cholesterol content. Beans and peas also contain lecithin, and their inclusion in the diet, coupled with the regular use of whole grains, is effective in reducing serum cholesterol levels.

COOKING WITH FATS AND OILS

The choice and quality of oils or fats that are used in cooking have important health repercussions.

For general cooking purposes (except frying) we recommend using only the highest-quality fresh unbleached, unrefined vegetable oils of the type sold in natural food stores. However, these natural vegetable oils are most useful in the diet if they are eaten primarily in their uncooked state—for example, in salad dressings. They are high in natural preservatives such as vitamin E and lecithin, which provide protection against rancidity. If unrefined natural oils are used as a regular ingredient in the diet, their poly-unsaturates, vitamin E, lecithin, and other trace nutrients such as copper, magnesium, calcium, and iron can prove to be helpful in general health maintenance. This is not the case with heavily processed conventional oils (even the ones whose labels loudly proclaim that they are "poly-unsaturated" are suspect) as most of their nutritive value has been bleached, heated, and refined away.

Natural oils will keep from four to six months if they are stored in tightly sealed dark containers. To maintain fresh-ness and avoid rancidity, it is best to refrigerate oils. Rancid oils are extremely toxic and should not be eaten.

We believe that it is generally more healthful to fry foods only occasionally, and when you do so the choice of cook-ing oil is very important. However, most children enjoy fried foods, and while we caution against making fried foods a habit, we recognize the need to satisfy children's tastes to a certain degree.

Vegetable oils are not suitable for use in frying. When heated beyond 200° F (the normal frying temperature is 400° F), vegetables oils lose their integrity, rapidly caus-ing their oxygen molecules to become reactive. The result is that vitamins and other intrinsic molecules are burned up or changed, making them unusable in the body.

In addition, frying temperatures have been shown to cause unsaturated oils to become saturated and to raise the cholesterol level. Butterfat is not affected by heat in exactly the same way vegetable oils are, and may there-fore be preferable for frying. In experiments, animals fed foods fried in polyunsaturated vegetable oils sickened and eventually died, while the same food fried in butter apparently left no side effects at all.

Although in general fats and oils should be tampered with as little as possible, the example of Indian cooking habits may provide a clue to how butter may be used beneficially in cooking and frying. In Ayurvedic medicine, the traditional health system of India, many virtues have been attributed to ghee (clarified butter), and it has been used in India for thousands of years as a cooking oil as well as in the preparation of medicinal remedies. It is said that ghee has the ability to take on and magnify the properties of foods and herbs with which it is combined. Unlike butter, which bleaches and smokes when it is heated beyond a certain temperature, ghee remains quite stable and imparts a delicious, sweet taste and a pleasant smell to foods. Children love its taste. We have used it for over ten years and recommend it as a cooking and frying oil *par excellence*. In addition it keeps extremely well and need not be refrigerated.

HOW TO MAKE CLARIFIED
BUTTER (GHEE)

Place one pound of unsalted (sweet) butter in a saucepan and heat until the butter boils. Now lower the heat and allow the butter to continue to boil. Its water content will begin to evaporate. After a few minutes the milk solids in the melted butter will begin to accumulate on the top. Allow these solids to thicken and then begin to skim them off the top with a spoon. Allow the butter to continue boiling gently. Every few minutes skim the milk solids off the top. Some of the solids will fall to the bottom. When these solids are a golden-brown color and when the oily portion of the butter becomes clear, remove the pan from the heat. Let the ghee stand for a few minutes and then pour it into a glass or earthenware container. Ghee need not be refrigerated and can be kept near stove until ready for use.

The remaining milk solids can be mixed with the original skimmings and refrigerated for later use on toast. Children particularly love these lightly roasted skimmings.

FATS SURVIVAL PLAN

The points that follow summarize this chapter and are designed to help you make appropriate decisions about the use of fat in your family's diet.

1. As far as possible, avoid frying with oils. Ghee (clarified butter) is a superior fat for frying purposes, and is not subject to the same polymerization as vegetable oils.

2. For cooking and salad oils, use only natural, unrefined oils that are free of preservatives and chemicals. Such oils contain vitamin E, a natural preservative, and lecithin, a natural emulsifier.

3. Avoid margarine. Moreover, when purchasing prepared foods, check the label to be sure that margarine and other hydrogenated oils are not among the ingredients. Margarine is manufactured from vegetable oils that, in addition to being refined and bleached, contain chemicals and preservatives. When such oils are hydrogenated, the results for health are questionable indeed. Butter, although a saturated fat, is a natural product, unlike margarine. Several research studies suggest that unlike other animal fats (such as meat fat), butter actually has a protective effect on the heart.

4. Raw, unhomogenized whole milk, although rich in cream, a saturated fat, is much more healthful than skim milk. Homemade fresh yogurt made from such milk is easy to digest and contains helpful digestive bacteria. Moreover, milk products are particularly helpful to vegetarian children, especially ones who tend to be finicky eaters. For children who are allergic to milk products, soy milk and tofu are excellent substitutes.

5. Eggs do not constitute a cholesterol risk. Actually they are an extremely nutritious food, high in protein. They also contain large quantities of lecithin, which acts to dissolve excess cholesterol. Eggs can easily be "hidden" in foods for finicky eaters. Soy milk and tofu are, again, excellent high-protein substitutes for eggs if your children are allergic.

6. Include generous and regular amounts of whole grains, dried beans and peas, and fresh vegetables and fruits in your family's diet. These foods have been shown to reduce cholesterol levels as well as the risk of heart disease.

7. When fatty foods are eaten, be sure that they are as close to their natural form as possible. If fat is a part of a natural food, it contains valuable nutrients. However, fatty food should be eaten in moderation.

THE STAGES OF
GROWTH AND THE
VEGETARIAN CHILD

6.

FEEDING THE
UNBORN CHILD

FROM the moment of conception, a pregnant woman is called upon to give of herself to the new life in her womb. For this tiny being, she is literally the earth mother—the total environment in which he will grow strong enough to venture out into the world nine months later.

Through the fluid inside the womb, the developing fetus hears and feels the constant reassurance of the mother's heartbeat, the sounds of digestion, and, more distantly, the sounds of voices and music and the million other sounds of daily life. The rise and fall of the mother's breath and the movements of her body provide a gentle rocking motion to soothe and comfort him. And since the mother's heartbeat and the rhythm of her breathing will vary with the speed and grace of her movements and emotions, every mood she experiences will affect the atmosphere of her baby's world. Therefore from early pregnancy on, the ways in which a woman increases her own joy and contentment are inextricably bound to her child's healthy development.

This is not to imply that a woman can or should always be calm. A loving home is composed of many moods—not only happiness, peace, and laughter, but sadness, anger, and tears as well. The vast majority of us are not free from depression and irritability; these moods, like our positive emotions, are felt in our bodies and it is likely that they affect the developing child. Since a pregnant woman is frequently emotional and sensitive as a result of the dramatic hormonal changes taking place in her body, it is reassuring to view these ups and downs as a necessary ebb and flow in the fetal environment. Expecting herself to be more perfect than the world her child will have to live in will only add psychological pressure to the experience of pregnancy. She can, however, consciously nurture herself with soothing, strengthening activities, such as yoga and meditation, throughout pregnancy to enhance the experience of child-bearing.

Beyond the environment a woman provides for her unborn baby, she also is the sole source of the food he needs for healthy development. By nourishing her own body properly, she nourishes the baby, too. If she is not well nourished, he will take from her body, in total innocence, her vitality, strength, good humor, and enthusiasm, leaving her tired, irritable, and resentful. If she does not consciously take tender care of herself while pregnant, she will suffer and her baby will still be inadequately fed.

The potential consequences of inadequate nutrition are frightening. Some scientists estimate that one out of ten babies born in the United States at present is abnormal, either mentally or physically. Nearly every expectant parent feels at least occasional anxiety about the health of the unborn. A pregnant vegetarian may be further worried by the warnings of well-meaning relatives, friends, and "experts" who are concerned about the dangers of protein, vitamin, and mineral deficiencies to the baby. It may be difficult for a committed vegetarian to accept, but these fears are not without foundation.

We live in a society that has lost touch with the traditions known in simpler cultures, in which sensible, nutritionally sound eating habits and ways of preparing for childbirth and feeding infants are passed on from mother to daughter. In contrast, American mothers often give birth under sedation, artificially have their milk dried up, and feed their children commercial formulas. We have to establish a new wisdom based on our own methods of understanding our needs.

Since our food comes to us from large production "farms" whose soil is often depleted of natural minerals, it is not possible to follow strictly the example of traditional societies in which food is largely produced in a family garden without chemical fertilizers. We must rather combine traditional knowledge with Western nutritional research and study, to evolve our own tradition worthy of passing on to our children. This new heritage begins with the special dietary needs of pregnancy.

PROTEIN FOR PREGNANCY

Protein has become a byword for nutrition in recent years, and rightly so. Nevertheless, there is an unwarranted preoccupation with, and a gross overconsumption of, protein foods in North America. While responsible scientific and governmental agencies recommend 54 grams of protein daily for a 167-pound man, and less for a lighter woman, most Americans consume twice that quantity daily, mainly in the form of meat and eggs. This "normal" diet is actually an extreme diet, laden with health hazards that accompany any unbalanced way of eating. We vegetarians are often accused of eating an unbalanced diet, and thus we may overreact to the suggestion that we are protein-deficient. The result can be strict adherence to a diet that, however well intentioned, is highly risky during pregnancy. Raw-food, mucusless, and sometimes macrobiotic diets, to name only a few, when undertaken with little nutritional knowledge, can be severely lacking in the protein needed for a healthy baby's prenatal development.

Setting vegetarian prejudices aside and looking at the nature of protein with an open mind, we find that protein is as essential to a baby's development as sunshine is to the growth of a garden. If you were to dehydrate a human body, you would find that the weight of the muscles is 80 percent protein, the weight of the skin is 70 percent protein, and the weight of the blood is 90 percent protein. Every living cell depends on protein. While you are pregnant, protein is literally building every cell of your baby's body. It is truly the process of growth that takes a human being from his beginnings as a unicellular organism, to a jellylike mass, and then rapidly to an embryo before gaining the weight necessary for a healthy birth.

Let us pause briefly to look at this marvelous process. At conception two germs cells fuse to form a one-celled organism with forty-six chromosomes. Then this cell vibrates so intensely that it explodes into two cells. By the time you are seven days pregnant, your future child, who is merely a cluster of cells at this time, has attached himself to your uterine wall and has begun to feed himself.

By the second week he is using this nourishment to form brain, blood, and skin cells. In the third week, he develops a tubular shape as his spinal cord grows. Already his brain and nervous system, eyes and ears, can be differentiated. Then, not much more than four weeks after conception, blood begins pumping through his microscopic circulatory system. His digestive tract is a little tube running from his mouth to his stomach, and he is budding arms and legs. The tiny creature who will be your child is now about a quarter-inch long but is rapidly becoming a recognizable human fetus.

In one month, he will be four times his present size. At eight weeks of age he will be one inch long with internal organs formed, covered with a layer of tissue and transparent skin, and with a heart that is beating.

During the third month of life, he will triple in size, becoming three inches long—clearly a human child with a skeleton of bones, fingers, toes, ears, and eyelids, all well formed even though he weighs only an ounce! His umbilical cord has grown longer, and he floats freely within your womb, passively receiving his nourishment through the placenta.

Although his basic structure is now complete, with the passage of the fourth month comes his first extraordinary gain of weight. He will be six inches long and weigh seven ounces at the end of his next month's growth. His weight has increased sevenfold in four weeks. His need for body-building nourishment has obviously taken an extraordinary leap forward.

In the fifth month more body parts are differentiated: Nails become harder, nipples become visible, and he becomes sensitive to sound. His length is not quite doubled this month. He grows to approximately twelve inches.

During the sixth and seventh months, the baby sucks his thumb, stretches, kicks, and turns somersaults in the womb. His organs begin to function independently. At the end of this period he will weigh two and a half pounds. In three months his weight has increased from approximately seven ounces to two and a half pounds—nearly a fivefold gain.

In the eighth month, the organs become completely self-sufficient in their functioning. Though still frail, he is approximately sixteen inches long.

In the ninth month, the baby settles into a quieter life: sleeping and eating. He no longer has room to turn around and kick, but keeps his knees folded and his arms crossed much of the time. The movements you feel and see at this time are probably the minimal stretches of the elbows or knees. During this last month, the baby continues to grow, reaching his full length, approximately nineteen inches, and full weight, anywhere from six and a half to ten and a half pounds. In the last period he has gained weight at an astounding rate. Just two months before, he weighted two and a half pounds; now he weighs between six and eight pounds. During this last period your body supplies the infant with special proteins and antibodies to ensure his health when he comes in contact with the world.

The last week spent in the womb is one of rest: Growth ceases while the baby waits to be born. In forty weeks he has grown from a single cell into a fully independent human being. Through the nourishment you have provided, a microscopic organism has grown into a full-size baby.

How Much Do You Need?

Protein needs vary greatly with each individual, depending on weight, stress, and ability to assimilate protein. Estimates set forth by governmental agencies have tended to be high in order to be sure that each individual would get an abundant, rather than a deficient supply. It is estimated that a 128-pound woman (who is not pregnant) should eat 46 grams of protein per day. If you are heavier, your daily requirement would be more, and if you are lighter, somewhat less. If you are under a great deal of stress, your protein intake should increase. On the other hand, if you are experiencing a calm and serene period of your life, your need for protein may be lessened, depending on your body type.

Pregnancy is a time of special protein needs. Extra protein is required not only for building the baby's body, but also for producing the necessary hormones, enzymes, antibodies, and blood cells, as well as for forming new tissue in the uterus and breasts. Pregnancy is often a period of stress alternating with joy, and for this reason, too, an abundance of protein is beneficial. Generally it is recommended that 30 grams of protein be added to the diet; this estimation seems safe and reasonable to us considering the special needs of both mother and child. If you weigh 128 pounds at the time you become pregnant, it is safe to assume you need 76 grams of protein throughout your pregnancy, although you may actually require slightly less during the first trimester and slightly more during the last trimester. Again, needs will vary according to body type, weight, and the stress of your day-to-day activity.

It is not difficult for a pregnant vegetarian to consume daily 76 grams of protein. During the first trimester of Nina's second pregnancy, she was as nauseated and miserable as she had been during the early months of her first pregnancy. Worried that the snatches of food she was eating every thirty minutes throughout the day were starving her and the baby of protein, she kept a running account of her food intake. It was a relief to discover that her daily tally did not fall below 70 grams very often. Since her normal weight is 96 pounds, this supply was more than adequate.

Sources of Protein During Pregnancy

Even nonvegetarians, we believe, would be wise to eliminate meat from their diet during pregnancy. Although meat may have once had nutritionally redeeming features, present-day methods of cattle and poultry production have made it a highly undesirable food for pregnant women.

Today 2,700 drugs are available for use in cattle. Of these, 152 drugs are routinely used in the production of beef and poultry; many of them are known to cause cancer, birth defects, and/or mutations in laboratory animals.

The most widely known of these drugs is DES, which is used in the breeding of at least 80 percent of the nation's cattle. This drug was given to pregnant women to prevent miscarriages in the 1950s. Recently, it has been proved that the drug causes a rare vaginal cancer in the daughters of the women who took it, causing many young women undue hardship and ironically rendering them incapable of bearing children. No one knows what dosage of DES caused this disastrous effect. Also, no one knows how much DES is present in the meat of cattle that are bred with the help of the drug. Researchers do know, however, that some residue is to be found in both the muscle and liver tissues of these animals. Only time will tell whether women who have eaten meat from cattle that were bred with the aid of DES are unconsciously contaminating their unborn children. In the meantime, there is little doubt that the questionable nature of many of the drugs contained in meat make it a food that pregnant vegetarians can feel entirely safe leaving out of their diets.

There is a multitude of other sources of protein—including beans, grains, tofu, gluten, dairy products, and soy products. By combining complementary-protein foods, as explained in chapter 2, you can get complete protein in a vegetarian diet.

In addition, during pregnancy you can get a protein boost by simply adding a high-protein ingredient to your favorite dishes. Breads and crackers can be made with soy flour or dry milk powder. Soy grits or soy granules are easily hidden in casseroles and vegetarian burgers. Noninstant dry milk can be blended into whole milk, puddings, and desserts. Tofu can be blended into creamy salad dressings. If you eat eggs, they can be added to nearly every main dish, bread, dessert, and salad dressing you eat. Eggnog can become a regular snack. With high protein meals and snacks such as these, you can easily get enough protein during the nine months of pregnancy.

Avoiding Protein-Deficiency Anemia

Nearly two-thirds of American women are anemic during pregnancy. Their blood is unable to transport sufficient oxygen, making them tired, dizzy, and short of breath. This condition also causes the baby to receive a deficient supply of oxygen. A substantial undersupply of oxygen caused by severe, prolonged anemia can be the cause of brain damage to the growing fetus. Also, an infant born to an anemic woman may be anemic himself.

Although iron deficiency is routinely believed to be the sole cause of anemia, it is only one of several possible inter-related causes. Protein-deficiency anemia in combination with generally poor nutrition habits can be a problem for a pregnant vegetarian who has no knowledge of protein complementation and thus has an insufficient total protein or insufficient complete protein intake.

Another possible source of anemia that can be linked to protein deficiency is vitamin B_{12} deficiency, which results in an inability to utilize protein. Most people receive vitamin B_{12} from animal food sources. It is available in dairy products and eggs as well as meat. The pregnant woman who uses no animal products will find her vitamin B_{12} sources in miso, tempeh, spirulina, seaweeds, brewer's and nutritional yeast, and comfrey. She should eat sub-stantial quantities of these while pregnant. Even with these foods, it may be wise for the vegan to take B_{12} supple-ments while pregnant. Protein-deficiency anemia compli-cates iron-deficiency anemia since inadequate protein inhibits the absorption of iron into the blood.

If she is anemic, an expectant mother should be certain to get up to 100 grams of protein per day, from comple-mentary sources, until the weakness subsides. If the anemia is serious, caused by a deficiency of protein and complicated by a deficiency of vitamin B_{12}, she might well consider adding fish to her diet as a therapeutic measure. Fish is extremely high in protein and vitamin B_{12}. Depending on your reasons for being vegetarian, this advice may or may not be palatable. Otherwise strict vegetarians we have known have eaten fish during pregnancy, acknowledging that the life and health of their child were more important than their ethical reservations.

Adelle Davis reports a study which showed that babies born of mothers who carried them during the summer months were less healthy than those who were carried during the winter months. Analysis of the respective diets showed that the summertime menus tended to lack protein because the pregnant women were naturally attracted to large quantities of fruits and salads and neglected heavier protein foods. In summer then, a pregnant vegetarian should choose her food with care to make sure she receives enough protein.

CALORIES AND WEIGHT GAIN

For years, pregnant women who gained more than 20 pounds were criticized or ridiculed by their doctors, husbands, and parents. This was not only unfair to women who spent much of their pregnancy hungry and feeling guilty about sneaking snacks, it was also medically unwise. Recent studies show that the least risk occurs to babies whose mothers gain more than 30 pounds and that the incidence of toxemia is not reduced by limiting weight gain. Apparently the old proverb that the pregnant woman is "eating for two" is closer to the truth than many people think.

According to the prestigious National Research Council's Committee on Maternal Nutrition: "The idea that the limitation of weight gain by caloric restriction protects against toxemia goes back to the observed reduction in the incidence of eclampsia [a form of toxemia] in Germany and Austria-Hungary during World War I. Because of the war there was a scarcity of meat and fats; pregnant women, therefore, gained less weight and it was concluded without further study that a restricted diet was protective. Caloric restriction to limit weight gain during pregnancy became widely advocated as a means for preventing toxemia and many other complications. The idea found its way into textbooks of obstetrics and was widely accepted by the medical profession. Seldom has a medical idea with such a base [hearsay evidence] been applied so widely and subjected to so little scientific study." Moreover, the committee declared that "there is no advantage to be gained by prescribing weight reduction regimens for obese patients during pregnancy either for improving the course of pregnancy or for contributing to the woman's general health. The possible danger of inducing ketosis [a condition associated with starvation and diabetes, causing acid imbalances in the blood] with accompanying hazards to the neurological development of the foetus, must be borne in mind."

It is interesting to note that the medical profession did not infer from the World War I experience that the reduction of fats and meats during pregnancy might prove beneficial to the prevention of toxemia. If this hypothesis has been carefully researched, it is possible that an entirely different approach may have been espoused by medical textbooks.

Although you may need to take care to eat enough during the first trimester because of nausea and fatigue, after that you need only follow your appetite and you will be certain to consume more than an adequate supply of calories. The number of pounds gained during pregnancy is less important than the quality of food eaten in response to genuine hunger. Eating a variety of whole foods and fresh produce, while avoiding refined carbohydrates and processed foods, is the vital issue. One of our closest friends, a woman who is nearly six feet tall with a delicate frame, gained 50 pounds during pregnancy, was vibrantly healthy, gave birth at home to a 9-pound boy, and lost the weight naturally after a few months of nursing.

Pregnancy is a time of body-building for both you and your child. It is not a time for extreme cleansing or purification techniques. Fasts, enemas, astringent herbs, sauna baths, vomiting, and yogic kriyas should not be undertaken at any time during pregnancy. Even during the first trimester, when well-meaning, self-taught "healers" may encourage you to fast, use strong herbal remedies (such as ginger, golden seal, garlic, or cayenne), take enemas, or induce vomiting as cures for nausea, these should not be undertaken. The discomfort of the first three months of pregnancy is not an illness in the normal sense. It is caused, not by impurities, but by a normal increase in hormonal activity that accompanies pregnancy. Although there are safe and beneficial ways to end your discomfort, these must be undertaken with extreme caution. Certainly the thalidomide experience of the past has taught that at this crucial time in fetal development, what is convenient for Mom is not necessarily convenient for baby.

SPECIAL NUTRITIONAL NEEDS

Expectant mothers cannot live by protein alone. The need for vital nutrients also increases dramatically during pregnancy. If you are already following a natural, vegetarian diet, you are in a good position to begin a pregnancy. However, there are particular nutrients that you may neglect during pregnancy if you are unaware of the additional need you and your baby have for certain vitamins and minerals. If you fulfill these special nutritional needs, you may avoid the discomforts that many doctors and women consider "normal." Pregnancy need not be a debilitating condition that leaves a mother feeling weak and older that her years.

A brief study of the following table will make you quickly aware of the special nutritional needs of pregnancy.

	Daily Requirement for Women Ages 23–50 (Weight: 128 lbs.)	Additional Need During Pregnancy
Calories for light activity	2,000	+300
Carbohydrates	300 g	same
Fats	66 g	same
Protein	46 g	+30 g
Minerals		
Calcium	800 mg	+400 mg
Iodine	150 mcg	+25 mcg
Iron	18 mg	+30–60 mg
Magnesium	300 mg	+150 mg
Phosphorus	800 mg	+400 mg
Potassium	Average daily intake 1,950–5,850 mg	
Sodium	Average daily intake 2,300–6,900 mg	
Zinc	15 mg	+5 mg

	Daily Requirement for Women Ages 23–50 (Weight: 128 lbs.)	Additional Need During Pregnancy
Vitamins		
Vitamin A	800 mcg RE (4,000 IU)	+200 mcg RE (+1,000 IU)
Thiamine (B₁)	1.0 mg	+0.4 mg
Riboflavin (B₂)	1.2 mg	+0.3 mg
Pyridoxine (B₆)	2.0 mg	+0.6 mg
Cyanocobalamin (B₁₂)	3.0 mcg	+1.0 mcg
Folacin	400 mcg	+400 mcg
Niacin	13 mg	+2 mg
Vitamin C	60 mg	+20 mg
Vitamin D	5 mcg (200 IU)	+5 mcg (200 IU)
Vitamin E	8 mg α - TE	+2 mg α - TE

Source: Food and Nutrition Board, National Academy of Sciences—National Research Council, *Recommended Daily Dietary Allowances*, revised 1980.

Calcium

If your pregnancy is characterized by nervousness, headaches, leg or foot cramps, insomnia, and tooth decay, it is possible that your body is not receiving an adequate supply of calcium. Acquiring enough calcium during pregnancy is difficult since needs are so substantially increased and since calcium is so hard to absorb, especially in the final trimester. Your body normally absorbs only 10 to 30 percent of the calcium it receives.

Foods high in calcium, including milk, almonds, sunflower seeds, cabbage, broccoli, navy beans, millet, watercress, dandelion greens, sesame seeds, endive, lettuce, kale, and Brussels sprouts, should be eaten frequently. (See also the table on page 61.)

Calcium absorption depends upon adequate amounts of

vitamin A, C, and D. It is also aided by relatively high protein and moderate fat intake. Phosphorus should be present in similar quantities. Factors that interfere with calcium absorption are stress, lack of exercise, excessive fat intake, and oxalic acid (found in chocolate, spinach, rhubarb, beet greens, and Swiss chard).

It is routinely recommended that pregnant women drink one quart of milk (we recommend only high-quality raw milk) daily. If you eat dairy products, and if you can tolerate this quantity, it is an advisable practice. The calcium in milk is more readily absorbed than that in many other sources. Flavoring milk, eggnog, and high-protein milk-based drinks with blackstrap molasses will give these drinks a substantial calcium boost.

Even with a conscientious diet, obtaining enough calcium is difficult; therefore, most nutritionists and doctors will encourage you to take a calcium supplement. Supplementation is certainly advisable if you are a vegan.

Iodine

Extra iodine is needed during pregnancy to develop the baby's thyroid. An inadequate supply of iodine during pregnancy poses grave health risks. Iodine-deficient babies have been found to have a condition called cretinism, retardation which occurs when iodine deficiency is severe enough to cause hypothyroidism.

The soil in North America has been depleted of iodine through the use of fertilizers and the overuse of land, so it is difficult to obtain the iodine you need from land vegetables. Seaweeds such as kelp, dulse, wakame, hiziki, and nori are, however, excellent sources of iodine. In Japan, thyroid conditions are nonexistent thanks to the widespread use of sea vegetables. Iodized sea salt is another excellent source.

Sea vegetables can be eaten in soups and salads daily. Or a teaspoon of kelp powder can be mixed into vegetable juice to ensure that your daily need for iodine is met. Iodine is best obtained from these natural sources, since high dosages can be extremely toxic.

Iron

As we have mentioned, iron deficiency may be one possible cause of anemia. There are other causative factors that may occur in conjunction with iron deficiency. Chief among these are protein-deficiency anemia and folate-deficiency anemia.

Iron is available in many foods, including whole grain breads, green vegetables, soy flour, soy granules, millet, hiziki seaweed, prune juice, pumpkin seeds, black beans, chickpeas, pinto beans, and split green peas. Beef liver is highly recommended by nonvegetarian nutritionists for its high iron content. However, liver has also been found to contain the drug DES (see page 89).

Nutritional yeast, blackstrap molasses, rice polishings, and chlorophyll are all extremely high in iron content. Nutritional yeast can be added to drinks and food; rice polishings can be added to drinks; blackstrap molasses can be added to drinks and baked goods; and a teaspoon of chlorophyll can be stirred into vegetable juice, water flavored with lemon, or peppermint tea. Iron absorption is nearly doubled when a 500-milligram supplement of natural vitamin C is added to the daily diet.

If you are making use of all these iron sources but are still in need of some iron supplementation (according to a laboratory-examined blood sample), we recommend the use of ferrous fumarate or ferrous gluconate. When iron supplements are taken with meals, absorption can be improved by as much as 100 percent. Vitamin E and iron should never be taken together, because vitamin E impairs iron absorption. Vitamin C helps iron absorption and should be taken at the same time as iron supplements.

Magnesium

Many women feel irritable, nervous, and moody during pregnancy. Magnesium, which is necessary for protein synthesis, often helps alleviate these symptoms. With the increased need for protein, calcium, and phosphorus during pregnancy comes a greater need for magnesium. Magnesium is lost through perspiration. Therefore, if you are pregnant during extremely hot weather, your need for this mineral may be increased even more. Taken in a natural supplement, magnesium is a laxative of great benefit if you experience constipation during pregnancy.

Adding bran, wheat germ, noninstant milk powder, and black walnuts to baked goods is an excellent way to increase magnesium in your diet. Millet is the grain highest in magnesium and can be eaten regularly during pregnancy. Stewed prunes and prune juice are also very good sources of magnesium as well as age-old remedies for constipation. Organically grown green leafy vegetables are an excellent source of magnesium. Leafy vegetables grown in soils that have been depleted are often extremely low in this important mineral.

Phosphorus

Phosphorus and calcium often occur naturally in the same foods. They are complementary nutrients that work together in bone development. However, phosphorus is much more readily absorbed by the body than calcium. About 70 percent of the phosphorus you ingest is utilized by the body, while only 10 to 30 percent of the calcium ingested is absorbed. Therefore, as long as an adequate supply of calcium is taken, phosphorus intake should not be a problem during pregnancy.

Zinc

Zinc is essential to the formation of DNA, making it vital for healthy fetal development. In addition, it has been shown that pregnant laboratory rats who are receiving adequate supplies of zinc deliver their young after about thirty seconds to two minutes of labor, while rats deprived of zinc undergo thirty minutes of difficult labor.

Since most of the soil in industrialized countries is depleted of zinc, kelp is a more reliable source than land vegetables. It can be added to vegetable soups or juices.

Vitamin A

Fetal malformations occur when pregnant women are deprived of vitamin A. The universally known vegetarian source of vitamin A is carrots. It is interesting to note, however, that only 1 percent of the carotene (which the body converts to vitamin A) is absorbed when carrots are eaten raw, while 30 percent of the carotene is absorbed if the carrots are cooked.

During pregnancy it is advisable not to avoid butter and cream. These may be a vegetarian's best natural sources of vitamin A.

Vitamin B Complex

The whole range of B vitamins is necessary for the proper prenatal development of a baby's brain. An adequate supply of all the B-complex vitamins will help ensure your child's normal intelligence. However, some of the B vitamins should be given special consideration during pregnancy.

A deficiency in Vitamin B_6 during the early months of pregnancy has, in some cases, been linked to mental retardation in infants. Other studies indicate that vitamin B_6 deficiency in early pregnancy is a cause of vomiting and nausea. Research has shown that as many as 95 percent of pregnant women are lacking in adequate amounts of this essential vitamin. One or more of the symptoms of B_6 deficiency are common to nearly every pregnant woman: abdominal pain, heartburn, intestinal cramps, nausea, vomiting, headaches, dry skin, leg aches, nervousness, insomnia, fatigue, flatulence, dizziness, dandruff, and an inability to concentrate.

B_6 can be obtained by adding nutritional yeast, low-fat soy flour, brown rice, pinto beans, and wheat germ to the diet in abundant quantities. However, if symptoms such as nausea and vomiting persist and are severe, the most reliable cure we know of is recommended by Adelle Davis: Take 10 milligrams of a B_6 supplement every hour and eat small amounts of high-protein, natural carbohydrate food every thirty minutes for several days. The amount of B_6 should be limited to 240 milligrams a day since recent studies have shown that extremely high doses of B_6 (600 milligrams or more per day) can have detrimental side effects, including an inability to produce adequate milk for nursing. Homebaked bread (fortified with nutritional yeast, milk powder, wheat germ, and/or eggs), aduki-bean brownies, eggnog, protein-fortified drinks, and rice cream cooked in soy milk are all good possibilities.

Lack of folacin, another B vitamin, is a possible cause of anemia in pregnancy, and a gross deficiency can lead to toxemia as well as miscarriages, premature labor, congenital defects, and still births. Folacin is not readily obtained in foods, nonprescriptive dosages are small, and often vitamins labeled "prenatal" contain no folacin. Many natural food and health food stores do, however, carry folacin supplements, especially for pregnant women.

Although most foods contain a small fraction of a milligram of folacin, one teaspoon of fenugreek seeds contains 2.11 milligrams. These seeds can be readily sprouted to obtain an excellent quantity of folacin for your added need during pregnancy.

Vitamin C

As we have already noted, vitamin C assists in the absorption of iron and is therefore vital to the prevention of anemia during pregnancy. However, beware of extremely high dosages of vitamin C during pregnancy. A recent study showed that pregnant women who took very high dosages of vitamin C gave birth to vitamin C–dependent babies. These children needed a daily supplemental dosage of viatmin C or they developed scurvy. A 500-milligram supplement of natural vitamin C seems to be a safe dosage during pregnancy. Natural sources high in vitamin C such as green peppers, oranges, and lemons should be eaten in season.

Vitamin E

Gross deficiencies in vitamin E can cause miscarriage, premature birth, varicose veins, and anemia. Vitamin E is helpful in ensuring that an adequate supply of oxygen reaches the fetus. However, vitamin E deficiency is often overlooked. If varicose veins accompany anemia, there is a very good chance that the anemia is related to vitamin E deficiency. If varicose veins occur at all, vitamin E should be increased.

Food	Measure	Calories	Calcium	Iodine	Iron	Magnesium	Phosphorus	Protein
Daily total								
Pregnancy RDA		2,300	1,200 mg	175 mcg	78 mg	450 mg	1,200 mg	74 g
+ (amount exceeding RDA)								
− (amount less than RDA)								

Food	Measure	Vitamin A	B₁	B₂	B₆	B₁₂	Folacin	Niacin	C	E
Daily total										
Pregnancy RDA		1000 mcg	1.4 mg	1.5 mg	2.6 mg	4 mg	800 mcg	15 mg	80 mg	10 mg α - TE
+ (amount exceeding RDA)										
− (amount less than RDA)										

Using Supplements During Pregnancy

A conscientious pregnant vegetarian may well obtain all the nutrients she needs from food. Antivitamins such as sugar, refined foods, tea, coffee, chocolate, alcohol, and tobacco, and other drugs should, of course, be strictly avoided by the expectant mother.

Even with the assurances offered by a varied and conscientious diet, however, there may be deficiencies in your diet that are beyond your control. A program of natural vitamin and mineral supplementation may thus be advisable for the majority of pregnant women. You will probably do well to seek the advice of a nutritionally informed doctor or a nutritionist in choosing a well-balanced program. Pills, however, cannot be regarded as a replacement for a nutritionally sound diet.

Salt and Liquids

At one time salt and liquids were restricted routinely in the diets of pregnant women. It was thought that these restrictions would prevent the water retention associated with toxemia. Now research shows that such restriction is detrimental and may even contribute to the development of eclampsia. During pregnancy the blood volume increases tremendously, and for this you need extra liquid. You may crave liquids and salt soon after conception. These are natural desires that help to ensure your health. You should drink whenever thirsty and add moderate amounts of salt (especially iodized sea salt) to your food.

KEEPING A DIET SHEET

It may be helpful to spot-check your diet for one week at a time periodically, so that you can take note of any deficiencies there may be and make adjustments accordingly. Also, your records may help to assure a skeptical obstetrician that your vegetarian diet is healthful. Keeping a diet sheet is also an effective way to imbue yourself with a knowledge of nutrition that will become "spontaneous" later. The form on pages 100–101 is specifically designed for use during pregnancy. (To calculate the amounts, see the *Nutrition Almanac* by Nutrition Research, Inc., and *Laurel's Kitchen* by L. Robertson et al., both listed in the Bibliography.)

7.

BORN VEGETARIAN

IN a sense we are all born "vegetarian." Like other mammals, at birth we instinctively desire to nurse from our mother's breast. Even before the placenta comes out, if a newborn infant is lightly touched on the cheek by a nipple or a finger, he will turn and direct his mouth toward the side where he was touched. Upon finding a nipple, he will suck. And as he sucks, he will clench his fist, being comforted if a small finger or bit of cloth is available for him to hold. When satisfied, his grip will ease.

In those first moments after birth, a mother's instincts are awakened. It has been observed that a mother who is left alone with her infant immediately after birth will stroke, cuddle, and communicate with him. After nursing him for a half-hour, the new mother will then fall asleep with the infant nestled in her left arm, close to the reassuring beat of her heart. Mothers who are allowed this period of intimacy are more likely to nurse and to remain patiently responsible to their child's needs. They are likely to continue to sleep with their babies for the first month, and they learn that their little ones will instinctively wiggle their way toward the breast when hungry. The natural instinct of nursing is reinforced whenever mother and child sleep together.

If instinct is allowed to take its natural course, without the interference of hospital officials or protective relatives, most mothers will gladly endure the discomforts and insecurities of nursing as a response to their baby's obvious need. Simply put, your baby needs the human contact provided by nursing. Studies have shown that babies brought up in institutions where their physical needs are completely taken care of, but where no time for cuddling is set aside, become retarded in development by six months of age.

THE NUTRITIONAL VALUE OF MOTHER'S MILK

Breast milk provides perfect nourishment, and there is no disputing that it is the only "natural" food for infants. The National Academy of Sciences confirms the value of mother's milk. In fact, the Recommended Daily Allowances for infants are based on the nutritional content of mother's milk.

Despite the growing recognition of the superiority of mother's milk, many myths about nursing abound. Some ill-informed people will tell you that there is no physical reason to nurse your baby rather than give him a "good formula." Studies comparing breast-fed and bottle-fed babies present reassuring evidence to the contrary. Babies who have been nursed have a higher resistance to infection, greater immunity, and fewer allergies.

In a classic study of 20,000 babies quoted by Adelle Davis in *Let's Have Healthy Children*, it was found that twice as many bottle-fed babies as breast-fed babies developed infections. Of those developing acute infections, 96.7 percent were bottle-fed babies. This difference is due to the immunity babies obtain directly from mother's milk.

Among breast-fed babies, allergies are nearly nonexistent, while 66 percent of bottle-fed babies are likely to experience allergies of some kind. Studies show that allergies in breast-fed babies occur in direct proportion to the length of time they nursed. The longer a baby receives mother's milk, the more likely it is that he will not develop allergies at any stage of his life, even if there is a history of allergy in his family.

These studies plus the nutrient value of milk should allay any doubt that nursing is the most healthful way to feed your infant. Breast milk contains more vitamin C, eight times more vitamin E, many times more linoleic acid (an essential fatty acid), more calcium, less phosphorus, and five times less sodium than cow's milk. Vitamins C and E help fight infection. Linoleic acid is essential to the healthy functioning of every human cell. Calcium is, of course, essential to the health of the skeletal structure including the teeth. Since phosphorus occurs in lesser proportions to calcium in mother's milk, it aids the utilization of calcium, magnesium, zinc, and other minerals more effectively than cow's milk. Thus, breast-fed babies have greater amounts of magnesium in their blood. Additionally, breast-fed babies have a much greater concentration of B vitamins in their intestines than bottle-fed infants do, and since B vitamins play such a significant role in health and well-being, this fact is significant.

NURSING IS GOOD FOR THE MOTHER, TOO

Occasionally, women respond to the urgings of relatives, doctors, or nurses who tell them nursing will be physically debilitating. These warnings could not be further from the truth. A new mother does need time to sleep and relax to allow her body to recover from childbirth—but what could be more restful, satisfying, and revitalizing than to sleep with your newborn child, awaking only to guide him to your breast and then drifting back to sleep while he contentedly continues to suck? Compare such a leisurely way of being to the demands of bottle-feeding: mixing formulas, sterilizing bottles, washing bottles, holding a bottle in a baby's mouth, and burping a baby who is much more likely to develop indigestion than a breast-fed infant. It seems to us that any woman would choose nature's way of restoring her energy while establishing her bond with her newborn baby.

Nursing enhances rather than harms your health. Women

who breast-feed directly after birth are much less likely to hemorrhage after childbirth. The sucking at the breast releases a powerful hormone, oxytocin, which causes the uterus to contract.

Nursing may also diminish the possibility of developing breast cancer in later life. Karen Pryor, in her book *Nursing Your Baby*, reports that the likelihood of contracting breast cancer diminishes from one chance in twenty-five to one chance in one hundred and twenty-five by nursing one child for six months. In countries where several children may be nursed for over a year, cancer of the breast is unknown. We have known women who became terribly concerned that their breasts would begin to sag after nursing and refused to perform this natural function. It seems ironic, if not tragic, that such vanity increases the possibility that they might lose their breasts altogether after contracting breast cancer.

There are minor discouraging developments associated with nursing that can easily be overcome with a little forewarning. We sincerely believe that almost any woman who wishes to breast-feed can do so with very little problem. Women of our mothers' generation were discouraged from nursing, and many taught their daughters that only exceptionally strong women can produce sufficient milk of suitable quality to feed a rapidly growing infant. This is simply not true.

It is only in extreme cases of disease that nursing becomes either impossible or unwise. A woman's desire to nurse, coupled with a healthy diet, are the largest single factors governing her ability. That some women who truly want to nurse can is illustrated dramatically by a number of women who are able to nurse adopted infants without even having been pregnant. The first reports of mothers feeding adopted offspring come from New Guinea and Sicily. Women in both areas were able to produce enough milk to feed their adopted babies simply by allowing the infants to suck all they wished.

The La Leche League, long a support to nursing mothers all over the world, has helped American mothers who are unable to have their own children to have the gratifying experience of nursing their adopted infants. The mother patiently sits with a bottle of warm formula by her side while her child sucks. When the child becomes distracted or discouraged, he is encouraged to continue sucking by having formula dropped onto the nipple with a medicine dropper. Within two weeks many women are producing their own milk supply. As the infant continues to suck, the milk supply becomes sufficient to meet his total food needs.

MINUTES OLD: FIRST FEEDING

In spite of your best intention, you may encounter your first deterrent to nursing even before your child is born. You will be told that babies suck so hard and long that your nipples will be sore and inflamed. It's true! You can, however, prevent some of this discomfort by having your husband suck your breasts for extended lengths of time and/or by washing your nipples daily with a solution of a quarter teaspoon of sea salt to one cup water for one month before your expected date of delivery. A mixture of equal parts of lanolin and wheat germ oil rubbed on the nipples regularly may also be helpful in this regard.

Moments after your child is born, you may meet your second discouraging experience. If your baby is born in a hospital, you will want to nurse him immediately and the nurses and doctor may reluctantly place him in your arms. Then, in an attempt to "help" your infant, a nurse may place his mouth on your nipple. Often the infant will not respond, but instead will be confused. The nurse may confidently announce that most babies refuse the breast immediately after birth. You and your husband may have to tell the nurse directly to be patient and not to touch your child's face. Then you can practice your knowledge of an infant's instinctual need to "grasp" by touching his cheek with your nipple. He will begin to search for the nipple with his open mouth, and you can gently guide it between his lips. He will pull the nipple into his mouth, but he may not suck until his sucking instinct is stimulated by the touch of an object near the back of his palette. If your nipples are long and pointed, you are likely to stimulate the nursing reflex immediately in your infant. If they are rounded or inverted, your baby may need a little help. Simply insert your finger gently into his grasping mouth. When you touch the proper place, he will begin to suck. Replace your finger with your nipple and he will get his first taste of "natural food."

Interfering people may also discourage you from nursing for more than a few minutes directly after birth. They will warn you that your nipples will become sore and that "you don't have milk yet anyway." Depending on the preparation you have made for nursing and on the sensitivity of your skin, your nipples may be a little sore, but this soreness will pass as your nipples become accustomed to your baby's insistent sucking. Moreover, the food provided your baby in the first minutes, hours, and days is of the utmost importance to his future health.

Nature's Preventive: Colostrum

The claim that nursing during the first hours and days after birth is unimportant is based on a gross misunderstanding of nature's wisdom. Colostrum, the thick yellow liquid that the nipples can begin to excrete as early as the fifth month of pregnancy, is perhaps the most important food your baby will receive throughout his lifetime. It is the medicine that assures his health in infancy.

Babies are born without stores of vitamin A or E, which protect against infection, bronchitis, and pneumonia. Colostrum contains five times as much vitamin A, twelve times as much carotene (which the body converts to vitamin A), and seven times as much vitamin E as the mother's milk that replaces it in a few days. Colostrum also contains three to four times more antibodies and antitoxins as extra insurance against illness. Along with its impressive preventive qualities, colostrum contains six times more protein than ordinary mother's milk. The "mega"-nutrient quality of colostrum is the reason why many informed nutritionists and doctors say that even if you cannot nurse your baby later, you should nurse until your milk comes in.

Nursing on Demand

During the first month of life your baby will want to nurse frequently. Again, concerned relatives, some doctors, and outdated literature may suggest you feed your infant once every three to four hours. You will be told that both of you need rest as much as food, and that the infant's demands are emotional rather than physical. Many may even warn that an infant who is fed every time he cries will become spoiled and intolerable by the age of four months. Scheduled feeding during the first month of life is more likely to inhibit your ability to produce enough milk to meet your baby's needs than any other single practice. Early scheduled feedings are emotionally as well as physically unnatural for both mother and child.

The way that mother's and baby's need complement each other shows the innate wisdom of nature. The newborn stomach will only hold approximately an ounce of mother's milk. His first breast milk is low in fat content and can therefore be digested quickly. When the baby's stomach is empty, he experiences extreme hunger and demands more milk. Mother's milk production is stimulated by sucking. The more frequently you nurse, the more milk you will produce. In ten days, your baby's stomach will be able to hold 3½ ounces of milk and your glands will be able to produce that 3½ ounces. If you feed on demand, your milk supply will increase proportionately to your child's needs. By one month, your baby's stomach capacity will be 6 ounces, which you will easily be able to provide.

At one month, also, the fat content of mother's milk increases. With this change, the baby's ability to digest matures and slows down. By this time your milk production is well established and your baby's need for frequent feedings naturally diminishes. If, however, your milk supply begins to diminish, your baby will naturally demand to be fed more often, thus increasing your milk response once again. This natural law of supply and demand will continue throughout the period of nursing.

Nursing the Premature Infant

Frequent feeding of mother's milk is even more essential for the premature infant. Although Westerners tend to think that a premature birth should be compensated for by man's scientific knowledge, nature in her silent wisdom takes care of the premature infant's need for exceptional nutrition. At Duke University Medical Center in North Carolina researchers found that the milk of mothers who had delivered premature babies was 50 percent higher in protein than that of other mothers, while the concentration of natural antibodies was two to three times greater. Twenty-eight days after a premature birth, mother's milk remained 20 percent higher in protein, still giving infants the benefits of nature's compensation for their early birth.

THE WORKING MOTHER

Mothers who have an emotional or a financial need to work may feel a conflict between nursing a child and pursuing a career. There are no easy answers to this dilemma, but there are alternative approaches that can minimize both guilt and frustration for nursing mothers who work.

Perhaps the easiest compromise is part-time employment. If part-time situations are managed efficiently, they need not take much nursing time away from your infant. In the beginning the father or another caregiver can feed the baby from a bottle of expressed breast milk if he becomes hungry while you are at work. After a short time, your baby will probably adjust to your work schedule, nursing before you leave and demanding to be fed the moment you return.

For the woman who enjoys being at home, but who needs to make a supplemental income or who begins to "climb the walls" without creative expression, the whole range of at-home working possibilities can be carefully considered. Women who are talented in crafts or cooking could create a product to sell locally. Those who have secretarial skills might type student papers and manuscripts at home. Others who have been working professionally as editors, writers, or graphic artists can free-lance while the baby is still in the nursing period.

Mothers who feel the need for social contact and creative expression can form a cottage-industry crafts collective. They can meet in one another's homes, bring their babies, and work together to produce salable items.

There are also some jobs where babies can be brought

to work. These are not easy to find, but the number is slowly increasing as women become a more powerful part of the work force.

If none of these alternatives is feasible, some full-time working mothers arrange to breast-feed during lunch and coffee breaks. The logistics of finding a baby-sitter near your work place, making satisfactory arrangements with an employer, and scheduling your baby's hunger to coincide with your lunches and coffee breaks are exceedingly complex. Moreover, the demands of this kind of arrangement may be physically debilitating to all but the most robust of women. Therefore, unless you are truly a "superwoman," we suggest you postpone returning to full-time employment, if at all possible, until your little one is weaned from at least his daytime feedings.

POSSIBLE NURSING PROBLEMS

Infant Indigestion

If your baby is suffering from indigestion, you may feel there is something wrong with your milk and you may be tempted to substitute a formula. A formula will certainly complicate an already uncomfortable situation. Instead, it may be helpful to understand the main cause of indigestion in infants, due to the immaturity of a baby's digestive enzyme systems: Toxic bile from the liver is thrown into the baby's bowel system for elimination. This green-colored bile may cause even mother's milk to form irritating rubbery curds. If your little one is persistently uncomfortable, a recipe suggested by Gena Larson in *Better Foods for Better Babies and Their Families* may offer relief: Soak a half-cup of organically grown almonds and a quarter-cup of raisins in a quart of spring water for two days in the refrigerator. Strain it and feed it warm, to your child until his indigestion passes. This toxic bile can be the cause of the discomfort for children for the first three years of their lives.

Colic

Colic has always been a terrifying word for vegetarian and nonvegetarian mothers alike. Mothers are often told that colic is a reaction to their instability, nervousness, and general emotional state. Such talk can make a woman feel that a baby would be healthier if not held at her "neurotic" breast. Recently, however, every guilt-ridden mother with a colic baby has been vindicated.

It was found that colic is often avoided if the feet of a newborn baby are kept warm. This finding seems to indicate that a little one's sensitivity to temperature, not his mother's emotional shortcomings, are the major cause of colic. Evidently our great-grandmothers were wise in their custom of knitting warm booties for a new baby.

Certain foods eaten by the nursing mother may change the quality of her milk and affect the infant's digestion. According to Dr. Lendon Smith, the most commonly offensive foods in this regard are garlic, onions, cabbage, beans, chocolate, eggs, corn, and wheat. Paavo Airola also includes broccoli, cauliflower, and citrus fruits on his list of foods that may affect the nursing child.

Another extremely common cause of excess painful gas in young infants is gulping while nursing. If a mother has an abundance of milk, it is likely to pour out as soon as her baby begins to suck. In order to keep up with this flow, the infant has to swallow quickly, and he may swallow air as well as milk. This can be rectified either by beginning to nurse from the breast containing less milk or by expressing milk from overfull breasts just before nursing. Both methods will relieve some of the initial pressure of the letdown reflex.

Sore, Cracked Nipples

Sore, cracked, even bleeding nipples are common in light-skinned women, especially first-time mothers. This condition usually passes as the nipples become accustomed to nursing. In the meantime there are simple ways to relieve pain.

Lubricate nipples with a mild oil such as wheat germ oil.
Keep nipples dry (as free of milk or water as possible).
Nurse more frequently for shorter periods of time, about five minutes from each breast.
Begin nursing from the nipple that is less irritated.

If irritation persists, there is a possibility that it is being caused by thrush, a fungus infection in the baby's mouth. Check the mouth for milky-white spots. If they appear, consult your physician. A commonly recommended cure is to wash nipples with one teaspoon of bicarbonate of soda dissolved in one cup of water, dry them, and then apply a soothing mild cream.

Clogged Milk Ducts

If your breasts are tender and swollen, there is a strong likelihood that a milk duct is clogged. This common condition is not cause for alarm, but should be treated since it can lead to the breast infection called mastitis. If your duct is clogged, you will have a small, painful lump, which is usually red. Several simple steps will relieve this condition.

Wear a bra that gives comfortable support but is not too tight or binding.

Nurse more often and for longer periods of time to relieve pressure.

Change your position each time you breast-feed your baby.

If your child is fully satisfied and refuses to nurse, express milk by hand to relieve pressure.

Wash your nipples to ensure that milk can flow from them freely.

Offer your sore breast to your baby first.

Don't stop nursing; this will only aggravate the problem.

Mastitis

Mastitis is accompanied by headache, engorgement, hot breasts, fever, and a general flu-like feeling. It is generally caused by either a clogged duct that has not been relieved or a staphylococcal infection from your baby. If this condition develops, it should be treated seriously.

Keep nursing, offering the sore breast first.

Stay in bed and rest.

Apply heat to the breast with a hot-water bottle or heating pad.

Use a firm bra for support.
Consult your physician.

Abscesses of the Breast

The most serious condition of the breast for a nursing mother is abscesses, which usually result from untreated mastitis. Pus accumulates in the breast in a localized infection. A doctor should always be consulted in this case. Often he will surgically open the breast to relieve the buildup of pus. This procedure can be done in an office, and you need not discontinue nursing. If one breast is unaffected, it can be offered to your infant while the other heals. Milk can be expressed from the abscessed breast in order to prevent milk from drying up. Healing is quite fast, and normal nursing can then be resumed. If both breasts are abscessed, you can bottle-feed temporarily until you have recovered.

One-Month-Old Grouch

It is quite possible that your baby will become crabbier at one month to six weeks of age. You might be tempted to think that something is wrong with your milk since he may refuse your nipple but continues to fuss. Actually, many babies develop a case of the "grouchies" at this time. It is as though their honeymoon with life is over. They begin to be irritated by heat, cold, diapers, loud noises, and loneliness. They are beginning to grow up. If your baby becomes irritable, it is best to be patient; his mood will eventually improve.

Sleepless Nights

If by three months your infant is not sleeping for six hours during the night, you may feel your milk has inadequate nutritional content to keep him satisfied. By this time, night feedings may be exhausting you and you might be tempted to try a supplementary bottle. Every mother we have ever known has complained that her infant falls asleep while nursing but then awakes as soon as he is replaced in his own bed. One of our friends discovered a solution.

When she gave her baby his late-night feeding, she placed an electric heating pad in his crib. She removed it just before returning him to his bed. The child continued to sleep soundly. Obviously it was a cold and lonely bed that kept her infant awake and not a need for food. This same technique works well with a hot-water bottle.

WHEN TO WEAN?

At six months most babies develop a curiosity about solid food. They want to grab food and put it in their mouths. They are fascinated with taste. This is a sign to begin feeding solids, but it should not be a sign to eliminate nursing. Breast milk remains a child's most important food for at least twelve months and is extremely beneficial for the first two years. Therefore, it is best to nurse before feeding the infant a meal of solid foods. Otherwise, he might fill up on solids that do not meet his nutritional needs as well as breast milk.

The final decision about weaning will be reached when your little one is walking. People will begin to question at what age you intend to wean him totally. They will tell you that he will never stop nursing if you don't do something. In this instance they may very well be right! Our first child nursed until she was nearly three. Giving up the breast was a painful experience for her because she had come, in the last year of nursing, to associate it more with her need for love than with nourishment. Earlier weaning, between one and two years of age, seems to be less difficult for children and mothers. By then the nutritional need for mother's milk has passed and children are ready to experience love in new ways. We discuss the process of weaning in more detail in chapter 8.

NUTRITIONAL NEEDS OF
THE NURSING MOTHER

During the entire nursing period your nutritional needs will be enormous. You will be amazed by the sheer quantity of food you consume. Any attempt to diet at this time will only cause physical weakness and deter you from nursing. Instead, eat to your heart's content, but only wholesome foods. Despite your "truck driver" dinners, you are unlikely to gain weight, especially if you begin a regular, relaxing routine of exercise after giving birth.

Since you are continuing to provide the food for a growing infant, your nutritional needs while nursing are similar to your prenatal requirements. The most notable changes are an increase in calories and a slight decrease in protein. The following chart will enable you to review these requirements quickly.

	Need During Pregnancy (normal weight: 128 lbs.)	Need During Lactation (normal weight: 128 lbs.)
Calories for light activity	2,300	2,500
Carbohydrates	300g	300g
Fats	66g	66g
Protein	74g	64g
Calcium	1,200 mg	1,200 mg
Iodine	175 mcg	200 mcg
Iron	78 mg	78 mg
Magnesium	450 mg	450 mg
Phosphorus	1,200 mg	1,200 mg
Vitamin A	1,000 mcg R.E.	1,200 mcg R.E.
Thiamine (B_1) mg	1.4 mg	1.5 mg
Riboflavin (B_2) mg	1.5 mg	1.7 mg
Pyridoxine (B_6)	2.6 mg	2.5 mg
Cyanacobalamin (B_{12})	4.0 mcg	4.0 mcg
Folacin	.8 mg	.5 mg
Niacin	15 mg	18 mg
Vitamin C	80 mg	100 mg
Vitamin D	10 mcg	10 mcg
Vitamin E	10 mcg α - T.E.	11 mcg α - T.E.

Source: Food and Nutrition Board, National Academy of Sciences—National Research Council, *Recommended Daily Dietary Allowances*, revised 1980.

Any special food preparations using nutritional yeast, wheat germ, kelp, blackstrap molasses, wheat germ oil, and soy flour are recommended as long as you are nursing. Your protein consciousness can relax slightly during nursing, as long as you eat whenever hungry.

A vegetarian diet is especially advisable while you are nursing. Studies in both the United States and Canada show that the amount of DDT in mother's milk is substantially greater for meat-eaters than for vegetarians. In 1975 the Environmental Protection Agency reported that the milk of 99 percent of meat-eating nursing mothers contained levels of DDT unsafe for infant consumption. Two years later the same agency conducted a study of vegetarian nursing mothers and reported that their milk contained one-third to one-half the amount of DDT that was present in the milk of the meat-eating mothers. In citing similar studies, CBC, Canada's national radio network, suggested that nursing mothers eat no meat and maintain as much as possible a natural, pesticide- and chemical-free diet. This view was reiterated by Stephanie Harris of the Environmental Defense Fund, who said: "If you're planning on becoming pregnant, and especially if you plan on nursing, then become vegetarian." Her view was affirmed even further by the Environmental Defense Fund's recent study, which found that mothers who ate a conventional diet had two to three times greater concentrations of many more pesticides in their breast milk than vegetarian mothers. In view of studies such as these, one wonders why many doctors and nutritionists are still proselytizing about the value of meat, particularly liver, for nursing mothers.

INFANT FORMULAS

Although bottle-feeding is not a perfect substitute for the nutrition or the warmth of breast-feeding, there are situations when nursing may be impossible. Financial necessity may absolutely require you to work full-time away from home. If you are carrying an infectious virus, your doctor may advise you not to nurse.

In such circumstances, it may be possible to locate a

source of mother's milk or a trustworthy wet nurse through your local hospital or La Leche League. These alternatives are nutritionally more beneficial than using infant formulas.

Your baby will triple his weight and grow one and a half times his original length during his first year of life; therefore it is essential that his staple food be nutritionally capable of supporting his growth needs. Most infants thrive best on a dairy-based formula, diluted with water and with acidophilus culture or yogurt to increase digestibility. A small amount of nutritional yeast will increase the nutritional value. A general recipe would be:

1 quart boiling spring water
1 quart certified raw goat's or cow's milk
½ teaspoon nutritional yeast
½ teaspoon acidophilus or 4 tablespoons yogurt

Any formula should be considered carefully with the help of a physician who is well acquainted with your individual child's needs.

If you object to a dairy formula for some reason, or if your infant is allergic to milk, even greater care should be taken in formulating his food. Homemade soy milk is deficient in vitamin B_{12}, vitamin D, and calcium. Commercial soy drinks for infants are fortified with these and other nutrients but often contain sugar and other detrimental additives. Nut milks and vegetable juice formulas are likewise deficient in some essential nutrients. Therefore, the consultation of a nutritionally aware doctor or a nutritionist well versed in infant needs is advisable.

8.

FIRST FOODS

AT the age of about six months your baby will no longer be content to be just a passive observer who sits around waiting to be fed or entertained. He now wants to explore. He wants to grab every object within his reach, and practically everything must undergo his taste test. His awareness of and participation in the world around him are rapidly growing. At this stage he is ready to discover solid foods. His habit of grabbing and tasting everything on the table from the food on your spoon to the tea in your cup is not the only indication that he would like, and is ready to eat, more than just breast milk. About this time he will cut his first teeth, a sign in many traditional cultures that the time to begin eating solids has arrived.

IRON FOR INFANTS

Around the time when your baby cuts his first teeth you will undoubtedly begin to notice an increase in his appetite. His demand to nurse more frequently or for longer periods is a clue that he is not getting all the nutrition he needs from mother's milk.

TEETHING REMEDIES

The teething baby can be given finger foods for the comfort of his gums, but these should be firm. Any loose particles might cause choking. Carrot and celery sticks are old stand-bys. An excellent soother is a ball of tightly wrapped cloth soaked in a solution of 1 cup water and 3 tablespoons apple juice that has been boiled for ten minutes with three whole cloves. The ball is then frozen. The combination of cold and cloves gives much temporary relief when the baby sucks or gums the ball of cloth.

Another effective teether, used by Central American peasants, is a frozen scallion. The cold and the numbing effect of the onion juice provide relief for teething babies. The scallion also adds some vitamin C and a little iron to the nursing diet. If discomfort becomes prolonged and severe, many babies get sustained relief from the special tissue salt combination for teething found in most natural food stores.

At birth an infant's body generally stores about a six-month supply of iron, but as he reaches six months of age that supply begins to run out and he must receive the necessary iron for his growing needs from his food supply. In some babies the store of iron runs out before either his teeth come in or his interest in food develops. This can be largely prevented at birth by ensuring that the placenta cord is not cut before it stops pulsating. If the cord completely ceases to pulsate before it is severed, the iron stored in the infant's body is increased by 4.5 milligrams. This may seem like a minuscule amount, but actually it is twice the amount of iron the infant will receive from his entire food supply over the first six months of life.

Because of the infant's need for adequate iron from his food supply once this stage is reached, many physicians and nutritionists recommend an iron supplement for infants, even as early as four months of age. If the placenta has been properly "emptied," this should not be nutritionally necessary. Even at six months the wisdom of supplying a supplement may be questionable. Iron pills are usually difficult to absorb entirely even for the mature digestive system of adults. The immediate result can be blackened stools, constipation, and stomach irritation. In addition, iron salts can prevent the assimilation of vitamin E, causing vitamin E–deficiency anemia.

It should be stressed that iron is extremely toxic to children if taken in large doses. In Canada therapeutic doses of all iron supplements are kept behind the druggist's counter, so that he can reiterate the warning to keep them out of the reach of children. This precaution was instituted because of the numerous cases of early death attributed to childhood consumption of iron pills.

First foods should include natural sources of iron most easily assimilated by the infant. Diluted prune juice, diluted blackstrap molasses, Gena Larson's mineral-rich water (see pages 205–206 for recipe), or Floradix (a fruit-herbal tonic available at most health food stores) can be added to the baby's fruits, vegetables, and juice for the additional iron he needs.

BEGINNING FOODS

Begin to feed your baby solids gradually to allow his taste buds, his digestion, his swallowing reflex, and his desire for food to develop naturally. Breast milk is still the best food for a baby and will continue to be his most effective nourishment until he is between one and two years old, when his digestive system matures. Therefore, solids should not entirely replace mother's milk (or a well-balanced formula) until twelve months of age. Nurse your baby as you have done since his birth, but now feed him other foods directly after nursing or between usual feeding periods. You may wish to stop him from nursing a few minutes before he would normally be satisfied, to ensure that he still has an appetite for a new taste experience. If this sudden interruption perturbs him, you may need to wait an hour or two before introducing the new solid food.

For at least the first week of feeding, sit him on your lap with his head tilted back slightly. This position helps him to swallow more easily. Also, it is a familiar eating position providing security while he begins a new phase. Spoon or finger-feed small amounts of diluted food into his mouth, proceeding slowly so he can become familiar with the new taste and sensation.

His first food diluted with one of the iron-rich formulas mentioned previously should be repeated for all "meals" for five days before moving onto a new food. Each successive new food should be tested for five days before trying another. Adding foods one by one to the diet will allow you to see if any particular food causes digestive upsets, constipation, diarrhea, rashes, or other reactions. A food that seems to cause such reactions can then be easily identified and eliminated, perhaps to be tried again several months later. To adults this method of food introduction may seem painfully slow and boring, but to a baby whose entire diet has consisted of mother's milk for six months, it is a rapid succession of changing tastes.

The amount of food given for the first week is best limited to 1 to 3 teaspoons at each sitting. This quantity will enable the baby's digestive system to adjust slowly and naturally to the food. The amount of food can gradually be increased as your baby demands more, but as long as he is nursing regularly he will need only one-half to two-thirds cup whole, natural food daily.

The very first foods can be puréed ripe banana, smooth mashed avocado, smooth applesauce, and diluted carrot juice. Each food should be puréed with an iron formula and fed for five days, followed by the next food for a five-day testing period.

Fruit-based iron sources should only be added to fruit, while diluted blackstrap molasses can be added to vegetables. Gena Larson's mineral-rich water can be used to dilute any puréed fruit (see recipe on pages 205–206). One part prune juice and three parts water, or one part Floradix and four parts water, can also be used in fruit purées. One teaspoon blackstrap molasses dissolved in two cups water can be tried in fruits and vegetables. Whichever iron source you choose, be sure to use it consistently for five days or longer in order to be certain it is well tolerated by your little one.

Grain cereals and starchy vegetables (potatoes, yams,

and sweet potatoes) are not wise choices for first foods, unless you chew them first, as Eastern European grandmothers do. These complex starches require partial digestion in the mouth by the starch-digesting enzyme in the saliva called ptyalin, which does not develop until children are around one year old. Any complex starch fed directly to infants will not be digested well and may cause difficulties. If, however, you feel comfortable chewing infant grain cereals before feeding them to your baby, they will provide an excellent early source of iron. Rice is most easily digested, while wheat is often a source of allergies. Other grains, such as millet, oats, and buckwheat, can be introduced between rice and wheat. Every whole grain should be well cooked until soft, then puréed with water until smooth before being chewed and fed to an infant.

Certain vegetables should also be avoided as first foods. Spinach, beet greens, and Swiss chard contain oxalic acid, which interferes with the absorption of calcium, a nutrient that is extremely important to a growing baby. Spinach, carrots, and beets contain nitrate. In itself nitrate is harmless, but studies show that when these foods are puréed at home, the nitrate changes to nitrite, which can cause an infant blood disorder, methemoglobinemia. Care should thus be taken not to feed infants spinach or puréed carrots and beets. Carrots and beets can be made into juice instead and diluted with water for infants, or steamed until soft and fed as finger foods later.

Participating at Mealtime

As soon as your baby is able to sit comfortably in a high-chair, he can begin his participation in the social aspects of eating and join you in the kitchen while you are preparing meals. Although development varies from baby to baby, most infants will be able to join you at meals and in the kitchen around the time they start eating solid foods. Your baby can learn to be a part of family meals even before he actually eats with the rest of the family. He can be given suckable foods like carrot and celery sticks, or small portions of his puréed food can be placed directly on his highchair tray, although only a little may reach his mouth and much may reach the floor and his body. Put a large bib on him and surround his highchair with newspaper so that the inevitable mess he delights in making is easier to clean up. Family mealtime can be a new and pleasing adventure for the young baby. Although it may take him a little time to associate these family gatherings with eating, he will identify them with fun. This experience can be the beginning of a positive attitude toward healthful natural nutrition.

At the same time he begins eating with the family, he can begin to participate in cooking. Whoever is cooking can keep his highchair close to where food is being prepared and periodically hand him something safe to play with: a small wooden spoon dipped in juice, a jar lid, a plastic container, two spoons, or a small, tightly covered plastic jar with water or beans in it. During this time he can experience elementary lessons about food preparation. Hand him a whole apple and allow him to suck on it; then take it from him, cut it, and give him a piece. Since he will inevitably try to suck on both the whole apple and the pieces, he will learn that the skin of the apple seals in the juice. The same can be done with other fruits and vegetables.

SECOND FOODS

After approximately one month of eating solid foods, a second series of foods can be introduced to your infant. By this time he will probably be eating most of his solid meals while sitting in a highchair rather than your lap. His main foods should continue to be well puréed but can be made slightly thicker. They should still contain iron and be introduced at five-day intervals. If you eat eggs, you can now try boiling a free-range fertile egg for one minute and adding one-eighth to one-quarter teaspoon of the yolk *only* to his mashed fruits and vegetables. The preboiling makes the egg yolk easier to digest while keeping it liquid. The yolk is usually nonallergenic and is very high in iron and amino acids, making it a fine supplementary food for infants.

Egg white is often a cause of allergies in infants and should not be tried until the twelfth month.

Homemade yogurt and cottage cheese can also be added to the diet, one at a time. The cottage cheese can be puréed with a little blackstrap molasses and water or with yogurt sweetened with a touch of molasses.

It is not yet time to feed milk from a cup to your infant, since children who begin to drink milk from cups tend to reduce their breast milk intake. This decrease can be detrimental since they are still dependent on mother's milk or a nutritionally sound formula for the major part of their nutrition.

Puréed tofu diluted with mineral-rich water or with small amounts of spirulina or kelp can be introduced especially to vegan children or children who demonstrate an intolerance to dairy products.

Small amounts of kelp, nutritional yeast, spirulina, and seaweed can be added to puréed vegetables, such as romaine, collard, mustard greens, kale, and broccoli to provide a boost in iodine and other nutrients. These foods are wisely introduced while your baby is still open to new tastes. Green vegetables are especially beneficial since they are high in calcium, iron, folacin, and riboflavin.

Vitamin B_{12}–enriched nutritional yeast is especially important for the vegan infant since his supply of B_{12} is so limited. B_{12} deficiency can take as much as ten years to show any symptoms, but once it does, the nerve deterioration can be irreversible. Therefore, it is important, beginning with infancy, that vegetarian children who do not eat eggs or dairy products be conscientiously fed B_{12} foods regularly. A vegan can be given bits of comfrey or small quantities of spirulina in puréed vegetables. Comfrey and spirulina are the only vegetables known to contain B_{12}. Light miso soups can be introduced early to vegan infants. However, even with these precautions you might well wish to add a powdered B_{12} supplement regularly, though sparingly, to your infant's food.

The foods your baby has now been introduced to, one at a time, can be alternated freely or combined over the next few months to comprise his total diet. The content of his diet will not change considerably until he is about ten months old.

TEN MONTHS OLD: A NEW EATING PHASE

By ten months of age your baby's attitude toward food has changed considerably. He is able to distinguish food from other objects. Not everything goes directly to his mouth. By now it is likely that he crawls around, freely exploring here and there. He also knows by now that meal-times are for eating and he wants his share. No longer is he content to chew on a tasteless spoon or steamed whole carrots while everyone else eats. He wants some of what you are eating, and if he does not get it, he will try to climb onto the table or scream until he is allowed to taste some adult fare. It is time to put foods directly on his tray and allow him to eat it with his fingers. Mealtime finger foods need not be made especially and only for the baby. The whole family can eat at least one dish of slowly steamed vegetables at a meal. Then your baby will see that his meal resembles yours, at least in part. If he insists on some of your bean and rice casserole, however, you should chew it for him. The salad he wants to test should be in big pieces to prevent bits from getting stuck in his throat. At this stage, he should be very much included in the family mealtime, although the major part of his meal can continue to be mashed especially for him.

Anxieties surrounding your baby's food may begin to surface around this time. Some babies begin to take more interest in solids than in nursing, and you may wonder if enough good food is reaching his mouth on the way down to the floor. It doesn't make sense to carefully spoon-feed him to make sure he is getting what he needs, unless, of course, he loves being spoon-fed.

The best assurance comes from observing your baby. Remember that no infant would purposely starve himself. Babies are born with the instinct for survival, and when wholesome food is available, they eat all they need. If your baby is active, healthy, growing, and gaining weight; if he cries and laughs with enthusiasm; if he seldom has a fever, a cold, a running nose, earaches, constipation, diarrhea, or rashes, he is probably in better health than the vast majority of the world's children, including his meat-eating peers. But if you are still in doubt, you can chart your baby's weight gain and growth from week to week. If he shows a steady increase, even if it is slightly irregular, he is eating enough. (See growth and gain charts on page 139.)

Vegetarian parents, especially those with spiritual aspirations, sometimes equate a baby's placid, quiet behavior with good health. This equation can be nutritionally dangerous, especially if you are on a raw-food, fruitarian, low-protein, nondairy or mucusless diet and feed your infant according to your own dietary preferences. A "peaceful" baby who never complains may simply be too malnourished to make his needs known. If you eat from a limited range of vegetarian sources, you should make certain your baby is receiving an adequate supply of all essential nutrients, especially B_{12} and other B vitamins, protein, and iron.

Keeping Your Baby "Sugar-Free"

Most people, including grandparents and kindly ladies on the street, will assume that your ten-month-old is ready to eat anything, especially candy, ice cream, cookies, and other traditional goodies. Sooner or later your child is going to taste sugar, but the longer this experience can be delayed, the better for his health. Sugar is quickly addictive and has the power to subvert the young child's innate nutritional wisdom. Once a child, even a young child, has tasted a lollipop, for instance, he is likely to choose its empty calories over a nutrient-rich favorite food.

Grandparents can be told firmly that your baby is to receive no sugar, not even at holiday time. If told directly, they will likely abide by your decision, at least until your baby grows into a toddler and begins to ask for the mysterious foods that he sees in so many places. The storekeeper who offers sweets will accept your polite "We don't feed him sugar" with little objection. Again, the difficulty will arise later when your child wonders about the gift that he is not allowed to accept. Until he reaches this stage, keep him "sugar-free." It will be some time before he realizes that TV commercials are trying to sell something, that they are not simply interesting little stories. And, if he never tastes a candy rabbit or a chocolate Santa Claus, he will continue to think they are toys, at least for a few months. He will thus maintain his innate nutritional wisdom for a little while longer.

THE SECOND YEAR: MOBILITY, INDEPENDENCE, AND WEANING

First birthdays mark the beginning of a new stage of life for a child. During his second year, he ceases to be a baby and becomes a toddler. He becomes more independent, emotionally and physically. He learns to walk, and when he looks around the room now, he is not always pleased to find you watching him. Sometimes he wants you out of the room or at least your head turned so that he will be free to experiment without interference. Now he knows you might stop him from spreading the diaper-rash cream all over his face, or from climbing the stairs or dumping the wastepaper basket; therefore, he would just as soon make some of his discoveries without your watchful, protective eye intruding on his fun.

Luckily, this new independent attitude is accompanied by greater physical skill. Seldom does he hurt himself. He is a proficient crawler and learns to walk. His hands are able to perform more delicate tasks, and things are no longer inserted directly into his mouth.

Now he knows food well and insists on trying everything. At twelve months, he is ready to eat any foods he can chew. His digestive system is fully developed. Grains, beans, potatoes, wheat germ, and nut butters can be safely added to his meals. He can feed himself either with his fingers or a spoon. Of course, he still makes a terrible mess, but he enjoys his food thoroughly.

Foods can be as simple or as complex as is convenient. He can be given a variety of single foods or a portion of the family's casserole, whichever he and you find preferable. But until his back teeth come in, it may be wise to observe a couple of precautions. Either cook grains until very soft or purée them in a blender or food processor to aid digestion. Be careful to avoid raw vegetables and nuts that can easily get caught in his throat.

You can thrust your young child's desires to fulfill his

nutritional needs at this stage in his development. Particularly if he has not been introduced to sugar or refined food, his desires are probably a reliable guide to his needs. This view was confirmed by Dr. Clara Davis in 1939. In her well-known experiment she allowed babies to choose their own diets from natural sources. A large variety of natural foods were placed in front of the babies, and they selected the foods they wished to eat without either encouragement or discouragement. All of them thrived, even though one baby ate eleven eggs at one meal and another ate thirteen bananas. A baby allergic to egg whites separated the white from the yolk before eating the yolk. A child suffering from rickets drank cod liver oil 113 times until his bones returned to normal. Later analysis of the children's diets showed that each child ate a balanced diet over a period of time despite isolated binges. This experiment suggests that we should allow our young children to indulge their food whims as long as their desires are for natural, whole foods. If they are allowed this freedom, they will develop with healthy bodies and an enthusiastic love of good food.

WEANING

The decision to wean your infant is a very personal one. Nutritionally, your baby is ready to be weaned between twelve and twenty-four months of age, but emotional factors are different for every baby and every mother. Working mothers often continue to nurse in the evening, since it reestablishes the closeness they miss during their hours away from home. Other mothers find children becoming overdependent and wean them close to their first birthday.

Whenever weaning feels best, it should be approached slowly and gently:

1. Begin nursing after meals rather than before or midway between meals.
2. Give your baby certified raw goat's or cow's milk in a cup with meals.

3. Gradually reduce breast-feedings by offering cuddles or a favorite treat at the usual nursing times.
4. Eliminate before-bed nursing last, replacing it with storybook time.

Nursing After Meals

Nursing after meals will gradually cut down your milk production, since your child will be somewhat satisfied before he is offered the breast. Most babies are so enthusiastic about solid food when hungry that they won't even notice that they have not nursed.

Introducing Raw Milk

As long as you were nursing, it was preferable to keep goat's or cow's milk from your child, but now that the time to wean has arrived, milk can healthily become a part of nearly every meal. If at all possible, certified raw goat's or cow's milk is a better choice than boiled, pasteurized, homogenized, dried, or canned milk.

Pasteurized milk is undesirable for several reasons. The high temperatures used in pasteurization cause minerals in milk to be less soluble, so that they tend to become deposited in the pipes through which the milk passes during the bottling process. Thus valuable minerals never reach the carton or bottle you buy in the store.

Enzymes are also destroyed in pasteurization, among the most important of which are phosphatases, since they aid in the mineralization of bones. Heat also destroys hormones in milk that help prevent infection. This destruction of hormones may explain why so many more children appear to be allergic to commercial cow's milk now than were in the past, before milk was pasteurized. One of the eight essential amino acids, lysine, is also harmed in pasteurization, therefore causing milk to lose some of its natural protein balance.

Pasteurization was instituted largely because of fear of undulant fever and the consequences of unsanitary conditions in dairies. At one time these fears may have been justified, but with present-day methods of inoculation and sanitation, the production of safe, healthful raw milk is well within the scope of all conscientious farmers.

If no source of certified raw milk is available to you but you do know a local dairy that is willing to provide you with raw milk, you are taking a limited health risk. However, this risk can be minimized greatly if you make a personal inspection of the dairy, paying particular attention to these questions:

1. Are all calves inoculated against undulant fever?
2. Is there a closed circuit between milking machines and milk storage units?
3. Are all milking machine pipes sterilized daily?
4. Is the cows' feed free of pesticides and herbicides?
5. Do dairy workers stay away from work when sick?
6. Is the dairy farm regularly inspected by health authorities?

If you are satisfied that your raw milk is safe, it is a beneficial substitute for mother's milk. You can offer it to your child, beginning with weaning and continuing through his teenage years. If available in your area, fresh raw goat's milk is superior to raw cow's milk for young children, as it is easier to digest and is less mucus-forming. Try asking your local natural food stores to order some if they do not carry it.

Replacing Daytime Feedings with Cuddles and Treats

Around your child's usual nursing time, offer him a special treat to satisfy his appetite. If he loves mashed bananas and milk, offer him that; if he loves whole grain cookies, give him one. Or, if he prefers miso soup and tofu, make it especially for him. After he eats, spend a special five to ten minutes playing his favorite game. For most one- to two-year-olds this special time will be a favorable substitute for nursing.

Some young children, however, will not accept anything but the breast when they have come to expect it. In such a case, the father can be immeasurably helpful. If the mother disappears and the father offers treats and cuddles, the child entirely forgets about mother's milk. This period of time can enrich the father-child relationship as your growing child learns that his dad can also provide food and affection.

The Before-Bed Feeding

The enthusiasm your child has for books and quiet games may well determine how easily he is able to let go of his final daily feeding. If he becomes so absorbed in his story time that he forgets nursing, eliminating this last vestige of nursing will not be difficult. If, on the other hand, he merely looks at you and wants to nurse, it may again be time to enlist his father's help while you mysteriously disappear. You may find this difficult since you have become so accustomed to nursing him to sleep. However, you will be compensated by the pleasure of knowing that your husband now has the chance to enjoy rocking his child and then tenderly placing him under the blankets.

INTRODUCING FIRST FOODS

Age	Foods	Preparation	Method of Introduction
6 months	Banana Avocado Papaya	Mash until smooth and dilute with an iron supplement (see below).	Feed one food as prepared per day, once or twice a day for 5–7 days before introducing the next food. For the first week, only 3 teaspoons at a feeding, to be slowly increased.
	Applesauce	Purée until smooth and mix with Gena Larson's mineral-rich water.	
	Brown rice	1 part rice to 3 parts water, cooked for 2 hours. Purée with mineral-rich water or Floradix and chew to digest starch before feeding to infant.	
	Carrot Juice	Dilute with an iron supplement (see below).	

INTRODUCING FIRST FOODS

Age	Foods	Preparation	Method of Introduction
6 months (continued)	*Iron Supplements*		
	Gena Larson's mineral-rich water (pp. 205–206)	Use to dilute and add iron content to any first food.	Use only one iron-rich liquid for 5 days in succession before introducing another.
	Blackstrap molasses and spring water		
	Floradix and spring water		
7 months	Whole-milk yogurt	Preferably made at home and sweetened with Floradix or blackstrap molasses.	Continue to introduce each new food for 5 days to determine digestibility and allergies. Feed 5–10 teaspoons 2–3 times a day after or between nursings or both feedings.
	Homemade cottage cheese	Preferably made from raw milk, puréed, and diluted with an iron supplement (see above).	
	Tofu	Blend until smooth with an iron supplement (see above).	
	Romaine, collard, mustard greens, kale, broccoli, peas, comfrey	Steam on very low heat; purée or mash with pinch of kelp until smooth. Large amounts can be made and frozen in an ice-cube tray. One vegetable cube can be thawed and served per meal.	
	Egg yolk	Boil egg for 1 minute, and separate yolk from white. Serve ⅛ to ¼ teaspoon of yolk *only* in mashed vegetables or fruit.	
	Nutritional yeast	Add a pinch to puréed vegetables or fruit.	

Age	Foods	Preparation	Method of Introduction
7 months *(continued)*	Kelp powder	Add a pinch to puréed vegetables or prechewed grains.	
	Light miso	Dilute well and simmer without boiling for 10 minutes. Serve alone or purée with prechewed grain.	
	Millet	Slowly cook 1 part millet in 5 parts water until sticky. Purée and chew before feeding.	
	Oatmeal	Cook 1 part oatmeal in 4 parts water until sticky. Purée and chew before feeding.	
	Buckwheat	Prepare as for oatmeal.	
	Potato	Steam or bake until soft. Purée and chew before feeding.	
	Sweet potato	Prepare as for potato.	
10 months	Whole wheat	Chew bread before feeding. Cracked wheat or wheat cereal cooked until sticky; purée and chew before feeding.	Begin to serve child at regular family meals. Self-feeding with hands or spoon. Allow as much or as little as desired.
	Carrots, celery, eggplant, asparagus	Slice and slowly steam until soft and serve as finger food. Previously introduced vegetables can be served this way as well.	
12 months	Legumes, pinto beans, kidney beans, aduki beans, lentils, peas, etc.	Boil until soft. Serve as finger foods, or mashed. Part of family bean casserole can be puréed for child or served directly.	Allow amounts desired. New foods may still be tested alone for 3 days before being served in combination with other foods. All previously introduced foods can be served in digestible combinations since the digestive system has matured.

INTRODUCING FIRST FOODS

Age	Foods	Preparation	Method of Introduction
12 months *(continued)*	All grains	Purée and serve to child (prechewing not necessary).	
	Nut and seed butter	Use prepared butters available in health food stores.	
	Wheat germ	Added to fruits, yogurts, cereals, or baked goods.	
	Milk	Preferably raw goat's or cow's milk served in a spill-proof cup.	

9.

THE TIME OF
TEMPTATION: AGES
TWO TO FIVE

AS vegetarian parents you undoubtedly want your child to grow up with a natural and healthy attitude toward eating. You would like him to thoroughly enjoy whole, simple foods when he is hungry, and it would be ideal if he would never lose the instinctive ability to choose the foods his body needs.

However, your desire to preserve his innocence is inevitably thwarted by the influences of our culture and the growing-up process itself. Around the age of two, children begin to notice that Ronald McDonald is selling hamburgers, that Captain Krunch eats sugar-saturated cereal, that bubble gum balls are not the colorful marbles they once believed, and that Santa Claus gives other children sugar canes at Christmas. To make matters worse, Grandpa and Grandma desperately want to reward your two-year-old for every step, every new word, even every smile with something sweet. Also around this age, grandparents may become concerned about his protein intake and would love to secretly slip him an occasional piece of meat, "just to make sure."

All these influences coincide with the development of the two-year-old's willfulness. His life is now a series of isolated desire-filled moments—each moment either rewarded, and thus ecstatic, or frustrated, and thus painful. Dealing appropriately with the two-year-old will help him grow naturally into a reasonable preschooler who will understand the need to choose certain foods and avoid others. Unlike the two-year-old, who cannot conceive of a moment beyond his present desire, the preschooler can begin to exercise self-control and realize that food is a source of health, not simply a means of gratification. Until then, the problem of "temptation" must be met with conscientious parental understanding of and respect for children's physical, emotional, and intellectual needs.

Your own best protection against the onslaught of the "junk food" culture is the knowledge that you are not depriving your child of anything, but rather are providing him with the best possible opportunity to become a vital, healthy, happy adult by feeding him a diet of natural, whole foods. Having this assurance will enable you to set nutritional standards inside and outside the home with no sense of guilt, apology, or confusion. Understanding and adjusting to your child's changing nutritional needs and dietary preferences will help you to function from a place of security.

WHEN IN DOUBT . . .

Throughout the years from ages two to five, the health of your child will be an increasing concern. He is eating a varied diet, based to a large degree on his personal tastes, fluctuating appetite, and unpredictable whims, and you may well go through periods of wondering just what keeps him going.

As long as he "keeps going," he is probably a normal, healthy child. If you feel a need to have greater reassurance, there are several easy ways to keep track of his growth, development, and diet. Keeping a diet analysis sheet for him as you may have done during pregnancy and lactation makes little sense. At two he still feeds the floor as much as he feeds himself, so you cannot accurately measure the amount of food that actually reaches his tummy. But simple growth and gain charts, as you may

GROWTH CHART

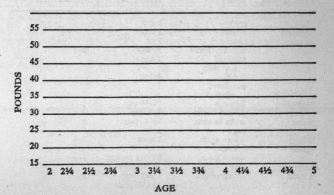

GAIN CHART

have used when your child was a baby, will show you whether or not he is maturing normally. Use the charts on page 139 or simply copy them.

Every three months, measure your child's height and weight. Plot these on the charts. If both charts show a somewhat steady, but sometimes irregular, increase, the child is growing well. Most children will gain 5 pounds between the ages of two and three, while growing about 3½ inches. During this time weight gain will decrease to approximately 4½ pounds annually, while height will increase by about 3½ inches per year. As these growth changes occur, your child's proportions will change accordingly. His head will become less dominant, his belly will protrude less, and his arms and legs will begin to appear less fragile. His whole frame will elongate.

In addition to keeping growth charts, be certain that your child's daily diet is adequate and balanced. As a general guideline, the following table, adapted from an article on feeding vegetarian children by Irma B. Vyhmeister and Lydia M. Sonnenberg, will ensure that your child receives the quality of nutrients, including calcium, iron, riboflavin, vitamin B_{12}, and protein, which are of special concern for vegetarians during the growing years.

This table consists of basic foods and does not take into account the extra nutrients you can slip into your child's

Food Groups	Foods	Serving Size	Number of Daily Servings for Children Aged 2–5
Milk products or soy milk	milk	1 cup	
	yogurt	1 cup	
	cheese	1 oz.	
	cottage cheese	¼ cup	2–3
	fortified soy milk	1 cup	
	fortified powdered soy milk	4 tbsp.	
Vegetable protein foods	legumes	¼–½ cup	1
	peanut butter	1–2 tbsp.	1
	seeds or nuts	½–1 tbsp.	1
	eggs	1	1
Whole grains	whole grain bread	1 slice	3–4
	whole grain	⅓ cup cooked	2–3
Vegetables & fruit	green leafy vegetables	½ cup cooked	
		1 cup raw ½ cup juice	2

Food Groups	Foods	Serving Size	Number of Daily Servings for Children Aged 2–5
	vitamin C—rich vegetables & fruit	1 cup raw, sliced or whole ½ cup juice	1
Fats	butter cold-pressed oil	1 tbsp.	1–3

meals in the form of supplemental foods such as brewer's yeast, nutritional yeast, wheat germ, blackstrap molasses, kelp powder, soy milk powder, and soy flour. For example, simply mixing a teaspoon of blackstrap molasses into a glass of milk or soy milk will increase the calcium content by over 10 percent, while adding much-needed iron as well.

If you occasionally feel a twinge of doubt about your child's diet, check that the food you are offering him is balanced and complete. To do this, a checklist like the one below may be used. Place a check mark next to the item when it is served. If you consistently notice that one item

DIET CHECKLIST

	Mon.	Tues.	Wed.	Thurs.	Fri.	Sat.	Sun.
Milk or soy milk product (You need 2–3 checks daily)							
Protein foods: beans, nuts, eggs, nut butter, tofu, cheese (You need 3 checks daily)							
Grain complement to protein foods (3 checks daily)							
Vegetables: some cooked, some raw (3 checks daily)							
Fruit (1 check daily)							

is not served regularly, try to correct this imbalance. By checking the list, you will get used to thinking in terms of serving a complete and balanced menu, and the need for such a list will fall away.

Although the checklist can reassure you that your child is being served the food he needs, you cannot force him to eat it. Once you serve his food, you will have to take a "leap of faith" and trust your child to know his own bodily requirements. Remind yourself once again that, left to his own instinctive wisdom, a child who is offered natural, whole foods free of sugar and chemicals will not suffer malnutrition. However, he may refuse beans when his digestion is weak, or milk when he feels a cold coming on. If we want our children to retain their inborn wisdom, we have to suspend our temptation to nag, coax, and punish and reward with food.

MEALTIME TACTICS

From the time babies begin to eat their first solids the pleasure of sharing meals can be a way of establishing their respect for the health-giving nature of food. This certainly does not mean that each meal should be accompanied by a righteous lecture on the virtues of a vegetarian diet and the evils of sugar-coated chemicalized food. It does mean that if meals are accompanied by cheerfulness and enjoyable family conversation, the mental association of pleasure with healthful foods will establish itself in a very natural way.

The greatest challenge to maintaining a pleasant mealtime atmosphere will come when toddlers enter the infamous "terrible twos." During this period your child becomes impressed by the control he has over his own body, and he seeks to explore new dimensions of personal power. He is quick to discover his parents' idiosyncrasies at the dinner table. Soon he may realize that mealtime is a wonderful opportunity to be the center of attention, either by demanding entertainment or by instigating a battle. The two-year-old can easily become a tyrant presiding over the table from his highchair throne with an iron hand, learning to play power games instead of enjoying the food his body needs.

This development, with its accompanying indigestion, can be prevented or easily corrected by a few mealtime guidelines.

1. *Don't try too hard to please your child.* Keeping mealtime peace can become a chore rather than a pleasure if you spend hours making up nursery rhymes to entertain your child, games to pacify him, or special treats to entice him. If you fall into this trap, he will quickly learn that he is in charge, and you will suffer his many despotic whims. Moreover, if he doesn't appreciate your efforts, you have set yourself up to feel resentful—after all, you tried so hard to please him. Do not give your child the opportunity to exert such power plays at mealtimes.

2. *Refuse to fight at the table.* At mealtime the small child would love to be the center of attention. If attention is not forthcoming in the measure he would like, he might try picking a fight to get what he wants. He might squeal or throw things, yell, fuss, or cry. If this attention-getting strategy works, the child's behavior is reinforced. Instead, the situation should be defused. Every parent has his or her own method of tricking children out of their cantankerous moods. One of the best is to change the subject. Without diverting the family's attention, simply surprise the child by giving him a toy or a new food. If his attention is drawn to something else, the chances are very good he will forget about his desire for attention. However, don't get tricked into trying too hard to please him.

If his concentration and resolve are strong, his disruptive behavior may persist despite all your attempts. In this case we believe your child should be told compassionately, "If you need to cry, that's fine, but you have no right to demand everyone's attention while you do it." He can then be picked up, gently removed from the table, and told, "When you feel better, we'd really like you to be with us." This treatment will teach him that personal power is for self-control, not for manipulating others. When our first daughter was a defiant two-year-old, we periodically employed this method. We were always amazed at how quickly her tears and sometimes her screams would turn to songs and giggles once she was alone. Then she would return to the table all smiles.

3. *Offer food; never force it.* Place small portions of a

balanced meal on your child's highchair tray. If he wants more, give it to him as he requests. If he refuses a certain food, say nothing. A child who is pushed to eat will soon realize that his refusal upsets you. Then he will use this refusal to punish you when he is angry with you.

4. *Give your child a choice of foods.* Before sitting down, show him his meal. Ask if he likes the foods. If he does not, offer him some *simple* alternatives: a piece of cheese, a little peanut butter, apple slices, tomato wedges or a piece of banana. Few adults are forced to eat exactly what is put in front of them, and your child deserves the same respect. But no child has the right to demand that you interrupt your meal to get him special foods. Once he says he is satisfied with his meal, you should not meet his demands for more or different foods. If you jump at his every food whim, he will learn a new power game, and you will resent not being able to enjoy a restful meal yourself.

5. *Let him feed himself in his own style.* Your child should, of course, continue to wear a bib until he is ready to sit at the table. Until then, protect the floor underneath his chair with newspapers to simplify your cleaning job. If he likes using a spoon, fine; if he finds eating with his fingers more efficient, wonderful. In time he will learn to eat like an adult; at this stage it is important that he simply enjoy eating.

6. *Let him eat his own food combinations.* Serve foods that are complementary during a single meal, but allow your child to eat them in combinations he enjoys, even if they seem repulsive to you. Remember, according to the "law" of the two-year-old, if he cannot dip his tofu in his carob pudding, he will not eat either. Such combinations are his original eating experiments; they should be encouraged as ways to learn about food.

7. *Don't insist on serving dessert last as a reward.* If desserts are withheld until your child has eaten a "good meal," he will quickly associate sweet tastes with rewards. His desire for them will thus be exaggerated. Rather, serve only nutritious, whole-food desserts whose value is equal to other parts of the meal. Put this dessert food on his tray

at the same time as the other foods. Allow him to eat it whenever he pleases; then he will not give it extraordinary importance.

8. *Let him tell you when he is finished eating.* There is no need to coax or force your child to eat a few final mouthfuls. He knows when he is satisfied. Too many adults eat a few more mouthfuls after they are full, much to their own discomfort. It is not a practice that should be encouraged at any age.

9. *Allow him to leave the table when he is finished eating.* A young child cannot be expected to behave at the table once he has eaten his fill. Forcing him to stay would only encourage a fuss. Once he leaves, however, his meal is finished. Do not allow him to eat and run, and then return to eat some more. This game would be disruptive to the family and to his digestion.

10. *Do not bribe, reward, or punish with food.* If food is to be kept as an honest, healthy, and enjoyable response to hunger, it should not be given or withheld as a response to behavior.

11. *Let him have regular snacks.* Most children need a snack at midmorning, at midafternoon, and sometimes before bed. These little meals should be simple and varied. If snacks are consistently sweet, your child may come to prefer them to other foods served at meals. Instead serve a variety of foods: a little leftover soup, bread and cheese, a cut-up vegetable, apple wedges and peanut butter, yogurt with honey and wheat germ, or a cookie made with malt, blackstrap molasses, eggs, milk powder, wheat germ, and whole wheat flour. The cookie is as nutritious as the other foods and therefore need not be held up as "special." It can be served sometimes at snacktime, sometimes at a meal.

12. *Let your child participate in cooking.* At two, he will be able to take a more active role as you cook. He can knead a piece of bread dough for his own roll. He can put cut-up vegetables onto a plate. He can stir a casserole. Participating in these tasks will give him a sense that he is actively responsible for his own diet and health, not merely a passive recipient of whatever is set in front of him. This

kind of helping can continue until he reaches school age, when he will be ready to make some foods on his own.

13. *Encourage your child to help clean up.* He can take unbreakables to the sink and plastic containers of leftovers to the refrigerator. He can wipe off the table and the counters. He can begin through these simple "chores" to have a sense of the family working together. These tasks can be encouraged regularly, but not increased greatly until his school years, when he will be able to handle breakables with no danger to himself or the dishes.

SETTING LIMITS FOR THE TWO-YEAR-OLD

One dreaded day, even if your child has never tasted sugar, he will see a lollipop and say, "I want dat." From that day on, Granny and Grandpa will no longer *have* to offer him treats—he will ask for them of his own accord. He will no longer passively accept what is offered him; instead, he will actively seek out his own desires. In short, he is ready to be caught by the "Sugar Demon"—the junk food culture's Boogeyman!

Now the temptations of junk food can no longer be subtly sidestepped; they must be confronted directly. As vegetarian parents, we need to establish limits on our children's consumption of undesirable foods. The limits you choose to set will depend on your particular nutritional, moral, and ethical viewpoint. The emotional appeals of your child, the slick advertising accompanying his favorite TV program, and the concern of grandparents need have no bearing on your limit setting. As a parent the health of your child is your primary concern. Therefore, both parents need to come to some agreement about the limits and consistently abide by it.

Some parents set rigid rules: No sugar, no chemicals, no refined or processed foods, and no meat. Others have guidelines with varying degrees of flexibility. Parents who refuse all sugar, chemical-containing, refined, processed foods, and meat to their children simply repeat consistently, "We don't eat that." Parents who occasionally give their child a food on the "generally avoided" list will respond to excessive requests with a firm "Not today."

Temper Tantrums in Public Places

Your two-year-old will try out various strategies until he is certain that the limits you have set are consistent. These sometimes take the form of obstreperous behavior in public places such as the grocery store or department store. This behavior should never be rewarded. It will pass quickly if you never give in, even to demands accompanied by tears, tantrums, whining, panting, or insults. Instead, you can good-naturedly change the subject to a piggyback ride, a colorful display, a trip to Grandma's, or what to buy for dinner. There is never any reason to feel apologetic, guilty, or embarrassed about a two-year-old's insistence on a sugar treat. After all, it is normal behavior. But if you give in to it, it will become more frequent.

Offering Alternatives

At this stage in your child's development it is unrealistic to expect him to think in terms of the long-range health effects of his eating habits. He is not likely to make reasonable dietary decisions once sugar has become an *alternative*. It is addictive and he likes it, and in order to get it he will pretend to be reasonable and try to strike up bargains with you. He may agree to one candy a week because he hears that "one candy" is part of the deal—but he cannot comprehend "five minutes," never mind a "week"; life is always only "right this moment" for him. The only deal that counts is the one that gets him his candy right now.

If your child is really deprived of sweet, pleasure-giving foods, he is likely to become obsessed with them. He can easily become like some of the children in the playschool for three- and four-year-olds that our daughter attended. All the children were from homes with a health-food orientation, and many of them were vegetarians. One day as we entered the school, we heard the sound of four or five children loudly chanting "Sugar, sugar, sugar . . ." as they pounded on the pans in their playschool kitchen. These children couldn't wait to free themselves from the austere restrictions their parents had placed on them. But perhaps they were rebelling against the rigid quality of their parents' restrictions, not simply against the prohibition on sugar. Children like sweet things, but the fact that sugar makes things sweet is something they learn from their parents. Yet "sugar" and "sweet" need not be confused.

With a little care, even a total prohibition against sugar need not seem like deprivation to your child. Most children will find a sweet strawberry appealing. If you carry a few carob malt lollipops (see page 309) in your bag, you won't always have to refuse polite requests for a lollipop. In summer, give your child a juice popsicle (see page 298) as you go outside, so that when he sees other children eating popsicles, you can remind him that he has already had one. If he receives healthful sweets without even asking, he will be much less likely to nag when he sees his peers with sugary snacks.

Grandma and Grandpa Are "Sugar Daddies"

Grandparents offer children a special quality of love. They have the wonderful luxury of sharing affection with children without the responsibility of raising them. For children, Grandma's and Grandpa's affection is free; they receive unbounded attention without discipline. This kind of acceptance and affection inevitably give grandparents a special place in children's hearts. But this poses problems for vegetarian parents when grandparents insist on lavishing candy, cookies, ice cream, and soda pop on their grandchildren as an expression of affection.

If your parents recognize that you are the final authority over your own children's health habits, restraining their sugar-giving hand will not be difficult. Although they may not be convinced of your nutritional expertise, they will accept that you are now making the decisions for your family. If you say "No sugar," then no sugar it will have to be. If you say one candy a day, one candy it will be.

If, however, your parents think of you as a faddist going through yet another phase and taking your reluctant child along for the ride, visits to Grandma and Grandpa can be problematic—not only because they may slip your child a little sugar behind your back, but because they may fuel the fire of your two-year-old's natural bent toward defiance. At this stage it is vital to work out a relationship in which your parents have respect, even if begrudgingly, for your parental authority. If they do not, you may have to limit the visiting time between them and your child to short periods when you can be present at all times. This pattern of activity may have to continue into the preschool and school years.

The Sweet Sell of the Boob Tube

If your two-year-old watches cartoons, he will likely be attracted to the cartoon characters who sell sugar cereals. Animated folk such as Tony the Tiger, Captain Krunch, and Snap, Crackle, and Pop visit with real children like him, and they are on the screen for thirty seconds, which well suits the normal two-year-old's attention span. Small wonder that even a two-year-old gets the commercial message: Mornings with Tony would be much more exciting than his usual breakfast.

In combating such effective advertising, you may have to play along to some extent. An obliging neighbor may be of some help in satisfying your child's desires without sacrificing his nutrition. Simply ask them if you can have their leftover cereal boxes—you see, your child really wants the box more than the cereal. The box is the symbol of the character he adores. Fill the boxes with granola or any other cold cereal suggested in chapter 13 of this book. Occasionally you can even stick a little surprise toy in the box. Do not deceive your child by pretending that granola is Sugar Frosted Flakes. Instead, explain that his box can be filled with all sorts of cereals.

THE VEGETARIAN PRESCHOOLER

When your child becomes reasonable more than 50 percent of the time, he has passed beyond the "terrible twos" stage and become a preschooler. With this jump in maturity comes a new attitude toward and awareness of food. The task of raising a vegetarian child becomes easier and more exciting as you begin to teach your child respect for the natural way of eating. The thoughtful, willing preschooler is open to learning and eager to understand and to please.

The preschooler is ready to leave his highchair and sit at the table. He wants mealtime to be a harmonious event at which the whole family comes together to share food and enjoyment. He wants less to be the center of attention than to be an equal participant. In every social activity the preschooler wants to learn proper behavior, and he brings this desire to meals. He will watch how you eat and imitate. If you chew well, enjoy your food, and eat a balanced meal, he will naturally take your lead.

Hurried meals cannot instill in a child a respect for the relationship between his food and his body. Yet many people have strenuous schedules that cause them to eat "on the run" much too often. Therefore, celebrating one meal a week as a formal time for the family to relax together, enjoy special foods, and remembering the earth's bounty will give your child a respect for food as the physical source of well-being. We ourselves are "half-Jewish," so we have chosen the traditional Friday-night Sabbath meal as our time to appreciate each other and our food with a feeling of peace. Whether or not your family mealtime celebration has any spiritual significance, the basics can be the same. Use a special tablecloth and your best plates, prepare festive food, and eat by candlelight. Your preschooler will love the festivities and will gladly join in preparing the food, setting the table and especially lighting the candles.

He is old enough now to eat all family fare, except whole nuts, which can easily slip down his throat. Even these can be served if they are soaked in water and juice long enough to make them softer. He may not, however, like the strong, unfamiliar taste of some adult foods. Instead of springing new surprises on him during the meal, let him taste each dinner dish before eating as you did when he was younger. If he honestly does not like a particular protein dish, substitute a slice of cheese on bread, some nut butter on toast, or a boiled egg. If he does not like your curried vegetables, give him a few slices of raw carrot, green pepper, cucumber, or celery. His nutrition will not suffer in the least, and he will be much more content during the meal.

LEARNING ABOUT FOOD: ACTIVITIES FOR THE PRESCHOOLER

Only a generation ago, every child understood that vegetables grow in the ground, fruits come from trees, and milk comes from cows. Mothers and fathers grew their own vegetables, picked their fruit, and knew the local dairy farmer. Today a vast majority of preschoolers believe their eyes: Food comes from the supermarket. They have no experience of foods as natural, growing, living things. To them, food comes from cans, plastic bags, or large bins. To teach your preschooler the connection between nature and food, give him some firsthand experience in growing food. Then the idea of "natural foods" will be meaningful to him.

Sprouting

Even if you live in a city, you can grow food with your preschooler. The easiest indoor food growing project is sprouting seeds, grains, or beans in bottles. It will give your preschooler the experience of the life in food, since he will see it growing from day to day.

Rather than give your child specific directions for his sprouting project, allow him freedom to experiment. He will then take greater pride in the results of his experiments and will have some sense of having grown his own food. He may "waste" a few beans, but the pleasure he will feel at his eventual success will be well worth a few initial failures.

However, to prevent failure after frustrating failure, you can work alongside him with your own seeds. Then he can take your lead if he wishes, ask questions if he is curious and learn by observation, while maintaining his own feeling of independent research.

For this project you will need the following materials:

½ cup alfalfa seeds, mung beans, lentils, whole wheat berries, radish seeds, fenugreek seeds, or unhulled sesame seeds
two wide-mouth canning jars.
two circles of wire screening, inserted into the canning jars' screw bands or two rubber bands and two 5-inch-square pieces of cheesecloth.

Step 1. Tell your child you are going to grow some food in a bottle. Invite him to join you.

Step 2. Divide the materials. Give your child a quarter-cup of seeds or beans and keep a quarter-cup yourself. Give him one jar and keep one. Give him one canning jar screw band with screening or a rubber band and cheese-cloth and keep the other.

Step 3. Put your beans or seeds in your jar and add about 1 cup of water. Place the screening on the lid or secure the cheesecloth with a rubber band over the lid. Pour off the water to rinse the beans or seeds clean. Watch and see what your child does, but do not interfere.

Step 4. Pour about 1½ cups of water into the jar. Set the jar near the kitchen sink in a shady spot. Again, let your child do as he pleases.

Step 5. Tell your child you are going to leave the seeds or beans alone until tomorrow.

Step 6. The next morning, invite him to join you again. Drain your seeds thoroughly and put the jar back in a shady, warm spot near the sink. Allow your child to do as he wishes.

Step 7. Each day rinse and drain your seeds or beans two or three times, perhaps when you wash the dishes. Invite your child to join you. Each day talk about the changes in the seeds and discuss whether or not they are ready to eat.

Step 8. When the seeds or beans are fully sprouted (in six days for most seeds, or three to four days for beans), offer them to your child to eat. If his are also sprouted, ask to taste some. If his growing experiment failed, ask him if he wants to start again. Go through the same steps, allowing him the same freedom. On a second try he is much more likely to follow your lead and grow a healthy batch of sprouts.

Step 9. Eat the sprouts together in a salad or sandwich.

Indoor Gardening

The easiest way to give your preschooler firsthand experience of food growing from the earth is to plant indoor buckwheat and sunflower salad greens. These have a delicious sweet taste and can be grown indoors all year round.

As with sprouting, allow your child to establish his own personal connection with his little patch of soil. Supply materials and then work alongside him with identical materials. You will be providing both freedom and an example. His success or failure will thus be his own.

For this project you will need:

½ cup hulled organic sunflower seeds
½ cup unhulled sprouting-quality buckwheat seeds
two pint-size jars or small bowls
two flat containers that will hold an inch of soil: plastic trays, old square cake pans (lined with wax paper), or shallow wooden boxes
a bag of potting soil or garden soil
plastic wrap

Step 1. Tell your child you are going to grow some salad greens in dirt, and ask him to join you.

Step 2. Give him a quarter-cup sunflower seeds and a quarter-cup buckwheat seeds and keep the rest. Give him a cup or jar and keep one. Give him half the soil and keep the rest. Each of you gets a flat container.

Step 3. Place all your seeds in your jar or bowl, cover them with water, and let them soak until next day. Explain that this is all you are going to do for a start and that you will use the soil on the next day. The soil may well be irresistible to him. If he wants to plant his seeds immediately, do not interfere. It might even work.

Step 4. The next day, plant your seeds. Invite your child to watch you. Place the soil evenly in your container and sprinkle the seeds evenly over the soil, without placing any soil over the seeds. Water the soil well, and cover the container with plastic wrap. Place the plastic-covered container in a dark, warm spot for two to three days without disturbing it. Of course, if your child wishes, he can look at it once a day without removing the plastic cover. Your child is, of course, continuing with his own experiment.

Step 5. When the seeds have germinated, remove the plastic wrap and place the tray by a sunny window. Ask your child what he is going to do next.

Step 6. Allow the greens to grow for three to four days, watering them from time to time, until they are 4 inches tall. Check your greens and your child's experiment every day and discuss the changes you see.

Step 7. Harvest your greens by snipping them off with scissors. Share them with your family at mealtime in a salad. If your child's greens have grown, he can harvest them also.

If your child's experiment did not work, start again. He needs to know he can grow his own garden too. These indoor projects are not only fun but are a wonderful way to have fresh, nutritious vegetables all year round at a very reasonable price. Therefore, continuing to grow sprouts and greens with your child after an initial experiment or two is a very practical way he can contribute to mealtime nutrition and to saving food money. He should, of course, be commended for the contribution he is making.

A Family Garden

A preschooler can start his own tomato, broccoli, cauliflower, cabbage, or lettuce plants in early spring. These tiny plants will be planted in the garden as soon as the threat of frost is past. He will take pride in seeing his plants growing in the family garden.

If you have sprouted seeds or beans and grown salad grasses together, your preschooler probably watches the way you grow things carefully. Now he follows your example, realizing that you seldom fail. Continue, however, to allow him to work independently alongside you without nagging or directing him. Plant several of each variety of vegetable in several containers to ensure greater success.

You will need the following materials:

8-oz. paper cups
potting soil
seeds (for tomatoes, broccoli, lettuce, cauliflower, eggplants, peppers, and/or cabbage)
saucers

Step 1. Punch an eighth-inch hole in the bottom of each of your cups.

Step 2. Fill each cup three-quarters full with potting soil.

Step 3. Plant two seeds in each cup according to package instructions.

Step 4. Place cups in saucers on a windowsill.

Step 5. Water as the soil becomes dry, but do not overwater. Soggy soil will rot the seeds.

Step 6. Wait for the plants to grow, and transplant them in the family garden after the last of the frost.

You will not be able to involve your preschooler in outdoor gardening in the same independent manner as your indoor experiments. He is not quite ready to have his own outdoor vegetable garden, nor is he ready to be a free participant in family gardening. Without specific instruction, it is unlikely that his own garden would grow. A vegetable garden takes time to grow and daily care. The preschooler has neither the patience to wait nor the interest to weed. When your vegetables are thriving, his will likely be a patch of weeds. The experience might be devastating to his pride. Nor can he be allowed to have free, full participation in planting and caring for the family garden. His interest is still in experimentation, but his understanding is not precise. Left to his own devices, he will plant seeds in 5-inch holes, water them six times daily, and step on all your carefully planted rows.

In the garden, the preschooler must be content to be a student, learning from you how to plant, where to step, how to weed, and what to pick. If he can accept your authority, gardening can be an enjoyable family affair and he will take pride in the family harvest.

EXPLAINING FOOD LIMITS TO THE PRESCHOOLER

The preschooler wants to understand the reasons for his family's rules and guidelines. He is ready for simple explanations without details or long discourses. He is also more aware of the vast variety of foods that he is discouraged from eating. At two he realized that meat and sugar are off limits. Now he notices a lot of other things in grocery stores and at Grandma's house. He wonders why his family does not eat them.

During this period of increased understanding, it is even more important for you to determine which foods are strictly off limits and which foods are generally but not rigidly avoided. Your child will notice any foods you eat. If a "forbidden food" ever enters your mouth, he will immediately ask you why. You must apply your own guidelines as strictly to yourself as to your child; otherwise, he will notice the hypocrisy and your credibility will suffer dramatically.

For most vegetarians or natural food enthusiasts, four food categories are avoided either totally or generally (with occasional indulgences): meat, sugar, refined foods, and chemicalized foods. You should tell the child why each category is avoided and make it clear whether each category is a "never food" or an "almost never" food.

For example, you might explain that you never or seldom eat meat because you believe that people should not kill or hurt animals. Most preschoolers adore all animals and will agree with this concept immediately. In fact, if you occasionally do eat fish or meat, it is liable to upset your child terribly. When our older daughter was three and a half, Nina became weak because of a heavy teaching schedule and decided to eat some fish. When she saw what Nina was eating, tears came to her eyes and she said, "Mommy, I'm a vegetarian and you're not, and I think it's sad." Your preschooler's conscience about nonkilling is likely to be better developed than your own.

If you occasionally eat fish as many "basic vegetarians" do, you may have some difficulty explaining this discrepancy to your three- or four-year-old. Gray areas don't make sense to his black-and-white morality. Again, this was brought home when our older daughter was four. We were camping out when a mosquito alighted on Nina's arm and she killed it. Immediately, our daughter asked, "Why did you kill that mosquito?" Nina replied, "Because it bites." There was a short silence before our daughter thoughtfully responded, "But Fenton at my school bites, and we don't kill him." Nina was forced simply to admit the discrepancy: "You're right. I guess I just care more about some living things than others." Children may not understand adult inconsistency, but if it is honestly admitted, they will accept it anyway.

Whether sugar is religiously avoided or very occasionally eaten in your family, your preschool child will probably have no moral objection to eating it as he will with meat. Convincing him that it is not good for him is not easily accomplished because he cannot see the immediate harm it inflicts on people. But he will believe you if you explain that sugar hurts our teeth, that eating too much sugar can make people sick later in life, and that sugar does not contain any of the good things our bodies need.

If you occasionally indulge in a sugar treat, your child may question you. Be honest and say, "I know it's bad for me, but sometimes I like it." Then, if you feel sick an hour later, tell him that you realize that you should not have eaten it. At some time later, when he wants a sugar treat, you can remind him how the one you had made you feel ill. There will be a camaraderie in your shared weakness, and he will learn to take personal responsibility for his own desires. However, if you and your child feel no effect from occasional sweets, simply remind him that it is unhealthy to make a habit of eating sugar-filled food.

Refined foods are not a major temptation for the preschooler. But prepare him for the encounters with white bread and white rice by offering this simple explanation: "We don't like to eat food when all the good things your body needs have been taken out." He will understand that the brown color in whole grain bread and brown rice is the sign that really good things for people are still inside.

The invisible additives and the chemicals in processed foods can be explained directly and simply: "They put little bits of poison in that food." If you occasionally eat a little of that "poison," explain to your child that you don't think a little tiny bit will hurt you once in a while. However, your aware preschooler may well think you are crazy for eating it and refuse to join you.

TEACHING SELF-DISCIPLINE

Your preschooler has a solid foundation for facing the onslaught of the junk food culture if he enjoys wholesome family meals, has grown some of his own food, and understands why junk food is detrimental. Although he is still far from ready to assume total responsibility for his eating decisions outside the home, he is ready to be encouraged to discipline himself.

Self-discipline is the proper aim of all parental guidance. Children should be encouraged not simply to obey but to think for themselves. Now that you want your child to use his developing reasoning power, your attitude toward the temptations of junk food may change slightly. You are still the judge of what is best, but now that he is able to act properly, he can be allowed a plea-bargaining position. If he asks nicely for ice cream or a piece of candy, you can ask him why he wants it and whether he thinks it is really a good idea. Listen attentively to his reasoning. Then suggest alternatives: "Wouldn't it be better to get a honey ice cream at the health food store?" Given this kind of respect, most preschoolers will agree. In any case you reserve the right, as a parent, to be final judge, but at the same time give your preschooler a chance to think about his motivations.

With this kind of openness, you are likely to encounter some surprises that make you very proud of your preschooler. Once, when our older daughter was four, she spent several days with three other children at a friend's house. A young woman who was visiting one day took all the children to the corner store for a "treat." The three other children, thrilled by this unusual opportunity to indulge in sugar, headed straight for the candy counter. Our daughter walked all around the store musing on what she really wanted. She decided on a small unsweetened apple juice.

The preschooler is a far more sophisticated TV watcher than the two-year-old. He no longer believes that the cartoon characters will really join him at breakfast, nor does he think a cereal box with a picture of Tony the Tiger is such, exciting company. He may even have had the disillusioning experience of receiving toys that did not live up to the promises of TV commercials. If your child has reached this stage, he is ready to hear that those TV characters are telling him stories just to make lots of money. By now, he can even enjoy watching the commercials while having the discrimination not to believe a word of them. He will thus begin to think of the animated sugar pushers as either dumb or dishonest, or both. Of course, this attitude will help him to grow up with the basic consumer wisdom that is so necessary in our culture.

The preschooler's visits with his grandparents will likely pose new challenges to maintaining a healthful diet when he starts having overnight vacations at their house. If your parents are willing and respectful of your food guidelines, there is no reason to outlaw these extended visits. Grandma, however, may have no idea what to feed your child. You can help her by supplying a weekend food parcel. In it you can include healthful treats and vegetarian protein foods. Send a few sugar-free candies, a cupcake or cookies, a breakfast cereal, some whole grain bread, and several easy-to-prepare individual servings of protein: a lentil burger, two slices of tofu, a soy patty, a few slices of soy sandwich filler. You can also leave simple instructions for serving your child fresh fruit, cheese, and unhomogenized, sugar-free peanut butter for snacks and fresh vegetables and milk meals. If she asks about buying treats on shopping trips, you can suggest a small toy instead. If your understanding with your parents was firmly established during your child's two-year-old phase, you can leave feeling fairly secure that your preschooler will not return home stuffed with junk food.

Your preschooler has begun to face the temptations of the junk food culture and has begun to take responsibility for his own eating. However, he has not yet had to face the authoritative personalities of teachers espousing nutritional "units" that are in conflict with the way he eats, and candy-loving peers with whom he will spend increasingly longer periods of time. He will face these challenges shortly.

10.

SCHOOL DAYS, SCHOOL DAYS— THOSE GOOD OLD LUNCH- AWAY-FROM-HOME DAYS

WHEN a vegetarian child enters school, he discovers a world that is distinctly different from his home—unless he attends a hand-picked private school with vegetarian leanings. It is true that most children experience play groups, nursery school, or day care prior to their formal schooling, but these are normally private situations where parents exercise influence and are able to control their children's diets. Preschool teachers are regarded by children more as adult friends than as educational authorities, and they normally say little or nothing about nutrition. Moreover, preschool snack and lunch times are relatively free of peer pressure since each child brings his own food. However, once his educational career starts, he will daily face an environment in which teacher authority and peer acceptance increasingly become major influences on his thinking.

Many vegetarian parents try to arrange schooling that is at least to some extent compatible with the home environment. Some parents, feeling that it is important to send children to neighborhood schools, make school the primary consideration in choosing a place to live. Others can find no satisfactory public school and, if they can afford it, send their children to private school. Relatively few parents elect to keep their children home and educate them themselves. Such parents avoid the difficulties of feeding a vegetarian child in an environment where the vast majority of children ingest not only meat, but a steady flow of sugary, refined, and processed foods. However, parents who keep their children home deprive them of the opportunity to learn from other adults and children who have completely different perceptions of the world. Certainly the vegetarian schoolchild faces innumerable new problems, of which his divergent eating habits are only one. We view these difficulties as challenges that bring not only strength to children, but a confidence that helps them to overcome differences and develop tolerance. Moreover, we believe that if vegetarian parents can help their children understand the confusing nutritional information they encounter at school and help them to deal with the pressure from their peers to conform, the parent-child relationship will be strengthened and the child's ability to make personal food choices will be enhanced.

MEETING NUTRITIONAL NEEDS

Many nutritional needs are similar for both the preschool and school-age child until the age of ten. The recommended quantity of the important childhood nutrients—iron, calcium, phosphorus, vitamins C and D—are unchanging; most of the B-complex and vitamin E needs increase only slightly, while B_{12}, folacin, niacin, iodine, and magnesium needs are substantially higher. The increased activity of the school-age child also requires more calories from carbohydrates, protein, and healthful sources of fat.

For the most part your child's increased appetite will naturally take care of his need for added nutrients as long as he is continuing to eat a balanced diet of natural, whole foods. If you have any doubts about the balance of your child's diet, you can use a checklist like the one on page 141. Adhering to these guidelines will no doubt give him the extra calories and most of the nutrients he now requires from the carbohydrates, fats, and proteins that are eaten in greater quantity.

	Ages 4–6	Ages 7–10
Weight	44 lbs.	62 lbs.
Calories for light activity	1700	2400
Carbohydrates	240 g	330 g
Fats	58 g	80 g
Protein	30 g	34 g
Calcium	800 mg	800 mg
Iodine	90 mcg	120 mcg
Iron	10 mg	10 mg
Magnesium	200 mg	250 mg
Phosphorus	800 mg	800 mg
Vitamin A	500 mcg R.E. or 1666 IU	700 mcg R.E. or 2333 IU
Thiamine (B_1)	.9 mg	1.2 mg
Riboflavin (B_2)	1.0 mg	1.4 mg
Pyrodoxine (B_6)	0.9 mg	1.6 mg
Cyanocobalamin (B_{12})	1.5 mcg	2 mcg
Folacin	.2 mg	.3 mg
Niacin	11 mg	16 mg
Vitamin C	45 mg	45 mg
Vitamin D	10 mcg	10 mcg
Vitamin E	6 mg α - T.E.	7 mg α - T.E.

Special attention, however, may be due to those nutrients whose requirements are substantially increased. B_{12} is always of special concern to the vegetarian child who eats no animal products. Parents of vegan children should take note of the substantial increase needed during the early school years. By conscientiously adding B_{12}-fortified nutritional yeast to meals and/or a B_{12} supplement, you will meet this need. The accelerated need for folacin can be easily accommodated by occasionally feeding your child hot or iced fenugreek tea or sprouted fenugreek seeds as well as plenty of salads. Niacin is available in peanut butter in large concentrations. Iodine needs can be easily met by adding kelp powder rather than, or as a complement to, salt in foods. Magnesium intake can be increased by adding blackstrap molasses to milk, as well as a palatable amount of nutritional yeast. If you are in any doubt as to whether your child is receiving all the necessary nutrients, you can add a daily children's vitamin-mineral supplement to the diet.

Breakfast at Home

The meals your child has at home will be more important both nutritionally and socially, now that he has his morning snack and lunch at school. Breakfast has to be served and eaten on schedule, since he has to be on time for school each day, and this new time pressure can easily turn an important mealtime into a hurried snack. Parents often have morning commitments themselves, making the preparation of an elaborate meal impracticable. Breakfast has to be a meal that can be quickly prepared and served and yet eaten at a leisurely pace. Nutritionally, breakfast should include a source of balanced protein, a grain, and a fruit or vegetable. There are a variety of simple ways these foods can be provided. Eggs, toast, and juice are the conventional way to meet the need for a good breakfast. But many children find eggs objectionable, unless they are well hidden in pancakes or French toast. Since making these favorites is time-consuming, most parents will make them only occasionally. Less conventional breakfasts may be more convenient and just as enthusiastically received. Cut apples and toast served with peanut butter, with a glass of carob milk on the side, are one possibility. Cold breakfast cereals like granola or other "flake" cereals (see chapter 13) can be prepared in large batches and served with fresh fruit and milk or soy milk. For children with a taste for vegetables in the morning, a quart of miso-tofu-vegetable soup, with a tablespoon of nutritional yeast added, can be prepared in advance and then refrigerated, reheated, and served with toast for several mornings. If none of these seem palatable, several more possibilities can be found in chapter 13.

Digestion is always as important as the food eaten. If food is not digested, it is unusable by the body no matter how conscientiously it has been prepared. Therefore, be sure your child is fully awake yet not hurried while eating his morning meal. Remember that this meal may have to last until lunch, since many schoolchildren choose play over food at midmorning snack time.

After-School Snacks

Since you may have little knowledge of your child's actual daytime consumption of food, it is wise to offer an afternoon snack that can make up for any deficiencies incurred during a busy school day. A hot carob-coconut milk or soy milk drink, laced with a pinch of nutritional yeast, may be welcomed in winter, especially if accompanied by a crispy cookie made with lots of wheat germ. In warmer weather, blender shakes of fruit, soy or dairy milk, a pinch of nutritional yeast, and perhaps an egg may be greeted with the same enthusiasm as an ordinary milkshake. As the weather becomes hotter, the same shake can be frozen in home popsicle makers, to the envy of the sugar-consuming kids in the neighborhood. Many more snack ideas with mealtime nutrition are found in chapter 17.

Dinner with the Family

Because dinner is likely to be the only meal that the entire family eats together, it should be a time for relaxed communication and for reinforcing the pleasurable experiences associated with food.

You will probably notice a marked decline in your school-age child's instinctual ability to choose a balanced diet if left to his own resources. At this point, it will be difficult to find a balance between allowing him the full freedom of food choices and forcing him to eat everything on his plate. If you allow total freedom, your child is likely to choose far too many sweet foods and far too little protein. If you force him to eat perfectly balanced meals, his displeasure may cause indigestion, resentment, and, worst of all, a rebellion against healthful food during his teenage years. A moderate approach may prove to be the best way of dealing with this type of situation. Most children will agree to three bites of almost anything. Sometimes they even find themselves enjoying the food by the third bite. If, after three bites, your child still "hates" food, he will probably need a quick replacement for that portion of the meal. At this age he can get such replacements himself without interrupting your meal, if your refrigerator is arranged for easy access and supplied with simple alternatives. If your child cannot bear a new vegetable dish, he can get some raw vegetables and cut them into sticks himself. If the protein part of the meal is truly unpalatable to him, he can get himself another glass of milk or soy milk, a piece of cheese, a hard-boiled egg, or some yogurt. For families who avoid dairy products, the last-minute protein substitute may be less orthodox. We know one child who will happily get himself a few pieces of cold tofu and dip them in nutritional yeast. Soy and nut yogurts are also handy alternatives to dinner protein dishes. When all else fails, there is always peanut butter on a spoon. It may not be the most balanced protein food, but it is better than untouched bean and barley stew. Allowing your child these alternatives will help ensure that his nutrition is up to par and that he feels respected in the household.

THE HOT LUNCH DILEMMA

When your child starts school, you will be confronted with the hot lunch program. Nearly all public schools in the United States, and many private schools too, serve hot lunches. This federally subsidized program began some twenty-five years ago in response to the need of children to receive a full meal while away from home. Like many federal programs, it was well intentioned at the outset. However, a candid inspection of most school cafeterias will reveal that children are in fact receiving food of questionable nutritional value. The menus are saturated with sugar, chemicalized food, saturated fats, and refined carbohydrates. A typical day's menu reported in our daily newspaper included pink lemonade (that translates into sugar, artificial lemon flavoring, and red dye), hot turkey and gravy over mashed potatoes (canned turkey and chemically colored "gravy" over instant potato powder and BHT with water stirred into it), buttered canned green peas (the devitalized, pale yellow-green kind), cranberry sauce (a canned product containing more sugar than cranberries), and frosted chocolate cake (as nutritionally beneficial as anything else on the menu). With such menus being served daily, even nonvegetarian families should be concerned about their children's diet.

It is ironic that a special committee of the U.S. Senate has found the national diet woefully inadequate and has recommended "dietary goals" including a reduction of sugar, fats, and processed foods—and yet that same Senate has approved funding for a school lunch program that promotes the gross overuse of sugar, fats, and processed foods! If the Senate had funded a program that adhered to its own committee's recommendations, the lunch program menu would be substantially different. A responsibly constructed school lunch program would do much to correct the nutritional deficiencies of children in this country.

At least one state government has begun to take a responsible stance toward school lunches. The New York Board of Education recently sponsored a seminar that was mandatory for all school food service managers. This seminar was designed to introduce whole foods into the school lunch program. Workshops on sprouting, whole bread baking, and soy foods were given. The board insisted on the elimination of all foods containing nitrate, nitrite, and chemical coloring agents since these additives have detrimental effects on students' behavior. Recently two consultants to the New York City Board of Education received a grant to study the potential of protein-complementary foods in school lunch programs. In New York City, at least, school may become the best place for many children to eat.

Apart from New York State, there are some grass roots movements toward changing the menus in schools. In some communities, parents can educate other parents, teachers, and cooks about the possibility of changing the school's menu to whole, natural food meals. As the general public becomes more aware of the detrimental effects of poor eating habits, such efforts become more fruitful. If you wish to instigate change in your child's school cafeteria, you can call on the resources of Sara Sloan, who instituted a program of healthful eating in the schools of Fulton County, Georgia. In accomplishing this admirable act, Sara Sloan published two practical books for use in any school. *Guide for Nutra Lunches and Natural Foods* and *From Classroom to Cafeteria* (for teachers and managers) are large loose-leaf manuals containing recipes for a school cafeteria's every need. These recipes meet all federal standards, are made only with natural ingredients, and cost less than usual school lunches. Armed with these resources, you can meet the challenge of people who doubt the feasibility of making a change.

You may well be able to replace white bread with whole grain bread, canned pears in sugar syrup with fresh fruit, and instant mashed potatoes with baked potatoes. It is unlikely that meat will be stripped from the school menu entirely. However, at twenty-five cents per meal, any parent can afford to send a child to school with a tofu or lentil burger and tell him to eat everything on the cafeteria menu but the meat.

LUNCH BOX PSYCHOLOGY

If grass roots organizing is not your style, or if your community is staunchly opposed to change, you will probably resort to packing a lunch every day, and your child will eat differently from most of the other children in the school cafeteria. Since most elementary school children greet the hot lunch with something less than enthusiasm, commonly referring to meat as "fried basketball" and shooting canned peas across the table, your child may well be viewed with envy rather than derision for bringing his own lunch.

To ensure that your child's lunch box is a source of pride and not embarrassment, it is necessary to employ a little lunch box psychology. Children will respect a lunch box filled with "normal" and "yummy"-looking food. They will tease your child if he brings "weird" food. We made the mistake once of packing nori (seaweed) rice rolls for our daughter's lunch. She loved them at the time. After being teased about them all day, she refused to eat them again for months. Whole grain bread sandwiches are always safe, as long as you leave out the alfalfa sprouts—kids may call them "hair" sandwiches or the like. Tortillas with grated cheese, carrot, and chopped tomatoes served with a sauce will be the envy of most classmates. In some areas, even pita bread sandwiches are enjoying popularity. If whole wheat pita is sold in your area, you can fill the pocket with humus, lettuce, and tomatoes, and your child will suffer no peer criticism. Soups in wide-mouthed thermoses are usually acceptable as long as they are devoid of seaweed. Nutritious sweet baked goods are often a source of wholesome nutrients. These should not look too brown or too heavy, or they will look strange to other children who expect cakes and cookies to be white and light. But carob looks like chocolate; cookies made with a goodly portion of wheat germ are "respectably" golden; and cakes made with half brown rice flour are light, golden, and moist, like the white-flour kind. (See chapter 17 for recipes.)

The foods that your child will be most proud of are those that appear extra-special: vegetables with dips, individual pies made with beans, grains, or nuts and topped with toasted bread crumbs, sandwiches or sesame buns, custard in cups, and chewy carob brownies. All these "specials" are easy to prepare. Even the pie is not difficult if you merely place an extra portion of your family's dinner loaf in a small, unbreakable ovenproof pie plate and top it with buttered bread crumbs before baking. The bread crumbs make it appetizing, and at school your child will gladly eat it cold. Many other suggestions for appetizing box lunches appear in chapter 19.

To be sure your child is receiving a nutritionally balanced and appealing meal in his lunch box every day, the following checklist may be a handy reference:

1. Does his lunch contain two complementary sources of protein (tofu and bread, cheese and bread, beans and grain, nut butter and grain, etc.)?
2. Does his lunch have a nutritious, appealing drink (nut milk, milk with molasses, fruit smoothie, vegetable juice)?
3. Does his lunch contain one enticing item (pie, cookie, cake)?
4. Does his lunch contain one fresh raw food (vegetable sticks with dip or peanut butter, a fresh fruit)?
5. Does his lunch box include an extra snack for eating at recess time (a piece of fruit or a nutritious treat)?
6. Does his lunch contain any "strange"-looking foods that other children might laugh at?

BEING DIFFERENT CAN BE PAINFUL

Few children make it through elementary school without being the target of somebody else's brutal sense of humor. Despite your attempts to cater to the schoolchild's mentality with "respectable" lunches, your child may be occasionally teased or tormented about being vegetarian. However, even if he were not vegetarian, children would find a reason to tease him: his haircut, his clothes, his reading, or his mannerisms. Children establish a pecking order, by testing each other's responses to "innocent" torments. The strength of your child's reaction will determine how much, how often, and how severely he is "picked on."

A child who responds with confidence, taking little visible notice of the "treatment," or who has a quick, nonemotional retort will seldom be the brunt of another attack. He has handled the situation well and passed the test. We have seen little vegetarian girls being teased by mischievous boys on the playground, but these girls had the self-confidence of prizefighters and instead of calling for the teacher or crying, they walked right up to the boys and said, "Look, we can handle you. Don't think you're so big." The boys, quite shocked by the challenge, backed off completely. Other children we have observed defuse such situations by looking unafraid into their tormentor's eyes and not saying a word.

If the vegetarian child responds to tormenting comments about his diet with tears or anger, or threatens to "tell on" his tormentors, he will gain little respect from his classmates. Instead, any child with a bully-like nature will learn that picking on him reaps an agitated response. Once this weak spot is found, he and his vegetarian ways will become an irresistible target, not because he is a vegetarian but because he is a satisfying person to tease.

A vegetarian parent needs to have a particularly willing and sensitive ear. If a child has no sounding board for the hurt inflicted on him because of his unconventional eating habits, he will need to express that hurt through tears or temper tantrums in the classroom. If parents are receptive listeners, the emotional baggage he carries home from a bad day can be put away without becoming a heavy weight.

Do not dismiss your child's concerns. Vegetarian parents

may have a particular difficulty "hearing" their children's complaints if they feel self-righteously superior about their diets. It gives a child little solace if, when he confides in you that "Johnny says I'm skinny and weak because I don't eat meat," you quickly dismiss the subject by saying, "Don't pay any attention to him. He doesn't know what he's talking about." Your child will feel isolated. He cannot talk with the kids at school about his feelings as a vegetarian child and he cannot talk with you either. It is a very lonely and unnecessary position for a child to be in. When your child complains about being ridiculed, follow these guidelines:

Listen and ask questions. If your child confides that "The other kids say I can't run fast because I don't eat enough sugar for energy," ask: "How does that make you feel? Do you really run slower than other children? Do you think they are right?" and listen to his responses.

Listen to empathize, not out of courtesy. Your listening should come from a real desire to understand your child's feelings and fears. He may not only hate being teased, but really be afraid that he is going to grow up weak and malnourished.

Be sure you understand his particular problem and his reaction as well. Each child has a personal response to any way of being teased or tormented. Be sure you know your child's individuality. Does he want to eat just like everybody else and "forget about the vegetarian trip"? Does he feel afraid that he is unhealthy, weak, or too small? Does he think that all the other kids are a bunch of goons? Does he feel embarrassed about being different? Offer advice or information appropriate to the situation and to his feeling. If he feels rebellious about your way of eating, let him know you understand. Then either loosen his dietary strings or explain to him without defensiveness the nutritional reason for maintaining the diet. If he has fear about his health, give him some facts. Explain that because he is a vegetarian and eats natural whole foods, he is much less likely to grow up to suffer from heart disease, cancer, or diabetes. If he is developing a defensive sense of superiority, you might point out that Saint Francis of Assisi ate meat and that Hitler was a vegetarian. If he feels embarrassed about his diet, tell him that everyone in the world is different from everyone else. Give him a sense that being different can be a source of pride. Whatever his emotional response, talk to him with compassion.

Do not be overprotective. No child entirely escapes being teased by other children or feeling left out occasionally. No parent can protect a child from these uncomfortable feelings; they are part of growing up. They are also opportunities to gain personal strength.

Do not dwell on a particular problem. Once you have had a talk with your child and he is feeling better, let go of the problem and do something else. Giving an incident too much attention is like encouraging a little scratch to develop into a major infection.

Since you and your child share a special status as vegetarians, you have the chance to cultivate a special bond with him by giving support and intelligent answers to his questions. If this attitude of comradeship is encouraged, you will develop a loving and strong relationship.

RESISTING PEER PRESSURE

Quite apart from intentionally being maligned by classmates, your vegetarian child faces a multitude of awkward social situations. He must tell the neighbor who offers him a pepperoni pizza that he does not eat meat, or explain to a friend who is having a McDonald's birthday party that he will eat only the French fries. He may have to bring a lentil burger to the school barbecue, or announce to his whole class that he does not have a favorite meat dish because he is a vegetarian. In all these situations the child is subject to peer pressure. Parents need to recognize this problem and be willing to make personal adjustments to accommodate their child's feelings.

As with overt teasing, listening with an empathetic ear to his feelings is the first step, if not the solution, to a happy conclusion. Parents need to weigh potential emotional damage against the possible ill effects of compromising diet in particular circumstances. Since children's emotional makeup and social involvement vary, compromise will be appropriate in some households and unnecessary in others. Some children feel self-conscious about being different, while others feel perfectly at ease. Most schoolchildren have active social lives. Others prefer to spend the majority of their free time alone.

Most active elementary school children encounter three categories of potentially embarrassing social situations: visits to friends' homes, parties, especially birthday parties, and holidays, especially Halloween.

In the early school years, visits to friends' homes will be for parts of the day, while in later years overnight excursions will become popular. Daytime visits pose little difficulty, but overnight visits usually involve full meals away from home. You can help your child by explaining to his friends' parents that your child does not eat meat. They can usually accommodate this dietary mode quite readily, but you cannot insist that they refrain from feeding him all sugar-containing refined foods. They may have nothing else in the house. If you are going to allow your child the fun of visiting friends, you will probably have to leave his choice of foods largely up to him and his hosts. These experiences may even have the positive effect of increasing his resolve to eat well. You may be pleasantly surprised by his report that "the grilled cheese sandwich tasted like rubber and the chocolate ice-cream sundae gave me a stomach ache, but I did not complain."

When your child enters school, he enters a party-going society. At first parties will be mainly for birthdays, but later there will be parties for Halloween, Valentine's Day, Easter, and the Fourth of July. Children's parties are synonymous with cake, candy, soda, and ice cream. Most children want desperately to be invited to their friends' parties. If left out, they feel like social failures. Here again it may be time to loosen the sugar restrictions for the sake of social growth.

Every holiday is advertised as a time to shower your child with sugary gifts. Christmas has its stocking full of goodies, Valentine's Day its chocolate heart, and Easter its candy eggs and chocolate bunnies. But the holiday that is worst for the conscientious vegetarian parent is Halloween, when children are expected to canvas the neighborhood for candy. Returning home from trick-or-treating, your child will have a sugar supply big enough to make him sick for a year, while tripling your dental bills. You may find it in his own interests and yours to make a deal with your child at Halloween. See if he would like a Halloween party in lieu of trick-or-treating. Or, if he really wants to join the neighborhood kids in his costume, he may be willing to give away his share of the candy as "payment" for his party. At the party you can serve malt popcorn balls, rice-flour cake, and hot apple juice. Not one child will notice the absence of sugar. (See chapter 17 for recipes.)

EDUCATING YOUR CHILD ABOUT NUTRITION

The possible compromises you make during the elementary school years may enable your child to begin to take personal responsibility for his own diet. If he begins to make his own choices, his decisions are more likely to stay with him during his crucial teenage growing spurts. One mother, a member of our food co-op, allows her son a great deal of freedom and is seeing the results. She interviewed him for the co-op newspaper recently:

Q: What about honey and sugar? Which do you prefer?
A: I think both are too sweet.
Q: Which cereals do you like the best?
A: Shredded Wheat. I like brown rice.
Q: What kind of cookies do you like?
A: Um . . . I don't really like cookies. I like juicy stuff like an apple.
Q: Why do you always want to buy candy when we go downtown or gum from a gumball machine?
A: It's 'cause maybe we'll get thirsty on the bus, or hungry.
Q: Why not eat something better for you?
A: We can, maybe, if we get some bananas or apples or something like that.
Q: Do you like potato chips?
A: Sort of. I like them a little bit. I like carrots a lot.
Q: What do you think about being vegetarian?
A: I think it's a better way to be. It's much more healthy. Sugar ain't good for your blood. You know

what it does? It clogs up your blood if you eat a
lot of sugar. I don't want that to happen to me.
[from *Sprouts*, newsletter of Western Mass. Co-ops, Spring
1980]

Although this boy's understanding of sugar may not be
entirely accurate, he does show clearly the enthusiasm that
schoolchildren have for learning about the effects of food
on the body. Nutrition units are among the most popular
subjects presented in public schools. Eating food is, after
all, a real and daily experience for children, much more
tangible and interesting than learning spelling rules.

The difficulty you may encounter in teaching your child
about wholesome nutrition will not be his lack of enthusiasm, but his confusion. At school his teacher, the
supreme educational authority, will teach a brand of nutrition that bears as much similarity to your vegetarian,
whole-food philosophy as a stick of bubble gum to a pinto
bean. If you are lucky, the school curriculum will define
four food groups: Meat, Dairy Products, Fruits and Vegetables, and Bread and Cereals, and the teacher will say
that every meal should contain something of the four
groups. If your child does not eat dairy products, he may
be left worrying that his diet is lacking in an essential food
group. But things could be worse: Some school curriculums
add a fifth group called "Fats and Sweets" and still assert
that a balanced meal should comprise all five groups.

Explaining your own view of nutrition without under-
mining the authority of the teacher should be your goal. It
is important that your child respect his teacher; he cannot
learn reading, writing, and mathematics if he does not trust
his teacher's ability to tell right from wrong in these areas.
It is difficult to contradict a teacher in one area without
seeming to question his ability in all areas. Children like
consistency. But nutrition is one area in which you and the
teacher will have different viewpoints, and this should not
be denied. The simplest thing is to say honestly that the
teacher has one point of view and you have another. You
will need to add that the teacher has little knowledge of
the special needs of the vegetarian. Since you will probably
choke on a literal statement like "Both points of view are

valid," you are best off not pretending to be so magnanimous. It is much better to say, "I think I'm right, and I'll tell you why. . . ."

If your school has a policy of testing and grading nutritional units, this problem can become further complicated. Your child can memorize the required information, but giving answers he does not believe in may strike him as hypocritical. Or he can give answers according to his own understanding and, probably, fail the unit. It is best to approach the teacher directly and explain the problem as politely as possible. You can suggest that your child have a special independent library period during the nutrition unit. Explain that he gets a good grounding in nutrition at home, and perhaps suggest that he bring in some special nutrition projects instead of working on the school's unit. If your child is a well-behaved student, most teachers will respond positively to your suggestion. Your child can make a demonstration display of alfalfa sprouts or sunflower or buckwheat greens he grew in the activity suggested in the previous chapter. His classmates and teacher will enjoy the novelty of indoor food growing and will delight in tasting the sprouts and greens. His grade will likely be very respectable.

Once you have cleared up the school problem, you can continue to teach your child about his body and his food. He is now ready for more detailed explanations of his diet than you gave him during his preschool years. He needs to understand why the products he does not eat are detrimental. This can be taught to him slowly and naturally or more formally, depending on your relationship and desire.

Your child should come to recognize that he needs protein foods, whole grains, and vegetables or fruit at nearly every meal. He should learn what foods contain protein and which protein foods complement each other. This learning can take place during dinner conversations, or you can search out children's books and draw little charts and pictures with your child.

He should learn that these foods are responsible for the growth, maintenance, and health of his body, just as water, soil, and sun are necessary for healthy plants to grow. The way in which foods are used by the body can be taught in as much detail as fits your child's curiosity.

Understanding why your family avoids certain foods will be the most interesting aspect of nutritional education at home. Children really want to understand in detail why meat, sugar, chemical additives, and refined foods are bad for them when everybody else eats them constantly.

He is ready to understand the process of meat production and its effect on world hunger. He can learn about feed-lot procedures in which cattle are bred with the aid of dangerous drugs, kept in small cubicles, and forced to overeat. For information, you can refer to *Diet for a Small Planet* by Frances Lappé, *The New Vegetarian* by Gary Null, or the introduction to our cookbook *How to Make All the Meat You Eat Out of Wheat*. Report your findings in informal conversations with your child. Draw pictures and make charts together.

He will welcome some "good" reasons why he should not eat sugar. Get a copy of Rudolph Ballentine's *Diet and Nutrition* and show your child the pictures of traditional people's teeth before and after they were introduced to sugar. These pictures will provide an indelible imprint about dental care and tooth decay, and their relationship to sugar and refined foods. You can explain that sugar is addictive because it gives a burst of energy for a short time, then leaves you wanting another burst of energy. Also explain that sugar has nothing in it to help him grow or even maintain his health. It has only "empty" calories. Your child is also ready to understand that when he eats sugar, the sugar acts as an "antivitamin" that destroys the good nutrients, including calcium, phosphorus, and B vitamins that his teeth and bones need to prevent decay and disease.

He will want to understand how you know that the chemical additives in processed foods are dangerous to his health. You should simply explain honestly that scientists are not yet sure that all these additives are dangerous to humans, but that most are under suspicion. Tell him that laboratory animals, like rats, monkeys, and cats that are fed BHA, BHT, nitrites, and many other food additives get very sick and die. You can add that you would not want that to happen to him.

He probably is wondering why white bread, white rice, and white spaghetti are so different from whole grain products. If he is old enough, show him a comparison on a nutrition chart like the one on page 38. He will be impressed by the superiority of whole grains. Tell him about the factories with their large refining machines that take the vitamins out of the flour and rice. Explain that they take so much goodness out that the government makes them put some of it back in. He will find it very funny that manufacturers do not just leave the vitamins and minerals alone in the first place. Children generally have a good measure of common sense.

Since little responsible educational material on vegetarian and natural foods has been published for children, you will have to interpret information for your child. Try to make your child's nutritional education a lively and enjoyable experience. If you feel that educating your child is a chance to enjoy learning together, not merely an opportunity to indoctrinate him with your values, he will learn and adhere to these lessons of his early school years.

Food Fun with Your School-Age Child

Your school-age child should have ready access to the kitchen and, if you have one, the garden. The knowledge he has gained through studying with you is only one aspect of nutritional education. He needs to be able to get his hands wet and dirty as well! Most school-age children love to experiment, and what better place than in the kitchen? Some of your child's cooking efforts may end in disaster, but others will be a satisfying success. The successes will give him an appreciation of his special relationship with food.

The garden is another area where your child's independent relationship with food can easily be established. After several years of working together in the garden, or when your child can read the seed packet, he can be encouraged to plant and maintain his own garden. Growing and harvesting the food that grows there will give a sense of pride about the work he has accomplished in cooperation with the earth, the sun, and the rain.

Particularly as schoolchildren mature, it is important that they establish a clear sense of their own food priorities. The years will quickly pass, and soon your child will be a teenager who will perhaps need, more than anything else, your trust and respect as he deals with some of the most stressful years of his life. Nothing prepares teenagers for this intense period so well as the relationship you and they have enjoyed up to this state, especially the knowledge of sound vegetarian eating habits you have taught them throughout their early school years.

11.

THE VEGETARIAN TEENAGER

AS the school-age child approaches puberty, his needs are vastly increased, not only nutritionally, but also emotionally and intellectually. These aspects of his being are inextricably intertwined, and their tremendous new demands place great stress on the young person. Parents who wish to maintain a close relationship with their rapidly changing children must reach into their own reserves of understanding and tolerance to cope with this unpredictable and trying phase.

Adolescence begins with a youngster who basically thinks and eats as you have taught him to think and eat, but ends with a young adult who thinks as he wants to think and who eats more or less as he wishes. Teenagers can become deeply, even passionately committed to their own understanding of the ethical, ecological, economical, or nutritional aspects of vegetarianism—or they can take an attitude of disgust toward people who are "hung up" about food. Or they might position themselves somewhere in between these two extremes. The choices a particular adolescent makes will depend on how parental attitude and authority mesh with his maturing individuality, as well as on the food and nutritional information fed to him daily.

All consideration of teenage diet, therefore, must proceed against a background of rapid growth, sexual change, extreme moodiness, increasing intellectual capacity, and a march toward independence that even very secure parents may, from time to time, find too rapid.

A TIME OF SUDDEN GROWTH

Adolescence is ushered in with a dramatic growth spurt. For several years your child has been gaining 4 to 5 pounds a year. Suddenly, when a boy reaches the age of eleven, twelve, or thirteen, he will gain a fantastic 13 to 14 pounds in only one year, while a girl will gain about 11 pounds. A boy will sprout 4 to 5 inches and a girl 3 to 4 inches in their first growth spurt. This dynamic pattern will continue until puberty and then slow gradually until the young person, no longer a child, reaches his full adult height and weight near the end of the teenage years.

The demands this period of sudden growth make on the body and the mind are obvious, and both body and mind will suffer greatly if the teenager's nutritional needs are not met abundantly. Although youth and sheer energy in some cases may mask the long-range physical effects of poor dietary habits during the teens, these effects can show up later in the form of ailments such as arteriosclerosis, cancer, diabetes, hypoglycemia, or arthritis. On the other hand, the mental-emotional consequences of an inadequate diet will be visible almost immediately. The young person who lacks calcium, phosphorus, and B vitamins will be highly susceptible to the emotional turmoil that accompanies his sudden growth into adulthood.

The adolescent needs as much calcium, with its calming effect on the nervous system, as a pregnant woman needs. Without at least 1,200 milligrams a day, the teenager may be thrown into extreme mood swings, accompanied by poor bone and teeth development. Raw milk is the easiest way to supply a finicky teenager with calcium. It can be used in fortified shakes, custards, baked goods, and soups and fed to your teenager regularly as one of his many daily snacks. Vegan parents may have a more difficult time serving sufficient calcium-rich foods to meet their adolescent's needs. However, a calcium lactate powder can be stirred into nut-milk shakes to provide a good boost to the teenager's diet.

The teenager's need for B-complex vitamins, especially B_{12}, also increases. The parents of a vegan teenager should take special care to provide enough B_{12} supplement such as spirulina to his food. Other parents should make sure that enough dairy products and/or eggs are eaten regularly.

The need for iron as adolescence approaches almost doubles, making iron-deficiency anemia, especially among girls, a common problem. Iron-rich foods such as wheat germ, blackstrap molasses, and fortified nutritional yeast can be hidden easily and palatably in cookies, soups, and milkshakes.

Since vitamin A needs are increased greatly during adolescence, remember to simmer carrots gently for a few minutes before serving, since the available carotene increases substantially when carrots are cooked. Butter is high in vitamin A, but if your diet excludes butter, do not substitute margarine; use the nondairy spread recipe on page 351 for a generous portion of vitamin A. All fats, however, should be eaten sparingly. Your teenager's need for fat will decrease slightly during these growing years.

As a teenager grows, his need for body-building protein steadily increases, but this need is well supplied by the teenager's insatiable appetite for protein-rich foods. Adequate protein intake is therefore usually of less concern than other nutrients.

The need for magnesium is of particular concern to the adolescent boy. Magnesium is readily available in whole grains, raw wheat germ, almonds, green leafy vegetables, and a number of easily available foods that teenagers enjoy. (See page 60 for sources of magnesium.)

THE AVERAGE AMERICAN TEENAGE DIET

Despite their special nutritional needs most American teenagers have completely lost their instinctive dietary wisdom. Many teenagers, largely unaware of the effects of food on their bodies and minds, consume adequate or excessive calories in the form of refined carbohydrates and animal

THE NUTRITIONAL NEEDS OF TEENAGERS*

	Age (years)	Weight kg	Weight lb	Height cm	Height in	Protein (g)	Vitamin A (mcg RE)	Vitamin D (mcg)	Vitamin E (mg α-TE)	Vitamin C (mg)	Thiamine (mg)	Riboflavin (mg)	Niacin (mg NE)	Vitamin B6 (mg)	Folacin (mcg)	Vitamin B12 (mcg)	Calcium (mg)	Phosphorus (mg)	Magnesium (mg)	Iron (mg)	Zinc (mg)	Iodine (mcg)
Males	11–14	45	99	157	62	45	1000	10	8	50	1.4	1.6	18	1.8	400	3.0	1200	1200	350	18	15	150
	15–18	66	145	176	69	56	1000	10	10	60	1.4	1.7	18	2.0	400	3.0	1200	1200	400	18	15	150
	19–22	70	154	177	70	56	1000	7.5	10	60	1.5	1.7	19	2.2	400	3.0	800	800	350	10	15	150
Females	11–14	46	101	157	62	46	800	10	8	50	1.1	1.3	15	1.8	400	3.0	1200	1200	300	18	15	150
	15–18	55	120	163	64	46	800	10	8	60	1.1	1.3	14	2.0	400	3.0	1200	1200	300	18	15	150
	19–22	55	120	163	64	44	800	7.5	8	60	1.1	1.3	14	2.0	400	3.0	800	800	300	18	15	150

* These figures are repeated for the reader's convenience, from the table on page 48. See the footnotes to that table for International Units equivalents for vitamins A and D.

Source: Food and Nutrition Board, National Academy of Sciences—National Research Council, *Recommended Daily Dietary Allowances,* revised 1980.

NUTRITIONAL ANALYSIS OF A TYPICAL TEENAGE DIET

	Calories	Carbo-hydrates	Protein	Fat	A	B_1	B_2	B_6	B_{12}
1 doughnut	125	16.4	1.5 g	6 g	26 IU	.05 mg	.05 mg	—	—
1 sweet roll	179	19.4	3.1	10	130	.03	.06	—	—
1 hot dog	140	.8	5.7	13	—	.07	.09	.06 mg	.6 mcg
8 oz. cola	94	19	—	—	—	—	—	—	—
1/6 apple pie	410	61	3.4	17.8	48	.03	.03	—	—
1 roll	119	21.2	3.3	2.2	—	.11	.07	—	—
1 chocolate bar	147	16.1	2.1	9.2	80	.02	.1	—	—
1/4 lb. hamburger	304	—	20.2	24.5	40	.08	.18	.37	1.6
20 french fries	274	36	4.2	13.2	—	.12	.08	.18	—
2 slices Italian bread	110	22.6	3.6	.6	—	.12	.10	—	—
1 cup canned green beans	32	7	1.9	.3	630	.04	.07	.054	—
1/2 cup lettuce	5	1.1	3.5	.5	125	.025	.025	.014	—
1 piece chocolate cake	450	69.4	3.5	17.25	213	.024	.052	.102	—
1 cup milk	159	11.4	4.4	8.15	350	.093	.395	—	.871
3 chocolate chip cookies	153	18	1.65	9	30	.03	.03	—	—
Totals	2,701	319.4	63.9	131.7	1,672	.772	1.332	1.56	3.071
RDA for adolescent girls % obtained	2,100 128%	345 92%	46 139%	80 164%	4,000 42%	1.1 70%	1.3 102%	1.3 120%	3 103%
RDA for adolescent boys % obtained	2,800 96%	345 92%	56 114%	80 164%	5,000 33%	1.4 55%	1.5 89%	1.7 92%	3 103%

	Folacin	Niacin	C	E	Phosphorus	Calcium	Iron	Magnesium
1 doughnut	.003mg	.4 mg	—	.81 IU	61 mg	13 mg	.4 mg	7 mg
1 sweet roll	—	.3	—	—	46	21	.4	8
1 hot dog	—	1.2	—	—	60	3	.86	—
8 oz. cola	—	—	—	—	35	1	.5	14
1/6 apple pie	.006	.6	2 mg	.32	34	30	.8	16.2
1 roll	.002	.9	—	—	65	65	.3	19.3
1 chocolate bar	.008	.1	—	.308	177	11.25	—	—
1/4 lb. hamburger	.004	4.9	—	—	172	26	3.05	—
20 french fries	.016	9.6	—	—	34	18	1.9	28
2 slices Italian bread	—	1.0	—	—	7	61	.8	—
1 cup canned green beans	—	.4	5	—	213	18.5	2	—
1/2 cup lettuce	.01	.1	5	—	—	—	.4	—
1 piece chocolate cake	.012	.25	2.29	—	—	74	1.21	—
1 cup milk	—	.205	—	.293	228	291	.12	33
3 chocolate chip cookies	.003	.3	—	—	30	10.5	.6	—
Totals	.064	20.26	14.29	1.731	1,162	643.25	13.34	125.5
RDA for adolescent girls	.4	15	60	12	1,200	1,200	18	300
% obtained	16%	135%	24%	23%	96%	54%	74%	42%
RDA for adolescent boys	.4	20	60	18	1,200	1,200	18	400
% obtained	16%	101%	24%	9.5%	96%	54%	74%	31%

protein while ignoring nearly every other category of food. The resulting nutrient debt becomes magnified as body growth accelerates. An analysis of an average day's food consumed by an American teenager, based on the work of Dr. Rudolph Ballentine as described in *Diet and Nutrition*, reveals some alarming facts (see table, pages 184–85): Too many calories (for girls), far too much fat, and an inadequate portion of carbohydrates are consumed. Most of the carbohydrates consumed are highly refined, offering little nutritive value.

Adolescent girls are typically deficient in eleven of thirteen vital vitamins and minerals. Although adolescent boys generally obtain adequate calories, their diets are excessively high in fat, and deficient in all but two essential vitamins and minerals. In some cases the deficiencies are dangerously extreme. The average teenager receives only 15 percent of the recommended folacin requirement, 26 percent of the recommended vitamin C allowance, and 14 percent of the vitamin E requirement. In addition, the only iodine-containing food eaten in a typical diet is iodized salt, so that the teenager is grossly deficient in this essential mineral, just when his need for it increases rapidly.

A recent study of fifty Oklahoma teenagers by Dr. W. W. Brentlinger confirms the poor quality of the teenage diet and points to its ominous consequences. In a typical sample group he found signs of malnutrition in diets that average only fifteen different food items per week. His study shows the early signs of hypertension, hypoglycemia, diabetes, allergies, and arthritis. Twenty percent of all teenagers tested exhibited four degenerative illnesses concurrently. In addition, Dr. Brentlinger found that almost none of the minerals needed for vital cell metabolism were present in sufficient quantities to maintain health. Sustained lack of these minerals will lead to serious health consequences. As Dr. Brentlinger states, this is a form of "involuntary suicide." Even the teenager's normal overconsumption of protein is detrimental since it is accompanied by large quantities of refined carbohydrates. The combination of high amounts of protein with refined carbohydrates is extremely difficult to digest, causing an accumulation of toxins that can result in acne, a strain on the kidneys and liver, and constipation.

PREVENTING THE JUNK FOOD TAKEOVER

Most American adults eat similarly to their teenage children, acquiring 45 percent of their calorie intake from fat and 17 percent from sugar. It is unlikely that the parents described by the statistics feel any dissatisfaction with their children's diet, whereas most vegetarian parents would probably be horrified in the face of these facts. If you have conscientiously guarded your growing child from the "Sugar Demon" and guided him away from Ronald McDonald and his fast-food friends, it is unlikely that you will want to surrender him into their clutches now without putting up a fight.

Preventing your adolescent from going the way of the junk food crowd is a complex matter that depends to a large extent on his nutritional knowledge, internal security, peer group, and personal taste preferences. An adolescent who wants to avoid the nutritional ruin of so many of his peers needs to understand his own dietary requirements, to be supplied with nutritious foods, to be respected as a maturing person, and to have the strength to be different. He does not need, and indeed will rebel against, orders, lectures, preaching, and criticism. Most teenagers will respond to helpful suggestions, enjoyable food, a listening ear, trust, respect, and support.

KITCHEN COMMUNICATION

Before your child entered adolescence, you were his main teacher, a trusted source of information, but now he would rather "find out for himself." It is not so much that he questions your credibility; rather, as his cognitive development proceeds, he is capable of higher levels of abstract thought and reasoning, and naturally he wishes to exercise his new abilities. Now the world at large is his teacher. If his abilities are respected, he may ask for assistance in his research, but he will seldom ask for answers. The time for parent-structured nutrition lessons has passed. You should proceed gently, tactfully, and with detachment when offering nutritional advice or information.

In many homes the refrigerator serves as a family

DIET AND NUTRITION FOR HEALTH AND BEAUTY*

For:	You Need:	Found In:	Some Serving Suggestions:	Lack Can Cause:	Foods to Avoid:
Shining beautiful hair	Protein	Milk products, eggs, beans, whole grains, nuts, seeds, tofu, soy products	Blender shakes, complementary-protein dishes, natural cakes and cookies	Dull hair Split ends Thin hair Dry hair Hair loss Premature graying	Sugar Refined carbohydrates
	B-complex vitamins	Whole grains, wheat germ, bran, nutritional yeast, blackstrap molasses, nuts, eggs, milk products, soy products, peanut butter	Whole grain sandwiches, wheat germ in soy or milk yogurt, blender shakes with blackstrap molasses and nutritional yeast		
	Vitamin A	Alfalfa sprouts, avocados, green beans, squash, tomatoes, beet greens, apricots, yellow peaches, cream, butter	Sprout, avocado, and tomato salads, peaches and cream		
	Vitamin C	Green peppers, citrus fruit, broccoli, papaya, strawberries, rose hips, acerola cherries	Papaya and strawberry shakes, fruit salads, green peppers in salads		
	Iodine	Kelp, other seaweeds	Use kelp powder to replace salt		

* It should be noted that while it is important to consume the nutrients listed here and on the following pages, to be effective these nutrients must be part of a well-balanced diet.

For:	You Need:	Found In:	Some Serving Suggestions:	Lack Can Cause:	Foods to Avoid:
Healthy teeth and gums and sweet breath	Vitamin A Vitamin C	(See above.) (See above.)	(See above.) (See above.)	Tooth decay Bad breath Bleeding gums Pus around gums Tooth loss	Refined carbohydrates Sugar
Beauty sleep	Vitamin B₆ Pantothenic acid Calcium	Whole grains, nutritional yeast Brewer's yeast, egg yolks, whole grains, wheat germ Milk products, green vegetables, navy beans, almonds, sunflower seeds, walnuts, sesame seeds, millet	Whole grain breads, soups, shakes with yeast Eggnogs with nutritional yeast, wheat germ cookies Shakes, green mixed salads with tahini dressings, mixed fresh nuts and seeds	Bags around eyes Listlessness Rings around eyes Lack of energy Insomnia	Coffee, tea, cola drinks
	Magnesium Potassium	Whole grains, wheat germ, soy products, corn, apples, leafy vegetables, alfalfa sprouts, lemons, peaches, nuts and seeds Green leafy vegetables, oranges, bananas, potatoes, seeds and nuts, whole grains, milk	Whole grain bread sandwiches with sprouts and lettuce, soy shakes, mixed fresh nuts Vegetable and fruit salads, mixed seeds and nuts, shakes, whole grain crackers		
Clear, soft skin	Calcium Vitamin A B-complex vitamins Vitamin C	(See above.) (See above.) (See above.) (See above.)	(See above.) (See above.) (See above.) (See above.)	Acne Blackheads Scaly skin Pimples Large pores	Fatty foods, sugar, other refined carbohydrates, oxalic acid in chocolate,

DIET AND NUTRITION FOR HEALTH AND BEAUTY (continued)

For:	You Need:	Found In:	Some Serving Suggestions:	Lack Can Cause:	Foods to Avoid:
	Vitamin E	Cold-pressed vegetable oils, wheat germ, whole grains, wheat germ oil, nuts and seeds, soybeans	Wheat germ oil added to salad dressings, mixed nuts and seeds, whole grain and wheat germ cookies	Oily skin	cocoa, spinach, and rhubarb
Attractive body	Nutrition-filled foods	Whole foods	Balanced diet	Overweight from empty calories Flabby thighs and arms Thick waist	Sugar, fatty foods, refined carbohydrates, white breads
Vitality and strength	B-complex vitamins	(See above.)	(See above.)	Anemia Listlessness Lack of enthusiasm Excessive need for sleep Weakness	Sugar, coffee, tea, soda, refined carbohydrates, chocolate
	B_{12}	Milk products, eggs, fortified nutritional yeast	Blender drinks containing all sources		
	Folacin	Green leafy vegetables, brewer's yeast, milk products, whole grains, dates, fenugreek seeds	Salad, blender drinks, sprouted fenugreek seeds		
	Vitamin B	(See above.)	(See above.)		

bulletin board. Introducing the fridge as a medium of information exchange may be helpful early in adolescence. It can be used in several ways, by all the members of the family:

1. Articles of interest from newspapers or magazines can be posted for the family to read at will. Many of these can be nutritionally oriented, but your child should not be made to feel that the bulletin board is simply a convenient substitute for a lecture on diet. All articles that anyone sincerely wants to share can be used.

2. Notes can be attached to the refrigerator door with magnets. These can be informational or personal. For example: "Did you know that the average American eats the equivalent of 1 tablespoon of sugar every hour, 24 hours a day, 365 days a year?" or "Did you know that Virginia Satir says a person needs 12 hugs a day from his loved ones to function optimally?"

3. Appearance and vitality are extremely important to nearly every person as he or she approaches sexual maturity. Along with the discovery of the opposite sex comes a desire to be attractive and, if not athletic, at least vibrant. The chart on pages 188–91, based on the nutritional needs of skin and hair care, can be copied and posted as an incentive to maintaining a sound diet.

4. If you all agree, post a family checklist listing each family member's daily needs. Each member can check what he has eaten as the day passes, but no one should be allowed to chide anyone else for not fulfilling his daily requirements. Ideally, each person will notice his deficits, and rectify them. Also, you can take note of your teenager's diet and try to rectify it with more attractive alternatives in the missing categories. If he is not drinking enough raw milk or fortified soy milk, blend a pitcher of strawberry or banana shakes and leave it in the refrigerator. A sample checklist follows.

5. All the snacks in your house can be listed, along with their location and simple suggestions for eating. If the list is long and complete, including the most obvious foods, your teenager cannot complain that there is "nothing to eat." All family members should have the responsibility for maintaining the list. When any member finishes a particular snack, he should cross it off. Teenagers should

| | | Servings of | | | | |
Day	Protein (3–4)	Whole Grain (3–4)	Vegetables (3–4)	Milk or Calcium Food (3–4)	Fruit (1–2)	Kelp (3)
Dad Mon. Tues. Wed. Thurs. Fri. Sat. Sun.						
Mom Mon. Tues. Wed. Thurs. Fri. Sat. Sun.						
Teenager Mon. Tues. Wed. Thurs. Fri. Sat. Sun.						

be required periodically to contribute to the reservoir of snacks by making cookies, cake, pie, popcorn, or shakes.

FEEDING THE FINICKY TEENAGER

There are some dietary idiosyncrasies that are common to a vast number of adolescents. You may have experienced them when you were a teenager: hating breakfast, berating school lunches, and desiring particular foods in frequent repetition. With some intelligence and imagination, vegetarian parents can effectively deal with these food fads without any detriment to health.

If your adolescent cannot face breakfast in the morning, make a supernutritious shake for him. If you use raw milk and eggs in your diet, blend these ingredients along with fruit, an imperceptible amount of nutritional yeast, a teaspoon of blackstrap molasses, and a tablespoon of raw wheat germ. If you do not use eggs or milk, blend almonds or cashews, fruit, calcium lactate powder, yeast, blackstrap molasses, and wheat germ. Either drink will be as nutritious as any conventional breakfast but even easier to swallow, especially for the teenager on the run.

Your teenager may never have participated in the school lunch program, but if his friends are content to berate it, consider yourself blessed. Their distaste for the school food will make it easier for him to accept taking a packed lunch. When packing his bag (he has outgrown lunch boxes), be sure to pay the same attention to peer-group acceptability as you did when he was in elementary school.

If he loves ice cream, make it yourself from wholesome ingredients like whole raw milk, eggs, carob, malt, and mineral water. If he hates overcooked vegetables, steam them lightly or serve them raw. If he desires a particular food often, serve it frequently but vary the ingredients. You can satisfy a teenager with a pizza fetish, for example, by making the dough out of varying combinations of whole wheat flours: sometimes whole wheat and brown rice flour, sometimes seven-eighths whole wheat and one-eighth soy flour, sometimes three-quarters whole wheat and one-quarter buckwheat flour. The toppings can be varied by using different vegetables and a variety of cheeses. By using your imagination you can easily make the "same old food" provide balance and a variety of nutrients.

THE VEGETARIAN SNOB

Some vegetarian teenagers will have no attraction at all to junk food or meat. Often these teenagers are a part of a small high school subculture: all vegetarian, all against nuclear power, and all with some sort of spiritual inclination. They usually consider themselves an intellectual elite. While you may be proud of your adolescent's choice of friends, you may also want to ensure that he does not develop an inflated sense of his own superiority.

Although he may retain his respect for his family, a teenager member of such an elite group may be belligerent toward all meat-eaters, including teachers, other parents, and other students. This is an unfortunate but commonly held attitude among immature vegetarians. Discussion of the true motives behind vegetarianism may help such a teenager learn to respect all human beings, whatever their preferences. You most likely made your decision to become vegetarian because of the ethic of nonviolence, a concern for ecology, a desire for health, an awareness of world hunger, or the rapidly escalating price of food. Your decision was a life-affirming choice, not an attempt to show disdain for the views of your neighbors, colleagues, or acquaintances. It is this attitude of positive discrimination that you want your teenager to inherit, not an attitude of superiority. If your vegetarian son or daughter is guilty of such snobbery, you may need to ask yourself whether he or she has been following your own example. Perhaps you yourself have communicated an attitude of superiority, judgment, and alienation from society. If so, you must pay particular attention to the unconscious messages you are sending your teenager.

DEALING WITH REBELLION

The phenomenal physical growth of the teenager is accompanied by a dramatic increase in intellectual capacity. Even teenagers who "hate school" welcome a stimulating discussion about values, politics, or religion. Often this emerging intellectual ability goes without notice by parents, and teenagers are treated like overgrown children rather than emerging adults. The natural reaction of the still-dependent young person is rebellion. If you are a vegetarian parent with a whole-foods orientation and your child feels the need to exhibit his independence, he may defiantly gravitate toward a junk food diet.

Even if you feel you show your teenager loving respect, he may feel differently. He is often extremely sensitive to your insensitivities, however innocent, and equally observant of your inconsistencies. Although his insight may be colored by the emotional and physical pressures of his growth, they are his experience of you as a parent and as a person. If you can listen openly, this attitude will translate into his making personal food choices that are rational, not choices that are simply contradictory to yours. In short, if you respect him, he is more likely to respect your values, including your understanding of the nutritional, ecological, and ethical reasons for a vegetarian diet.

Having your child answer a simple questionnaire early in his adolescence will give you a clear view of his ability to approach you with his concerns, including his concerns about your family's nonconforming diet. Honest talk may prevent him from rebelling against the dietary standards in his home. The questionnaire is designed to let you know how your teenager sees you, thereby giving you the opportunity to become a more open, emphatic, respectful, and tolerant parent. The questionnaire was designed by Millard J. Bievenue and appeared in the *New York Times Magazine* under the title "Why They Can't Talk to Us" (September 14, 1969). Although the article appeared more than ten years ago, its relevance seems just as timely today as it was then.

Do your parents wait until you're through talking before having their say?
Do your parents seem to respect your opinion?
Do your parents tend to lecture and preach too much?

Do you discuss personal problems with either of your parents?

Do your parents talk to you as though you were much younger?

Do they show an interest in your interests?

Do they trust you?

Do you find it hard to say what you feel at home?

Do your parents have confidence in your abilities?

Do you hesitate to disagree with them?

Do you fail to ask your parents for things because you feel they'll deny your request?

Do they really try to see your side of things?

Do they consider your opinions in making decisions concerning you?

Do they try to make you feel better when you're down in the dumps?

Do your parents explain to you the reasons for not letting you do something?

Do you ask them their reasons for the decisions they make concerning you?

Do you help your parents to understand you by telling them how you think and feel?

Talking It Over

Even if the way is cleared for your adolescent to approach you with his personal and intellectual concerns, he may still feel ultimately that a diet vastly different from yours is more appropriate. If this occurs, his way of eating will have come from a thoughtful decision-making process, not from an act of defiance. As a responsible parent, you can help him look honestly at every angle, discuss a myriad of possibilities, and gradually decrease the limits on his behavior until he can be intelligently and securely independent.

Teenagers need to talk, discuss, argue, and debate. They are forming personal values. No longer are they willing or able simply to accept the family's moral stance without questioning and contemplating. In politically active families a teenager will question the "system"; in religious households an adolescent will want to understand the meaning of God; and in vegetarian households the young person will want to debate the ethics, economics, and ecology of diet. Nina's teenage years were marked by nightly talks, sometimes calm, sometimes very heated, with her father. They discussed religion and politics for hours, and, usually, if her homework was not complete, it was because her father and she had talked late into the night. The feeling that her father was extremely interested in her thoughts, reading, and viewpoints gave her confidence that she had value as a thinking, intelligent person, and seldom did she need to "go along with the crowd." A young vegetarian who talks for hours with you is certainly less likely to run off to the local pizza parlor just because everyone else does.

If you are interested in your teenager's thoughts, it is not necessary to wait for him to initiate a discussion about the ramifications of meat and junk food consumption. Try to elicit his thoughts and values. It is always a danger, of course, for parents at this time to want to teach rather than to attempt to learn together with their child. For years you have been teacher, and now slowly you must learn to be equal. One way to learn an attitude of equality is to ask your teenage son or daughter about matters that have no easy solution, things that you yourself are unsure of. Here are some sample "value" questions with no easy solutions.

1. If everyone suddenly stopped eating meat, would it be a good or bad thing? What would happen to all the livestock? What would happen to the ranchers and chicken and hog farmers? What about the truck drivers, butchers, meat packers? How would they earn their living?

2. Do you think there is a moral difference between eating cattle that are bred by artificial insemination in feed lots and raised on chemically treated feed, and eating animals that live on small farms, grazing naturally until the age of slaughter?

3. Can you understand how Hitler could be a vegetarian?

4. Do you think it's strange that a great saint like Francis of Assisi ate meat?

5. Is it better to eat fertilized free-range eggs or un-fertilized commercial eggs? Fertilized free-range eggs come from chickens who live a natural life outdoors. The eggs have, however, the potential to become chickens and therefore we are eating something living. Unfertilized commercial eggs are not embryos, so eating them is not the same as eating a living thing. However, the hens that lay them live their whole lives in cages, barely large enough to hold their bodies.

6. Some people say that if man did not hunt deer, they would multiply so rapidly that they would die slow deaths by starvation. Does that make hunting all right?

7. Conservationists want to ban the killing of whales, but the Eskimos say if they are not allowed to kill a few whales, they will die of starvation. Who is right?

8. Some people point out that plants are living things that have been shown to be very responsive to the world around them. Does that mean that eating them is no different from eating animals? Does that make any sense to you?

9. If someone raises an animal from its birth, supplying all its physical needs, does he have a right to kill it to feed his family?

10. Do you think as many people would eat meat if they had to slaughter the animals themselves?

11. Food manufacturers say they put sugar, chemicals, and dyes in food because customers like it better that way. Is their responsibility to give people what they like or what is good for them?

12. Do you think parents should give children what they want or what is good for them? At what age do you think kids should be allowed to do exactly as they please?

In discussing all of these issues, you need not agree with your adolescent, but you should respect and carefully reflect upon his viewpoint. As an adult, you have likely thought about these moral considerations and established workable answers to them, but your teenager is only now ready to resolve these kinds of questions for himself. Being open to this process may give you new insights and a fresh approach.

The Teenager's Need to "Belong"

Even if your teenager can freely talk with you about the values of vegetarianism and even if he has a strong sense of individuality, he may honestly enjoy congregating with his friends at the junk food hangouts that are so popular with teenagers. Peers are extremely important to the adolescent. He is widening his experience and growing increasingly independent, and to do this he needs the input of a circle of trusted friends. Being accepted by such a peer group may become even more important to your child than his relationship with you.

However, recognizing the importance of your teenager's peer group does not mean abdicating complete control of his diet. Especially during early adolescence, parental guidance is a needed source of security for the young person. It is easier for a twelve-year-old to say, "I can't go to McDonald's after the game because my mom won't let me," than to admit he thinks the food is "plastic." Later, however, he will have to let go of the parental security blanket. He will be of the age when he begins to make his own choices, and you will have to trust him implicitly. At this stage he will weigh his desire for social conformity with his own values and perceived nutritional needs. Sometimes his need for "fun" will win, but through the adult process of making decisions, and seeing results, he will ultimately achieve his own balance.

Other questions that require his discrimination and strength will also surface during adolescence. His friends may pressure him to try tobacco, alcohol, marijuana, or other drugs. The response he makes to such invitations will, of course, have tremendous repercussions on his future health. As with the question of diet, he needs your ready and willing ear, as well as an honest discussion of your own experience with these substances. This is a delicate area, and ultimately the healthy functioning of the family as a whole will be a deciding factor in determining how a teenager handles it.

Making Compromises

You may be as perfect a vegetarian parent as possible, but despite your best efforts, your teenager may turn his back on natural foods. If this happens, you will have to do some personal soul searching as well as some defining of family values to come up with a solution that satisfies everyone concerned. Does your teenager have the right to bring junk food and meat into the house, particularly if younger brothers and sisters might be influenced? Would you rather have him eating hamburgers at home with the family than sneaking out to a fast-food place? Is it fair for him to spend more than anyone else in the family on expensive packaged foods and meat? Must you cook or even smell meat cooking in your own kitchen, when you have taken a moral stand against it? Where does your parental responsibility to protect his health end? Where does this need to take personal responsibility begin?

If these questions are discussed openly, presupposing a willingness on everyone's part to compromise, a solution can be found that will not disrupt family unity. Some families decide to allocate equal portions of the family's food budget for their teenagers' use. The teenagers then take responsibility for buying and cooking their own food, while still eating with the family. In other families, especially when other siblings object to having meat or junk food in the house, teenagers are allowed to eat out occasionally, rather than bring such foods into the house. Still other families allow a teenager to have a personal "stash" in his room, but he cannot eat junk food at family meals. Some parents agree to let the teenager cook one family meal of his own preference per week. There may or may not be stipulations on the meal, but most vegetarian parents place one rider on such a compromise: "No meat in mine, thank you."

Whatever compromise you choose, you will likely feel uneasy about the results. Allowing an adolescent to embark on any adventure against your better judgment is never comfortable. There will inevitably be a touch of fear involved, but the parental strings must eventually be untied. If we want our children to grow into independent adults, we have to trust them, and have sufficient faith in the foundations we laid when they were much younger.

VEGETARIAN CHILDREN'S FAVORITE RECIPES

12.

VEGETARIAN FOOD
FOR BABIES

DRINKS FOR INFANTS AND TODDLERS

Gena Larson's Mineral-Rich Water

This wonderful drink appears in Gena Larson's book *Better Food for Better Babies and Their Families*. Although rich in iron and other minerals, it is so easy to digest that you can feed it to an infant to relieve stomach distress. If you use organic almonds, the drink will protect your infant from worms. The skins of almonds contain a natural enzyme that protects the nut from insects. As a result the drink will not only be an insurance policy against worms, it can also eliminate worms. If your child does become infected, feed him 6 tablespoons a day. This procedure can make the use of antibiotics unnecessary in some cases.

½ cup organically grown unskinned almonds
¼ cup coarse oatmeal

¼ cup organic raisins
1 quart spring water

Combine ingredients in a covered jar and allow to soak for two days in the refrigerator. Strain and return liquid to the refrigerator. Soaked remains can be used in cereals or cookies. The warmed liquid can be given to your infant directly, by spoon or bottle, or can be added to any mashed or puréed baby food.

Iron-Rich Drinks for Baby

Since a nursing infant's store of iron is depleted at six months, easily digested sources of iron should be mashed into his first foods. Here are three drinks that can be served directly or used to dilute puréed vegetables or fruits.

⅓ cup prune juice   *1 cup spring water*

Combine juice and water and refrigerate. Warm to body temperature just before serving as a drink or added to puréed fruit.

¼ cup Floradix (a mineral- *1 cup spring water*
 rich tonic found in health
 food stores)

Combine juice and water and refrigerate. Warm before serving as a drink or added to puréed fruit.

1 tsp unsulfured blackstrap *2 cups water*
 molasses

Combine and refrigerate. Warm before using as a drink or added to fruit or vegetable purées.

Green Mineral Drink

Green vegetables are an excellent source of minerals. At seven months your infant can be introduced to the strong flavor of kale, parsley, and comfrey. This drink may help him develop a taste for vegetables.

1 cup mixed greens (kale,   *¼ cup grated cucumber*
* parsley, comfrey, romaine*   *1 cup spring water*
* and/or collard)*

Purée all ingredients in an electric blender. Strain through several layers of cheesecloth. Refrigerate the drink if you are not going to serve it directly. If a juicer is available, you can juice the greens and cucumber and dilute with water before serving.

Fresh Seed Drink

The seeds of summer melons (cantaloupe and honeydew) and of winter squash (pumpkin, Danish, acorn, and butternut) are rich in vitamins and minerals. They can be put to good use in the following baby drink.

1 cup seeds and pulp from   *1 cup carrot juice*
* melon or squash*   *1 cup spring water*

Blend all ingredients until smooth. Strain through several layers of cheesecloth. Refrigerate. Warm to body temperature before feeding to an infant.

Super Vegetable Shake

At seven months your infant can acquire the habit of taking nutritional yeast and kelp powder in his food. Such a habit can ensure a lifetime of healthful eating.

½ cup alfalfa sprouts   *⅛ tsp nutritional yeast*
½ cup fresh juicy tomatoes *¼ cup grated carrots*
½ cup grated cucumber   *¼ cup chopped green*
⅛ tsp kelp powder   * pepper*
2 tbsp chopped parsley   *1½ cups spring water*

Blend all ingredients in an electric blender. Strain through several layers of cheesecloth before serving. Or, if a juicer is available, juice all vegetables and stir in yeast, kelp, and water.

Quick Nut or Seed Milk

Young children can become accustomed to the taste of brewer's or nutritional yeast if it is added in small quantities to this easy "milk."

1 tbsp smooth nut butter
  (cashew, almond, sesame,
  or peanut butter)

½ cup water
pinch nutritional yeast

Blend ingredients until smooth. Serve slightly warmed or at room temperature.

INFANT DRINKS WITH MILK

All milk-containing drinks are best avoided until you wish to wean your baby. Your own milk is ideal for him; therefore there is no need to introduce an alternative source until you are ready to stop nursing.

Infant Smoothie

Every child loves a smoothie. Your baby can begin to enjoy them soon after weaning has begun.

¼ cup fresh ripe banana,
  avocado, strawberries,
  blueberries, or fresh
  orange juice
⅛ tsp nutritional yeast
1 cup certified raw goat's
  milk (or ½ cup cow's
  milk diluted with ½ cup
  water)

¼ cup water or Gena
  Larson's mineral-rich
  water (see pages 205–6)

In an electric blender, blend all ingredients until smooth. Serve at room temperature.

Milk and Molasses

This drink with its high calcium, mineral, and vitamin content will become a staple for your child throughout his growing years.

1 cup certified raw goat's
milk (or ½ cup cow's
milk diluted with ½ cup
water)

1 tsp unsulfured blackstrap
molasses
⅛ tsp nutritional yeast

Combine all ingredients and serve. In the early stages of weaning, it is advisable to dilute cow's milk to give it the consistency and digestibility of mother's milk.

INFANT DRINKS WITH EGG YOLK

Although children are often allergic to egg whites, yolks generally cause no difficulty if introduced after an infant has become accustomed to solids, generally sometime in the seventh month. Egg yolks are a rich source of iron, other minerals, and protein. If separated from the whites after one minute of boiling, they are well tolerated.

Molasses Eggnog

This pleasant-tasting shake is extremely rich in nearly all the essential nutrients a young baby needs. However, it should not be introduced until weaning has begun.

1 fertile free-range egg yolk
(separated from the white
after 1 minute of boiling)
¼ tsp vanilla extract
1 tsp blackstrap molasses
pinch kelp powder

⅛ tsp nutritional yeast
1 cup certified raw goat's
milk (or ½ cup cow's
milk diluted with ½ cup
water)

In an electric blender, blend all ingredients until smooth. Serve while still frothy from blending.

Milkless Eggnog

If your family eats eggs, you may want to introduce egg long before you introduce milk into your child's diet.

1 fertile free-range egg yolk
  (separated from the white
  after 1 minute of boiling)
½ ripe avocado or banana
½ cup spring water

½ tsp unsulfured
  blackstrap molasses
⅛ tsp nutritional yeast
pinch kelp powder

In an electric blender, blend all ingredients until smooth. Serve at room temperature or slightly warmer.

PURÉED INFANT FOODS

Banana Avocado Lunch

After your first month of introducing one food at a time, you can begin to combine foods that are already a part of your baby's regular diet. Bananas and avocados are a natural combination.

½ ripe banana
½ ripe avocado
pinch nutritional yeast
  (optional)

2 tsp Gena Larson's
  mineral-rich water or
  iron-rich drink (see
  pages 205–6)

In an electric blender or baby-food mill, purée ingredients until smooth. If there are leftovers, squeeze in a touch of lemon and refrigerate. The same dish can be tried later that day.

Vegetable Grain Dinner

Grains should not be fed to infants less than one year old, since their saliva does not have the necessary enzymes to digest them. (For fuller explanation, see chapter 8, "First Foods.") If, however, you are willing to chew his food before feeding your infant, he can enjoy the benefits of grains earlier in life.

¼ cup soft steamed vegetables (peas, broccoli, turnip, collard, asparagus, kale, cauliflower, or green pepper)

¼ cup soft grain (rice, millet, oatmeal, or buckwheat)
½ tsp nutritional yeast
pinch kelp powder

In an electric blender or baby-food mill, purée all ingredients until smooth. Chew to mix with enzymes from your saliva before feeding your baby.

Apple Banana Lunch

This is another dish that can be an early item on your infant's solid-food menu.

3 tbsp applesauce
½ ripe banana
pinch nutritional yeast (optional)

2 tsp Gena Larson's mineral-rich water or any iron-rich drink (see pages 205–6)

In an electric blender or baby-food mill, purée all ingredients until smooth.

Green Vegetable Dinner

Puréed vegetables should be lightly steamed before processing to ensure a smooth texture. Green vegetables are a good source of calcium as well as other minerals and vitamins. It is wise to introduce them early. Their texture will be more appealing to a baby if they are blended with avocado initially.

¼ cup soft steamed broccoli zucchini, kale, peas, collard, or romaine

¼ ripe avocado
pinch nutritional yeast
pinch kelp powder

In an electric blender or baby-food mill, purée all ingredients until smooth.

PURÉED FOODS WITH EGG YOLKS

First Egg Food

Egg yolks are a rich food and should be introduced slowly to ensure that your baby is digesting them easily. This banana or avocado dish is a good beginning.

½ tsp fertile free-range egg yolk (separated from the white after 1 minute of boiling)
pinch nutritional yeast (optional)

½ ripe banana or avocado
1 tbsp Gena Larson's mineral-rich water or other iron-rich drink (see pages 205–6)

In an electric blender or baby-food mill, purée all ingredients until smooth. As your baby becomes more accustomed to eating and digesting egg yolks, the amount can be gradually increased to one yolk.

Pear Egg Cream

The egg yolk makes this dish especially smooth and creamy.

1 fertile free-range egg yolk (separated from the white after 1 minute of boiling)

½ ripe pear
pinch nutritional yeast (optional)

In an electric blender or baby-food mill, purée all ingredients.

Egg Vegetable Dinner

Egg yolks added to vegetables will make your baby's purée smoother and more nutritious.

½ cup soft steamed
  vegetables (kale, broccoli,
  cauliflower, green pepper,
  peas, or collard)
pinch kelp powder

1 fertile free-range egg yolk
  (separated from the white
  after 1 minute of boiling)
⅛ tsp nutritional yeast

In an electric blender or baby-food mill, purée all ingredients until smooth.

Vegetable Custard

Although especially smooth and creamy, vegetable custards make an excellent main dish for the whole family to share with the baby.

4 fertile free-range egg yolks
2 cups certified raw goat's
  milk or soy milk (or 1
  cup cow's milk diluted
  with 1 cup water)
2 tbsp soy flour

¾ cup puréed kale, broccoli,
  cauliflower, peas, green
  pepper, or collard
1 tsp nutritional yeast
½ tsp kelp powder

Blend all ingredients. Pour into oiled casserole or soufflé dish. Set in a pan of hot water and bake for 45 minutes at 350° until firm.

FINGER FOODS FOR INFANTS AND TODDLERS

Finger foods should be juicy, as they are more often sucked than chewed. They should not form little hard chunks that might easily be caught in an infant's throat. The best finger foods for children under one year are fruits and vegetables; babies cannot digest cookies, crackers, or cakes at this early stage. After one year, grain snacks can be added.

Stewed prunes. For the very young child the prunes can be peeled. Usually by seven to eight months your baby will be able to handle the skins easily.
Watermelon chunks. If you remove the seeds, this will be

a favorite juicy snack. In summer the chunks can be frozen on a popsicle stick for a cooling treat.

Steamed peeled apple wedges. Cored and peeled apple wedges can be steamed in a vegetable steamer to make the juice of the apple more available to your baby.

Berry cubes. Blueberries, strawberries, seedless grapes, or cantaloupes can be blended until smooth in an electric blender, frozen in an ice-cube tray with sticks in each cube, and served as a finger food on hot days.

Whole strawberries are large and juicy enough to be a great finger food.

Avocado wedges are smooth enough not to become caught in an infant's throat.

Steamed carrot sticks. When carrots are cooked, not only do they become softer, but the amount of available vitamin A increases tremendously.

Steamed whole string beans are fine if they are the stringless variety.

Ripe peeled pear wedges are a good soft fruit.

Finger Foods with Dairy Products

Yogurt fruit dip. Any fruit can be dipped in yogurt as a finger food.

Yogurt vegetable dip. Combine yogurt with a pinch of kelp powder and a pinch of brewer's yeast as a dip for any of the above vegetable finger foods listed above.

Cottage cheese fruit dip. Cottage cheese can be puréed with a little water and a small amount of blackstrap molasses for dipping finger fruit.

Cottage cheese vegetable dip. Purée cottage cheese with a pinch of kelp powder and a pinch of nutritional yeast and use as a dip for vegetable finger foods.

Cheese cubes are an excellent finger food all by themselves.

Finger Foods with Egg Yolks

Hard-boiled egg yolks can be finger-fed to babies once they have become accustomed to egg yolks.

Yolks in dips. Any of the above dips can be made with the

addition of ½ teaspoon egg yolk (separated from the white after 1 minute of boiling).

Tofu egg dip. Tofu and egg yolk (separated from the white after 1 minute of boiling) can be blended until smooth. For a vegetable dip, flavor with kelp powder and nutritional yeast. For a fruit dip, flavor with blackstrap molasses.

13.

BREAKFAST RECIPES

NONDAIRY BREAKFAST RECIPES

Oatmeal Breakfast Balls

These crunchy sweet balls are one way to make breakfast as much fun for your child as it is for his peers who expect Snap, Crackle, and Pop to stick their heads out of their bowl of breakfast cereal. They can be made ahead of time and stored in a cookie jar.

2 cups oatmeal
½ cup chopped nuts
¼ cup sesame seeds

3 tbsp melted butter
⅓ cup liquid malt

Combine oatmeal, nuts, and seeds. Spread mixture on a cookie sheet and bake at 200° for 15 minutes or until lightly browned. Melt butter over medium heat. Stir in malt. When malt and butter begin to boil, add the toasted oatmeal mixture and stir until it is well coated with malt. Remove from heat and cool. Dampen hands and squeeze the coated oatmeal into balls. Makes 12 balls.

Peanut Butter and Malt Dip

This nutritious mixture can be used either as a dip for cut-up apples and bananas or as a spread for toast, but it is so good that your child will probably be glad to eat it directly from the spoon.

¼ cup malt *½ cup water*
¾ cup peanut butter

Blend the malt, peanut butter, and water with a spoon. Stir until the mixture is smooth.

Tahini Custard

This breakfast pudding is high in calcium. It will be an especially important breakfast treat for the child who does not drink milk.

3 tbsp agar agar flakes *1 tbsp arrowroot starch*
3½ cups apple juice or cider *¼ cup tahini*

Sprinkle agar agar flakes over 3 cups of the apple juice in a saucepan. Bring to a boil, then reduce heat to simmer. Mix arrowroot starch into the remaining ½ cup apple juice. When agar agar flakes are completely dissolved, stir in arrowroot mixture and cook for 3 minutes, stirring occasionally. Remove from heat and blend in tahini with an electric blender. Allow to sit for 1 hour in the refrigerator or 2 hours at room temperature until custard is smooth and thick.

Baked Stuffed Pears or Apples

Serve these pears or apples warm to begin a cold winter's day.

4 apples or pears *2 tbsp raisins or currants*
½ cup peanut butter
1 tbsp liquid barley malt or
  1 tsp blackstrap molasses

Halve apples or pears and remove cores. Mix peanut butter, malt or molasses, and raisins together. Spoon into the center of each piece of fruit. Bake at 375° for 50 minutes until fruit is soft.

Cereal Cupcakes

1 cup leftover oatmeal, corn
   meal, or other cooked
   cereal
½ tsp vanilla

¼ cup carob powder
½ cup raw cashews
1 cup water
¼ tsp blackstrap molasses

Combine cereal, vanilla, and carob powder until well distributed. Pack into well-oiled custard or cupcake cups. Cover and refrigerate overnight.

Grind nuts in an electric blender or food processor. Slowly add water and molasses. Continue to blend until smooth. Unmold cereal and serve with nut topping.

Fruity Oatmeal Pudding

This dish is another way to make oatmeal interesting and to use leftovers.

2 cups leftover oatmeal
1 cup diced pear, apple,
   melon, or strawberries

½ cup raisins
⅓ cup apple juice
½ cup chopped nuts

Combine ingredients and pour into a well-oiled casserole dish or individual custard cups. Bake at 375° for 15 minutes until well heated. Serves 4.

Second-Day Fried Cereal

Children who hate cereal the first day may love it the second day when it is sliced and fried.

2 cups any leftover cooked   1 tsp sesame or sunflower oil
   cereal
½ cup raw wheat germ or
   corn meal

Pour cooked cereal into a loaf pan, cover, and refrigerate until the next morning. Unmold and slice. Dip slices in wheat germ or corn meal. Fry in oil until crisp on both sides and serve with any pancake topping (see pages 226–28).

HEALTHFUL COLD CEREALS

Although children may like granola, they sometimes reject it as too much a "health food." We offer these cold cereals as more acceptable alternatives to the commercial packaged cereals that many children demand. Prepare them ahead of time and occasionally add a surprise prize to the jar. These cereals can be eaten with milk or soy milk, depending on your child's preference.

Whole Wheat Soy Flakes

3 cups whole wheat flour   1 tsp vanilla
1 cup soy milk powder   6 cups water

Preheat oven to 300°.
In a large bowl, mix all ingredients until well combined. Pour 1 cup batter onto each of six well-oiled cookie sheets. Bake for 45 minutes until dry and crisp. Crumble between fingers and store in a wide-mouth jar or airtight canister. Makes 1½ quarts.

Crispy Corn Flakes

3 cups corn meal   ½ tsp cinnamon
2½ cups water

Preheat oven to 300°.

Combine ingredients in a large bowl. Pour 1 cup batter onto each of four well-oiled cookie sheets. Bake for 1 hour until dry and crisp. Crumble between fingers and store in a wide-mouth jar or airtight canister. Makes 1½ quarts.

Sweet Malted Puffed Rice or Wheat

1 6-ounce package puffed brown rice or wheat

½ cup liquid barley malt

Preheat oven to 300°.

Heat malt in a saucepan until thin. Pour over puffed wheat or rice and toss until well coated. Distribute over three well-oiled baking sheets and bake for 20 minutes until toasted. Makes 2 quarts.

Nutty Shredded Nibbles

1 box bite-sized shredded wheat
⅔ cup chopped nuts

2 tbsp butter or oil
⅓ cup malt

Preheat oven to 300°.

In a bowl, mix shredded wheat and nuts until well distributed.

Heat butter or oil and malt in a saucepan until well combined and thin. Pour over shredded wheat mixture and toss until well coated. Pour into a well-oiled baking dish and bake for 20 minutes until shredded wheat is toasted. Store in a wide-mouth jar or airtight canister. Makes 1½ quarts.

Peanut Butter Flakes

1½ cups whole wheat flour
½ cup soy milk powder
½ cup raw wheat germ

½ cup peanut butter
4 cups water

Preheat oven to 300°.

Beat all ingredients until smooth. Pour 1 cup batter onto each of four well-oiled baking sheets. Bake 1 hour until dry and crisp. Store in a wide-mouth jar or airtight canister. Makes 1 quart.

Malt and Molasses Granola

4 cups rolled oats
½ cup wheat germ
½ cup kasha (buckwheat groats)
½ cup chopped almonds
½ cup sunflower seeds

½ cup unsweetened shredded coconut
⅓ cup sesame or safflower oil
¼ cup liquid barley malt
1 tbsp blackstrap molasses

Preheat oven to 325°.

In a bowl combine oats, wheat germ, kasha, almonds, sunflower seeds, and coconut. Heat oil, malt, and molasses in a saucepan until thin. Pour over oat mixture and toss until well coated. Pour into a shallow baking dish and bake, stirring occasionally, for 20 minutes until oats are toasted. Makes 1½ quarts.

BREAKFAST RECIPES WITH DAIRY PRODUCTS

Stuffed Melon

This summer breakfast will be greeted with as much enthusiasm as an ice-cream sundae.

½ cantaloupe, honeydew, or musk melon
1 fresh cherry

1 ice-cream scoop cottage cheese
1 tbsp chopped nuts

Remove pulp and seeds from melon. Place a scoop of cottage cheese in the center. Top with a cherry and sprinkle with nuts.

Carob Pudding Cereal

This corn meal cereal will be as much fun as dessert for your child.

2 cups milk
2 tbsp noninstant powdered
 milk
¼ cup roasted carob powder

⅓ cup white corn meal
¼ cup chopped nuts
¼ cup raisins

Combine all ingredients in a saucepan. Cook over medium heat, stirring occasionally, for 10 minutes until cereal thickens. Serve alone or topped with whipped cream for a special treat. Serves 4.

Chilled Rice Cereal

2 cups apple juice
¼ cup brown rice flour

½ cup noninstant powdered
 milk

Combine ingredients in a saucepan. Cook over medium heat, stirring occasionally, for 10 minutes until thickened.
　Beat with a rotary or electric beater for 5 minutes until cereal is smooth and creamy. Chill and serve with milk and fruit, if desired. Serves 4.

Fruit Cream Cereal

This simple cereal is like fresh-fruit pudding.

1 cup cooked oatmeal,
 millet, or barley cereal
1 cup milk
1 ripe banana

1 tbsp fresh lemon or
 pineapple juice
1 cup fresh berries or
 chopped fresh melon

In an electric blender or food processor, purée cereal, milk, and banana until smooth. Stir in lemon or pineapple juice and fresh fruit. Serves 4.

Bread Blintz

This simple, quick breakfast is rich in protein.

4 slices whole grain bread *with crusts removed*	*1 tbsp butter* *½ cup applesauce*
½ cup cottage cheese	*¼ cup raisins*
½ cup milk	*½ tsp cinnamon*

Roll bread with a rolling pin until flat. Spread 2 tablespoons cottage cheese in a line down the center of each slice. Fold each slice in half over the cottage cheese. Dip in milk.

Melt butter in a frying pan and fry blintzes on both sides until lightly browned. Put two tablespoons applesauce and one tablespoon raisins on each blintz. Sprinkle with cinnamon. Serves 2 to 4.

Cardamom Rice Pudding

Rice pudding makes a palatable and nutritious breakfast. A properly prepared rice pudding cooks for hours, so make it the evening before you intend to serve it, and make plenty so it will last.

1½ cups brown rice	*20 cardamom pods or 1 tsp*
3 cups water	* ground cardamom*
9 cups milk	*4 tbsp liquid malt*

Bring rice to a boil and then simmer for 45 minutes. Add the remaining ingredients to the cooked rice and simmer for at least 2 hours, allowing the milk to evaporate. The pudding is done when the texture is smooth and the taste is rich. Serves 6.

Peanut Butter Custard

Serving custard is a sneaky way to encourage your child to eat enough protein in the morning even if he normally hates eggs and milk.

2 cups warm milk
¼ cup noninstant powdered
    milk

2 eggs, beaten
3 tbsp liquid barley malt or
    1 tbsp blackstrap molasses
3 tbsp peanut butter

Preheat oven to 325°.

Blend ingredients until well combined. Pour into lightly oiled custard cups or a soufflé dish. Place in a pan of hot water and bake for 30 minutes if using custard cups or for 45 minutes if using a soufflé dish, until lightly browned and firm. Refrigerate and serve cool. Serves 4.

Mary Janes

This old-time favorite of children is an interesting variation of fried egg and toast. Your child may love dunking the "hole" in his yolk.

1 slice whole grain bread

1 tsp butter
1 egg

Cut out the center of the bread with a cookie cutter (any shape) or a glass. Melt butter in a skillet. Fry both the bread and the cookie shape in butter on one side. Turn both pieces. Carefully break an egg into the hole in the bread. Allow white to set. Turn and allow to set on second side.

French Toast

French toast is an easy favorite with many children. It can be served with any pancake topping (see pages 226–28).

3 eggs
⅓ cup milk

⅛ tsp vanilla
8 slices whole grain bread
1 tsp butter

Beat eggs, milk, and vanilla. Dip bread in egg mixture. Melt butter in a heavy frying pan and fry bread on both sides until golden brown. Serves 4 to 6.

Pancakes

Seasonal fruits can be added to any of the following recipes for a special treat of blueberry, strawberry, apricot, melon, peach, apple, or pear pancakes.

Rice Flour Pancakes

These pancakes are so light and fluffy that your child may think you have reverted to using white flour.

¾ cup brown rice flour
¾ cup whole wheat pastry
  flour
2 tbsp raw wheat germ

1 tsp aluminum-free baking
  powder
1½ cups milk
2 eggs

Combine dry ingredients in a bowl. Beat in milk and eggs.
  Heat a lightly oiled griddle or heavy frying pan over medium heat. Drop batter onto hot griddle by spoonfuls. When surface of batter is covered with bubbles, turn and brown other side. Makes 12 3-inch pancakes.

Buckwheat Pancakes

1 cup buckwheat flour
¾ cup whole wheat pastry
  flour

1 tsp aluminum-free baking
  powder
1¾ cups milk
2 eggs

Combine dry ingredients in a bowl. Beat in milk and eggs.
  Heat a lightly oiled griddle or heavy frying pan over medium heat. Drop batter by spoonfuls onto hot griddle. When bubbles cover the surface of the batter, turn and brown other side. Makes 15 3-inch pancakes.

Nutty Pancakes

¾ cup brown rice flour
¾ cup whole wheat pastry flour
¼ cup noninstant powdered milk

3 tbsp raw wheat germ
1 tsp aluminum-free baking powder
1 cup chopped mixed nuts
1¾ cups milk or buttermilk
2 eggs

Combine dry ingredients well. Beat in milk or buttermilk with eggs.

Heat a lightly oiled griddle or frying pan over medium heat. Drop batter by spoonfuls onto hot griddle. When bubbles cover the surface of the batter, turn and brown other side. Makes 15 3-inch pancakes.

Old-Fashioned Corn Cakes

Your child will enjoy knowing that these breakfast cakes are like one of the first foods the early settlers learned to make from the Indians.

1 egg
¾ cup milk, buttermilk, or yogurt

¾ cup corn meal
¼ cup whole wheat pastry flour

In a bowl, beat egg and milk, buttermilk, or yogurt until well combined. Stir in corn meal and flour.

Heat a lightly oiled griddle over medium heat. Drop batter by spoonfuls onto hot surface. Brown on one side, turn, and brown on the other side. Makes 10 corn cakes.

PANCAKE TOPPINGS

The simplest topping for pancakes is butter and pure maple syrup. However, you can increase the nutritional

value of your child's breakfast by making your own topping
from one of the following recipes.

Fruit and Yogurt Topping

1 cup chopped fresh fruit: *1 cup yogurt*
  apple, banana, pineapple,
  orange, peaches,
  strawberries, blueberries,
  or raspberries

In an electric blender or food processor, purée fruit and
yogurt until smooth. If necessary, sweeten with honey or
maple syrup.

Molasses Raisin Syrup

2 tbsp blackstrap molasses   *¼ tsp cinnamon*
1 cup water   *1 tsp arrowroot starch*
¼ cup raisins   *dissolved in 1 tsp water*

Heat molasses, water, raisins, and cinnamon in a saucepan
until they begin to boil lightly. Stir in arrowroot paste.
Continue stirring for 3 minutes until sauce thickens. Serve
hot.

Dried Fruit Pancake Topping

1 cup dried fruit   *1 tsp arrowroot starch*
1½ cups water   *mixed with 1 tsp water*

Soak dried fruit in water overnight. Purée in an electric
blender or food processor until smooth. Heat in a saucepan nearly to boiling. Stir in arrowroot paste. Continue
stirring for 3 minutes until sauce thickens. Serve hot.

Peanut Butter Syrup

¼ cup peanut butter   ¾ cup water
¼ cup liquid barley malt   ½ tsp arrowroot starch
                             dissolved in 1 tsp water

Beat peanut butter, malt, and water until smooth. Heat in
a saucepan nearly to boiling. Stir in arrowroot paste. Continue stirring for 3 minutes until sauce thickens. Serve hot.

14.

SOUPS

NONDAIRY SOUPS

Alphabet Soup

Here is a soup that is every bit as attractive as—and more nutritious than—the canned kind.

½ cup whole wheat alphabet pasta	¼ cup finely chopped carrot
2 cups boiling water	1 cup tomato juice
¼ cup finely chopped celery	½ tsp blackstrap molasses
¼ cup finely chopped green pepper	½ tsp kelp powder

Add alphabet pasta to boiling water and continue to boil for 12 to 25 minutes until well cooked. Reduce heat to medium-low and add celery, green pepper, and carrot. Cook without boiling for 10 to 15 minutes until carrots are soft. Stir in tomato juice, molasses, and kelp powder before serving. Serves 4.

Noodle Soup

This simple soup is designed to taste like the popular canned variety but at the same time makes a wonderful disguise for nutritional yeast.

4 ounces udon (Japanese whole wheat pasta)	¼ tsp thyme
	½ tsp cumin powder
3 cups boiling water	½ tsp coriander powder
2 tbsp nutritional yeast	½ tsp turmeric
½ tsp sea salt	2 tsp chopped fresh parsley
½ tsp celery seeds	2 tbsp chopped scallions
¼ tsp sage	1 tsp corn oil

Break up the pasta and add it to the boiling water. Boil for 12 to 15 minutes. Reduce heat to low. When boiling subsides, stir in remaining ingredients. Allow to simmer for 5 minutes before serving. Serves 4.

Tomato Soup

This simple soup is a good source of vitamins A and C if it is not boiled (boiling destroys the vitamins).

1 6-ounce can unsalted tomato paste	1 tsp liquid barley malt
	1 tsp arrowroot starch
2 cups water	mixed with 2 tsp water
½ tsp sea salt	

Combine tomato paste, water, and salt in a saucepan. Heat over a medium flame. Stir in malt and arrowroot paste. Cook for 10 minutes until slightly thickened. Serves 2.

Miso Soup

There are many kinds of miso. Some are dark and extremely salty, while other, light-colored varieties are almost sweet in flavor. All miso contains valuable digestive enzymes and should not be boiled. Children love its taste no matter what the variety.

2 tbsp miso	*1 tbsp nutritional yeast*
3½ cups water	*¼ cup chopped scallions*
	2 tbsp chopped parsley

In a saucepan, dissolve miso in water. Add yeast, scallions, and parsley. Simmer on low heat for 10 minutes. Serves 4.

Tamari Broth with Dumplings

DUMPLINGS

⅓ cup buckwheat flour	*½ tsp kelp powder*
⅓ cup whole wheat flour	*⅓ cup water or vegetable*
2 tbsp soy flour	*broth*
	3 cups boiling water

To make dumplings, combine flours and kelp powder in a mixing bowl. Stir in water or broth to form a soft dough. Form dough into ¾-inch balls. Drop in boiling water and cook, covered, for 3 minutes. Drain and set aside.

BROTH

1 tbsp corn oil	*½ cup sliced string beans*
2 onions, chopped	*or celery*
1 garlic clove, chopped	*4 cups water*
½ cup sliced mushrooms	*2 tbsp tamari soy sauce*
	1 tbsp nutritional yeast

In a heavy-bottomed kettle, heat oil over medium heat. Stir in onions and sauté until transparent. Add garlic, mushrooms, and string beans or celery and cook for 5 minutes. Add water, soy sauce, and nutritional yeast. Add cooked dumplings to soup. Cook over medium heat for 20 minutes until vegetables are tender. Serves 4 to 5.

Nondairy Cream of Vegetable Soup

This is a creamy, light-green soup—a texture and color children will like.

2 cups spinach, broccoli,   2 tsp nutritional yeast
    peas, chard, or mustard   1 tsp kelp powder or
    greens   ½ tsp salt
1 cup crumbled tofu   1½ cups water
2 tbsp tahini

Steam vegetables until soft. In an electric blender or food processor, purée steamed vegetables with remaining ingredients until smooth. Heat over medium heat until warm and serve. Serves 3.

Bean and Barley Soup

This hearty winter soup gives children the energy they need for playing outdoors in the cold.

¼ cup kidney beans or   1 tsp kelp powder
    pinto beans   1 tsp cumin seed
¼ cup aduki beans   2 tsp ground coriander
¼ cup navy beans   1 tbsp chopped parsley
¼ cup barley   2 carrots, chopped
2 onions, chopped   1½ tbsp tamari soy sauce
2 garlic cloves, chopped   5 cups water

Place all ingredients in a covered kettle or pressure cooker. In a kettle bring to a boil for 5 minutes and reduce heat to low for 4 hours or until beans and barley are soft.

In a pressure cooker, increase pressure to 15 pounds over high heat. Reduce heat to low and cook for 2 hours. Decrease pressure according to manufacturer's instructions. Serves 6.

Nondairy Chowder

Chowders are an all-American favorite that children who do not eat dairy products can enjoy if made with a combination of soy flour and whole wheat pastry flour.

1 tbsp corn oil
2 onions, chopped
3 potatoes, diced
1 cup corn kernels, chopped
   celery, or sliced
   mushrooms
3 cups water

2 tbsp tahini
¼ cup soy flour
¼ cup whole wheat pastry
   flour
½ tsp salt
½ tsp black pepper
1 cup water

Heat oil in a heavy kettle. Sauté onions until transparent. Add potatoes, vegetable of your choice, and water. Cook over medium heat for 30 minutes until potatoes are soft. In a small bowl, combine tahini, soy flour, whole wheat pastry flour, salt, pepper, and 1 cup water to form a paste. Stir into cooking vegetables. Cook over medium heat for 15 minutes until soup thickens and there is no taste of raw flour. Serves 4 to 6.

Summer Cucumber Tofu Soup

Cold soups are a refreshing quick lunch for busy children. Cucumber soup can be made creamy and light with tofu for children who do not eat dairy products.

1 tsp safflower oil
2 onions, chopped
3 cucumbers, sliced
2 tbsp chopped fresh parsley

1 pound tofu, crumbled
4 cups water or vegetable
   stock
½ tsp sea salt
2 scallions, finely chopped

Heat oil in a heavy skillet. Sauté onions until transparent. Add cucumbers, parsley, tofu, and ¼ cup water or vegetable stock. Cover and simmer for 10 minutes.

   Remove from heat, add remaining water or stock, and purée in an electric blender or food processor until smooth. Pour into a serving bowl, sprinkle with scallions, and refrigerate until cool. Serves 4 to 6.

Gazpacho

This summer soup will delight children who enjoy Mexican food.

4 tomatoes, peeled and
    chopped
1 onion, finely chopped
½ cucumber, finely
    chopped

1 green pepper, finely
    chopped
¼ tsp dried crushed red
    peppers
2 cups tomato juice

In a bowl, combine tomatoes, onion, cucumber, and green pepper. In an electric blender or food processor, purée dried peppers with tomato juice. Add tomato juice and chilies to tomato-and-vegetable mixture. Refrigerate for at least 2 hours before serving. Serves 4.

SOUPS WITH DAIRY PRODUCTS

Chowder

Traditional chowder can be made with corn, celery, or mushrooms—whichever appeals most to your child.

1 tbsp butter
1 onion, chopped
2 potatoes, finely diced
1 cup corn kernels, chopped
    celery, or sliced
    mushrooms

1 cup water
2½ cups milk
¼ tsp black pepper
½ tsp sea salt
2 tsp arrowroot starch
    dissolved in 1 tbsp water

Melt butter in a heavy kettle. Sauté onion until transparent. Add potatoes, vegetable of your choice, and water. Cover and cook over medium heat for 25 minutes until potatoes are soft. Add milk, black pepper, and salt. Heat to scalding and stir in arrowroot paste. Continue stirring until soup thickens slightly. Serves 4 to 6.

French Onion Soup

Many children love the salty taste of miso and the texture of melted cheese. For them this can become a regular meal.

1 tsp safflower oil	3½ cups water
4 onions, cut into thin wedges	4 slices toasted whole grain bread
4 tsp dark miso	1 cup grated Cheddar cheese

Heat oil in a heavy kettle. Sauté onions until transparent. Dissolve miso in water and add to onions. Cook for 10 minutes and remove from heat.

Cut toast with a 3-inch round cookie cutter. Pour soup into individual oven-proof bowls or casserole dishes. Top each with a round of toast. Sprinkle with cheese. Place under a broiler until cheese has melted. Serves 4.

Cream of Tomato Soup

If your child loves the canned kind, this is another health-ful alternative that will make him pleased with your nutritious home cooking.

1 6-ounce can unsalted tomato paste	½ tsp salt
2½ cups milk	1 tsp nutritional yeast
	1 tsp liquid barley malt

Combine all ingredients in a saucepan. Heat over medium heat, being careful not to boil. The soup is ready to serve when hot. Serves 3.

Cold Potato Soup (Vichyssoise)

Your child may enjoy knowing that his summertime meal includes a soup served at the finest French restaurants.

2 tbsp butter	3 cups milk
2 onions, chopped	½ cup noninstant powdered milk
4 potatoes, diced	2 tbsp nutritional yeast
3 cups water or vegetable stock	1 cup yogurt or sour cream
½ tsp salt	½ cup finely chopped chives

Melt butter in a kettle and sauté onions until transparent. Add potatoes, water or stock, and salt. Cook over medium heat for 25 minutes until potatoes are soft. Purée in an electric blender or food processor until smooth.

Using a wire whip or blender, combine milk, milk powder, yeast, and sour cream or yogurt until smooth.

In a soup server, combine potato and milk mixtures. Stir in chives and chill before serving. Serves 6 to 8.

Summer Avocado Soup

This simple soup is hearty enough for a summer meal. It provides ample energy and protein for any active child.

1 ripe avocado, pitted and peeled	*½ cup sour cream or yogurt*
2 cups milk	*½ tsp salt or kelp powder*
	1 tsp nutritional yeast

In a blender or food processor, purée all ingredients until smooth. Serves 2 to 4.

SOUPS WITH EGGS

Egg Swirl Soup

This simplified version of a soup served in Chinese restaurants will please any child who enjoys Oriental food.

1 tsp sesame oil	*1 tbsp nutritional yeast*
3 eggs, beaten	*¼ tsp turmeric*
4 cups water or vegetable stock	*¼ tsp powdered thyme*
½ tsp salt or kelp powder	*1 cup peas*

In a wok, heat oil over medium high heat and coat pan. Pour 1 tablespoon beaten egg into the bottom of the wok while turning it so that the egg forms a thin layer. As soon as the egg is solid, remove it from the wok. Continue until all the egg has been fried and removed from the wok.

Place fried egg, water or stock, salt or kelp, yeast, turmeric, thyme, and peas in a kettle. Cook without boiling until peas are tender but have not lost their bright color. Serves 4.

Egg and Lemon Soup

This soup, based on a Greek recipe, has a tangy, garlicky flavor.

6 cups water	*2 garlic cloves, pressed*
2 tbsp nutritional yeast	*4 eggs, well beaten*
½ tsp thyme	*½ cup lemon juice*
½ tsp tarragon	*¼ tsp sea salt*

In a kettle combine water, yeast, thyme, tarragon, and pressed garlic. Bring to a gentle boil and reduce heat to simmer.

Remove 1 cup of hot broth. In a bowl, beat together eggs and lemon juice until frothy. Beat in 1 cup stock with a wire whisk. Stir egg mixture and salt into kettle of stock.

Cook, stirring constantly, over low heat until soup thickens. Serves 6.

15.

ALL-AMERICAN COMPLEMENTARY-PROTEIN MAIN DISHES

BURGERS ON BUNS WITH RELISH AND KETCHUP

Every child wants an occasional burger, and there is no reason why a vegetarian child need be deprived. The following recipes offer three different types of burgers that can be served on sesame buns and topped with homemade relish and ketchup. Each of the burger recipes satisfies the need for protein complementation while allowing your child to satisfy his "burger" craving.

Soyburgers

1 cup soybeans
3 to 6 cups water
1 cup cooked grain or whole wheat flour
1 tbsp powdered cumin

2 tsp garlic powder
½ tsp black pepper
1 onion, finely chopped (optional)
4 tbsp butter or ghee (see page 78)

Cook soybeans in a pressure cooker with 3 cups water for 3 hours or in a covered pan with 6 cups water for 6 hours until soft. Drain and mash cooked soybeans with a potato masher. Add all of the remaining ingredients (except butter) to the mashed soybeans. Mix well to form a stiff dough. Wet hands and form into quarter-inch-thick patties. Pan-fry patties in melted butter or ghee on both sides until crisp or bake on a well-oiled cookie sheet at 350° for 30 minutes. Makes 8 burgers.

Lentil Burgers

1 cup lentils	*2 tsp ground coriander*
3 cups water	*1 tsp tamari soy sauce*
1 cup cooked grain or	*1 small onion, chopped*
whole wheat flour	*(optional)*
2 tsp ground cumin	*3 tbsp butter or ghee*
	(see page 78)

Cook lentils in water for 45 minutes until soft. Add the remaining ingredients (except butter) to the cooked lentils. The burger dough should be stiff. Add more whole wheat flour or grain if it is too sticky to form into patties. Wet hands and form dough into quarter-inch-thick patties. Fry patties on both sides in melted butter until crisp, or bake them on a well-oiled cookie sheet at 350° for approximately 30 minutes until a crust forms. Makes 8 to 10 burgers.

Mung Bean Burgers

1 cup mung beans	*2 tsp curry powder*
3 cups water	*1 tbsp butter or ghee*
1 cup cooked grain or	*(see page 78)*
whole wheat flour	

Cook mung beans in water for 45 minutes until soft. Add remaining ingredients (except butter) to the cooked mung beans. Mix well. The dough should be stiff. Form dough into quarter-inch-thick patties with moistened hands. Fry patties on both sides in melted butter until crisp crust forms, or bake on a well-oiled cookie sheet at 350° for 30 minutes. Makes 8 burgers.

Sugarless Ketchup

1 8-ounce can tomato paste	*½ tsp honey*
¾ cup water	*⅛ tsp onion salt*
	dash of salt

Combine all ingredients. Makes 1½ cups.

Quick Relish

1 cucumber	*4 stalks celery*
1 green pepper	*1 tbsp olive oil*
1 sweet red pepper	*1 tsp cider vinegar*
1 small onion	*¼ tsp black pepper*

Chop all the vegetables fine. Toss with oil, vinegar, and pepper. Store in the refrigerator; the flavor increases with time. Use on burgers and sandwiches. Makes approximately 3 cups.

Sesame Buns

2 cups milk	*¼ cup lukewarm water*
¼ cup oil	*2 tbsp dry yeast*
¼ cup liquid barley malt	*6 cups whole wheat flour*
	½ cup sesame seeds

Heat milk to scalding and pour into a bowl with the oil and 2 tablespoons of the barley malt. In a separate bowl, combine warm water and the remaining 2 tablespoons of barley malt. Sprinkle the yeast on top of the water-and-malt mixture. Let both bowls sit for approximately 5 minutes until the milk is cooled to lukewarm. Combine the yeast and milk solutions in a large bowl. Add 1½ cups flour to the liquid. Beat vigorously with a wire whisk. Allow to stand in a warm place for 15 minutes.

Add the remaining flour slowly. Beat it with a wire whisk until the dough becomes too stiff to be beaten with the whisk. Then stir in the last of the flour with a wooden spoon. Knead on a floured board for 10 minutes.

Put dough in a well-oiled bowl and let rise until double in bulk. Punch down and form into buns. Place buns on a well-oiled cookie sheet about 3 inches apart and allow to rise until double. Sprinkle the top of each bun with sesame seeds and bake at 375° for about 20 minutes or until the bottoms are browned and the tops are lightly browned. Makes 12 buns.

Spaghetti and Bean Balls

The grains, beans, and cheese that make up this dish will give your child a generous serving of protein and delight him as only a heaping plate of spaghetti can.

SPAGHETTI SAUCE

1 12-ounce can tomato paste	*1 tsp ground cumin*
3 cups water	*½ tsp garlic powder*
2 tsp oregano	*2 tsp olive oil*
½ tsp black pepper	*1 tsp tamari soy sauce*
	1 egg (optional)

Mix all ingredients with a wire whisk. Cook over medium heat for at least 15 minutes. Makes 4½ cups.

BEAN BALLS

1 cup cooked beans or lentils	*1 tsp tamari soy sauce*
1 cup cooked rice or millet	*1 tsp oregano*
2 tbsp soy flour	*1 tsp coriander*
1 tbsp ground cumin	*¼ tsp black pepper*
	¼ tsp onion salt

Mix all ingredients well to form a stiff dough. If the dough is sticky, add more grain. Form into balls. Brown on all sides in a hot, greased frying pan. Add balls to spaghetti sauce. Makes 12 balls.

SPAGHETTI

12 ounces whole grain spaghetti

Cook spaghetti according to package directions. Serve topped with sauce and bean balls. Serves 6 generously.

Barbecued Tofu Sandwiches

Fried tofu is a crispy, tasty addition to any sandwich, especially when it is topped with homemade barbecue sauce. We warn you to make a lot. Our experience is that children gobble up as much as you make.

FRIED TOFU

1 pound tofu　　　　　*1 cup water*
1 tsp tamari soy sauce　*2 tbsp butter*

Slice tofu into quarter-inch slices. Place slices in a shallow pan or dish. Mix tamari and water and pour over the tofu slices. Allow to marinate for a few minutes. Wrap wet slices in a cloth or paper towel until the excess moisture is absorbed. Melt butter in a heavy frying pan over medium heat. Fry tofu on both sides until light brown and crispy. Remove from pan and drain on a paper towel. Makes enough fried tofu to fill 4 sandwiches.

BARBECUE SAUCE

2 garlic cloves　　　　　　*1 tsp allspice*
1 tbsp butter　　　　　　　*1 tsp dried parsley or 1 sprig*
1 6-ounce can tomato paste　　*fresh parsley, chopped*
1 cup water　　　　　　　　*¼ cup fresh lemon juice*
½ cup liquid barley malt　　*1 tbsp arrowroot starch*
2 tsp dry mustard　　　　　　*dissolved in 2 tbsp water*

Mince garlic and sauté in melted butter. Add all ingredients except arrowroot starch. Simmer for 10 minutes. Increase heat. When sauce begins to boil gently, stir in arrowroot paste. Continue stirring for 2 minutes until sauce thickens. This sauce can be spread on sandwiches or used in any way you and your children enjoy barbecue sauce. Makes 1½ cups.

DINNER PIES

Individual Protein Pies

If your child loves pies, he will be delighted to have an individual dinner pie made especially for him.

PIE FILLING

1 tsp corn oil	*3 tbsp soy flour*
2 onions, chopped	*1 tbsp nutritional yeast*
2 potatoes, diced	*½ tsp black pepper*
2 carrots, diced	*1 tbsp tamari soy sauce*
1 green pepper, chopped	*1 pound tofu, cut into*
2 cups water	*half-inch cubes*
3 tbsp whole wheat flour	

Heat oil in a heavy frying pan or kettle. Sauté onions until transparent. Add potatoes, carrots, green pepper, and 1 cup water. Cover and cook for 20 minutes until potatoes are tender.

In a bowl, combine remaining cup of water, whole wheat flour, soy flour, nutritional yeast, black pepper, and soy sauce. Mix with a wire whisk until well combined. Add to cooked vegetables. Stir in tofu cubes. Continue to cook, stirring occasionally, until filling thickens. Remove from heat and set aside.

PIE PASTRY

1 cup whole wheat flour	*⅛ tsp kelp powder*
¾ cup whole wheat pastry	*⅓ cup corn, safflower, or*
flour	*sunflower oil*
¼ cup wheat germ	*3 tbsp ice water*

Mix dry ingredients together. Stir in oil with a fork until well distributed. Stir in ice water until dough forms a ball. If necessary, add one more tablespoon ice water.

ASSEMBLING PIES

Divide dough into eight small balls to fit four individual pie plates. Roll each ball of dough between two lightly floured sheets of waxed paper. Remove waxed paper and line each pie plate with dough.

Spoon equal portions of filling into each lined pie plate. Cover with remaining four rounds of pastry. Trim and pinch edges. Gently punch holes in each pie with a fork. Bake at 400° for 40 minutes until browned.

Lentil Pot Pie

Here is a biscuit-topped casserole that the neighborhood mothers would be proud to take to a church supper.

LENTIL FILLING

1 cup lentils	*1 garlic clove, minced*
3 cups water	*3 potatoes, diced*
1 tsp corn oil	*1 cup water*
1 onion, chopped	*2 carrots, diced*
1 green pepper, chopped	*½ cup green beans, diced*
	1 tbsp tamari soy sauce

In a pot, combine lentils and water. Bring to a boil for 5 minutes and reduce heat to medium low. Continue to cook, covered, for 45 minutes, until lentils are soft.

Heat oil in a heavy frying pan. Sauté onions until transparent. Add pepper, garlic, potatoes, and water. Cook, covered, for 10 minutes. until potatoes are easily pierced with a sharp knife. Add carrots and green beans. Cook for 10 minutes longer.

Combine lentils and vegetables and stir in soy sauce. Set aside.

BISCUIT TOPPING

2 cups whole wheat flour
4 tsp aluminum-free baking
   powder

½ tsp sea salt
¼ cup corn or safflower oil
¾ cup soy milk

Combine flour, baking powder, and salt until thoroughly mixed. Stir in oil with a fork until mixture resembles the texture of corn meal. Stir in soy milk to form a dough.

Roll or pat dough 1 inch thick on a floured board. Cut in rounds with a 3-inch cookie cutter or drinking glass.

ASSEMBLING CASSEROLE

Pour filling into a casserole or oven-proof dish. Top with biscuits and bake at 375° for 25 minutes until lightly browned.

Shepherd's Pie

A crusty topping, mashed potatoes, gravy, and corn are among a child's favorite things. This recipe for shepherd's pie is a tasty combination of them all.

¾ cup lentils
¾ cup brown rice
5 cups water
3 medium potatoes
¼ cup milk or water

1 tbsp butter or corn oil
1½ tsp tamari soy sauce
2 tsp ground cumin
¼ cup chopped onion
2 cups corn kernels

Gently boil lentils and rice in water for 45 minutes. While they cook, wash and dice unpeeled potatoes. Steam diced potatoes for 20 minutes until soft. Add milk and butter or water and corn oil to cooked potatoes and mash until smooth. Set aside.

Remove lentils and rice from heat and stir in tamari, cumin, and onion. Purée mixture in an electric blender or food processor. The puréed lentils and rice should have the consistency of gravy. If too thick, add more water.

In a mixing bowl, combine corn kernels and lentil purée. Pour into an oiled casserole dish.

Top with mashed potatoes. Bake at 375° for 45 minutes or until a light brown crust forms on potatoes. Serves 6.

Baked Beans on Toast

This well-known all-American dish is a perfect complementary-protein food.

1 cup navy beans	½ tbsp dry mustard
4 cups water	1 tbsp nutritional yeast
¼ cup chopped onion	½ tsp salt or kelp powder
1 tbsp blackstrap molasses	6 to 8 slices whole grain
2 tbsp tomato paste	bread

In a covered pot, bring beans and water to a boil. Allow to boil for 10 minutes. Reduce heat to medium and cook for 1 hour until beans are tender.

Pour beans into an oiled casserole dish. Stir in remaining ingredients and bake at 250° for 4 hours until beans are soft. Cook uncovered during the last hour.

Toast bread and serve topped with beans. Serves 4 to 6.

Lentil Gravy on Rice

Gravy can be made substantial and protein-rich by using lentils as its base.

1 cup lentils	1 tsp kelp powder
4 cups water	1 tsp cumin powder
2 tbsp tahini	1 tsp coriander powder
1 tbsp tamari soy sauce	½ tsp black pepper
1 tbsp nutritional yeast	3 cups water
	1½ cups brown rice

GRAVY

In a covered pot, combine lentils and water. Bring to a boil for 5 minutes. Reduce heat and cook for 45 minutes until beans are soft. Purée in an electric blender or food processor.

Return to pot and stir in tahini, soy sauce, yeast, kelp, cumin, coriander, and black pepper. Cook for 15 minutes on low heat before serving over cooked rice.

RICE

Fifteen minutes after lentils have begun cooking, begin to prepare rice. Bring water to a boil. Add rice and reduce heat to low. Cook covered for 45 minutes until light and soft. Serves 6.

Tofu Stuffed Tomatoes

This summertime main dish will have special appeal because of its festive look.

2 ripe avocados	¼ tsp sea salt or kelp
1 pound tofu	powder
1 tbsp tahini	4 large tomatoes
1 garlic clove	4 to 6 slices of toast or
1 tsp lemon juice	warm bread

In an electric blender or food processor, purée avocados, tofu, tahini, garlic, lemon juice, and sea salt or kelp.

Remove stems from tomatoes and make six cuts from stem bottom, leaving bottom intact. Tomato will fall open, taking on the appearance of a flower. Spoon tofu and avocado mixture into the opening and serve with toast or warm bread. Serves 4.

Three-Bean and Bulghur Salad

This makes a perfect single-dish, protein-high meal for warm weather.

1 cup chickpeas
1 cup pinto or kidney beans
6 cups water
1 cup bulghur
2 cups water
⅔ cup chopped onion
2 cups steamed cut green
  beans

½ cup chopped green
  pepper
½ tsp salt
¼ tsp black pepper
1 tbsp cider vinegar
⅓ cup olive oil

Place chickpeas and pinto or kidney beans in a covered pot with 6 cups water. Bring to a boil. Allow to boil for 10 minutes. Reduce heat to low and cook covered for 3 hours until beans are tender. Remove from heat and drain off any excess water. Save and use in soup stock.

Place bulghur in water and cook over medium heat for 20 minutes until light and fluffy.

In a large bowl, toss chickpeas, pinto or kidney beans, bulghur, and remaining ingredients until thoroughly mixed. Allow to marinate for at least 1 hour before serving. Serves 6 to 8.

Tofu Cheesie Macaroni

This dish is especially good for children who do not eat dairy products but who sometimes ask for "macaroni and cheese" as other children do.

4 cups water
8 ounces whole grain
  macaroni
1 pound tofu
1½ cups water

¼ cup tahini
2 tbsp nutritional yeast
1 garlic clove
½ tsp salt or kelp powder

In a covered pot bring water to a boil. Add macaroni and boil lightly for 15 minutes until tender.

While macaroni cooks, prepare sauce. Purée tofu, water, tahini, yeast, garlic, and salt or kelp powder in an electric blender or food processor until smooth.

Drain macaroni and return to pot. Stir in sauce and heat over low heat. Serves 4.

Tofu Noodle Casserole

This casserole with its crunchy topping may become a favorite—particularly with children who do not eat dairy products.

1 quart water	*2 tbsp nutritional yeast*
8 ounces udon (Japanese whole wheat noodles)	*1 tsp tamari soy sauce*
1 pound tofu	*1 tsp cumin powder*
⅓ cup tahini	*3 tbsp butter or oil*
1½ cups water	*¾ cup whole grain bread crumbs*

Bring water to a boil. Add udon and continue to boil for 10 minutes until tender. Drain noodles.

In an electric blender or food processor, purée tofu, tahini, water, nutritional yeast, soy sauce, and cumin powder until smooth.

Stir tofu mixture into noodles until well combined and pour into a well-oiled casserole dish.

Melt butter or heat oil in a heavy frying pan over medium heat. Add bread crumbs and stir until thoroughly coated. Pour over noodle mixture. Bake at 350° for 35 minutes until crumb topping is crisp. Serves 4.

Fried Tofu over Rice

This is a main dish for children who enjoy Chinese food.

3 tbsp ghee (see page 78) or butter	*¼ cup sliced water chestnuts*
2 pounds tofu, sliced	*1¼ cups water*
1 tsp oil	*1 tbsp tamari soy sauce*
2 onions, sliced	*2 tsp arrowroot starch dissolved in 1 tbsp water*
1 tsp finely grated ginger	*2 cups cooked brown rice*
¼ cup bamboo shoots	

In a frying pan or wok, heat ghee or butter. Fry tofu slices on both sides until golden brown and set aside.

Add 1 teaspoon oil to wok or frying pan and reduce heat

to medium low. Sauté onions until transparent. Add ginger, bamboo shoots, water chestnuts, water, and soy sauce. Return tofu slices to pan. When mixture is hot, stir in arrowroot paste. Continue stirring gently for 3 minutes until mixture thickens.

Place rice on a platter and top with tofu mixture. Serves 4.

Tomato Tofu Lo Mein

Here is another Chinese dish for children.

1 quart water	4 tomatoes, cut into thin wedges
8 ounces udon (Japanese whole wheat noodles)	2 pounds tofu, cut into small cubes
2 tsp oil	1 cup tomato juice
2 onions, cut into thin wedges	½ cup water
1 tsp finely grated ginger	2 tsp arrowroot starch dissolved in 1 tbsp tamari soy sauce
1 garlic clove, minced	

Bring water to a boil. Add noodles and boil for 10 to 12 minutes until tender. Drain and set aside.

In a frying pan or wok, heat oil. Add onions, ginger, and garlic and sauté until onions are transparent. Stir in tomatoes and tofu. Add tomato juice and water. Increase heat. When mixture is hot, but not boiling, stir in arrowroot-tamari paste. Continue to stir until liquid thickens.

Pour noodles onto a platter and top with tofu and tomato mixture. Serves 4.

Swedish Bean Balls on Mashed Potatoes

This imitation of a traditional Swedish dish is a perfect complementary-protein dish for the child who loves mashed potatoes and gravy.

1 cup cooked aduki beans	3 tbsp whole wheat pastry
1 cup cooked rice or millet	flour and 3 tbsp soy flour
3 tbsp tahini	dissolved in ¼ cup water
2 tbsp whole wheat pastry	1 tbsp tamari soy sauce
flour	1 tsp kelp powder
2 tbsp ghee (see page 78)	1 tbsp nutritional yeast
or oil	1 tsp cumin powder
2 onions, chopped	½ tsp coriander powder
2 cups water	¼ tsp black pepper
	3 cups mashed potatoes
	(about 6 potatoes)

Mash aduki beans and stir in grain, tahini, and flour to make an easily shaped dough. If too sticky, add more flour. If too dry, add 1 tablespoon water. Shape dough with moistened hands into tablespoon-size balls.

In a frying pan, heat ghee or oil. Sauté balls until lightly browned on all sides. Remove from pan and set aside.

Add onions to hot ghee or oil and fry until transparent. Stir in 2 cups water. Add mixture of whole wheat flour, soy flour, and water. Stir in soy sauce, kelp powder, nutritional yeast, cumin, coriander, and black pepper. Allow to cook over medium meat, stirring occasionally, until thickened. Stir bean balls and cook for 5 minutes. Serve with mashed potatoes. Serves 4.

Humus with Pita Bread

This traditional Middle Eastern dish makes a good summer treat or box lunch.

2 cups cooked chickpeas	2 tbsp lemon juice
1 garlic clove, minced	½ tsp sea salt
⅓ cup tahini	1 cup water
1 tsp cumin powder	½ tsp cayenne (optional)
2 tbsp olive oil	4 to 6 whole wheat pita
	breads, warmed

Purée all ingredients except pita in an electric blender or food processor until smooth. If necessary, add more water to achieve desired consistency. Serve as a dip for whole wheat pita bread.

Felafel with Salad and Tahini Sauce

This traditional Middle Eastern sandwich is a tasty and completely balanced meal.

2 cups cooked chickpeas
¾ cup cooked bulghur
1 tbsp whole wheat pastry flour
½ tsp cayenne or paprika
2 tbsp chopped parsley
1 garlic clove, finely chopped
¼ cup ghee (see page 78) or butter

½ cup tahini
¼ cup water
1 tsp fresh lemon juice
¼ tsp sea salt
4 to 6 whole wheat pita breads, warmed
1 cup alfalfa sprouts
⅔ cup chopped tomato
1 cup shredded lettuce

Mash chickpeas. Stir in bulghur, flour, cayenne or paprika, parsley, and garlic. Mixture should be stiff enough to shape with moistened hands. If too sticky, add 1 tablespoon flour, if too dry, add 1 tablespoon water. Shape into tablespoon-size patties.

Melt butter or ghee in a heavy frying pan. Fry chickpea patties until lightly browned and crisp on both sides.

Mix tahini, water, lemon juice, and sea salt until smooth.

Cut warmed pita in half, stuff with fried chickpea patties, add sprouts, tomatoes, and lettuce, and top with tahini sauce. Serves 4 to 6.

Tofu and Rice Seaweed Rolls

This variation of a Japanese treat is a wonderful way to add the mineral content of seaweed to a meal.

2 cups water
1 cup brown rice
6 sheets nori seaweed
1 pound tofu, crumbled

2 tsp tamari soy sauce
2 tsp nutritional yeast
1 tsp grated ginger
1 tsp kelp powder
2 tbsp oil

In a covered pot, bring water to a boil. Add rice. Reduce heat and cook for 45 minutes until soft.

Cut each sheet of nori in half lengthwise. Toast each half sheet by waving it gently over a flame until its color changes to green. Set nori sheets aside.

In a bowl, mix rice, tofu, soy sauce, nutritional yeast, ginger, and kelp powder. Heat oil in a heavy frying pan. Sauté rice and tofu mixture, stirring constantly for 3 minutes. Remove from heat and allow to cool slightly.

Spread rice-tofu mixture over two-thirds of each half-sheet of nori. Roll nori in jelly-roll fashion. Wet the edge of the nori with a finger moisted with water or tamari. Press dampened edges against roll to seal. Moisten and seal ends also. Serves 4 to 6.

MAIN DISHES WITH DAIRY PRODUCTS

Pizza

Pizza is such an all-American favorite food that it is sure to be requested in your home once your child is in school. This dough, which combines whole grain flours, is somewhat lighter and more acceptable to children than a purely whole wheat dough.

DOUGH

½ cup lukewarm water
1 tsp liquid barley malt
2 tbsp oil
2 tsp dry active yeast

¼ cup soy flour
1 cup whole wheat pastry
flour
¼ tbsp gluten flour

In a bowl, combine water, malt, and oil. Sprinkle yeast over warm liquid and allow to stand 10 minutes until mixture foams.

In a separate bowl, combine flours. Stir into yeast mixture to form a dough. Knead on a well-floured board for 10 minutes until smooth and elastic. Shape into a ball. Oil and place in a bowl covered with a warm damp towel. Allow to rise for 45 minutes.

Preheat oven to 400°.

Spread or roll dough onto a 12-inch-round pizza tray. Bake for 8 minutes and remove from oven.

SAUCE

1 6-ounce can tomato paste
⅓ cup water
½ tsp oregano

¼ tsp salt or kelp powder
½ garlic clove, minced
¼ tsp allspice

In a saucepan, combine all sauce ingredients and cook over medium heat for 5 minutes.

TOPPINGS

¼ cup sliced mushrooms
¼ cup sliced green pepper
2 tbsp chopped Greek olives

¼ cup sliced onions
1 cup grated mozzarella cheese
½ cup crumbled feta cheese

ASSEMBLING PIZZA

Spread sauce over partially cooked dough. Top with vegetables and cheeses. Return to oven and bake for 5 minutes until cheeses are thoroughly melted.

Vegetarian Stroganoff

Noodles with a rich dairy sauce are a favorite of gourmets. Children also love the combination.

1 quart water
8 ounces udon (Japanese
   whole wheat noodles)
1 tbsp butter
1 onion, chopped
1 cup sliced mushrooms

1 garlic clove, minced
1 tbsp chopped parsley
1 cup cottage cheese
½ cup milk
½ tsp sea salt
¼ tsp black pepper
1 tsp nutritional yeast

Bring water to a boil and cook noodles for 10 to 12 minutes until tender.

While noodles are cooking, prepare sauce. Melt butter in a heavy frying pan over medium heat. Sauté onions until transparent. Add mushrooms, garlic, and parsley. Cover and cook until mushrooms have decreased in size and darkened in color.

Purée cottage cheese, milk, salt, pepper, and nutritional yeast in a blender or food processor. Stir into mushrooms and onion and remove from heat.

Drain noodles and top with sauce. Serves 4.

Asparagus on Toast with Cheese Sauce

1 pound asparagus
2 cups milk
6 tbsp whole wheat pastry
   flour or 4 tbsp brown rice
   flour
2 tbsp noninstant powdered
   milk

¾ cup grated Cheddar or
   Monterey jack cheese
½ tsp salt
1 tsp nutritional yeast
8 slices whole grain toast

Break woody ends off asparagus. Steam tips until darkened in color but still crisp. Set aside.

In a saucepan, combine milk, flour, and noninstant powdered milk. Cook over medium heat for 5 minutes, stirring occasionally, until sauce thickens. Stir in cheese, salt, and nutritional yeast.

Place asparagus tips on toast and top with cheese sauce. Serves 4 to 6.

Cheese and Onion Pie

This is a special dish for the child who loves melted cheese.

PASTRY DOUGH

1 cup whole wheat flour
½ cup whole wheat pastry
flour

½ cup raw wheat germ
⅓ cup oil
3 tbsp ice water

Combine flours and wheat germ in a bowl. Stir in oil with a fork until mixture resembles coarse corn meal. Stir in ice water, one tablespoon at a time, until dough can be gathered into a ball. (If necessary, add up to one tablespoon water.) Form into two balls. Roll each ball between two pieces of waxed paper to fit a 9-inch pie plate. Set aside.

FILLING

2 cups grated Cheddar
cheese
½ cup chopped onion
2 tbsp whole wheat pastry
flour

1 tsp nutritional yeast
½ tsp salt (optional)
¼ tsp black pepper
(optional)

Combine all filling ingredients in a bowl.

ASSEMBLING PIE

Preheat oven to 400°.

Remove top layer of waxed paper from one round of pastry. Place over pie plate and remove second layer of waxed paper. Gently press pastry into plate.

Pour filling into shell. Cover with second pastry round. Tuck in edges and pinch. Make fork holes before baking. Bake for 45 minutes or until lightly browned. Makes one 9-inch pie.

Lasagna

Here is a classic Italian favorite for the vegetarian table.

2 quarts water
10 ounces whole grain
   lasagna noodles
1 6-ounce can tomato paste
⅓ cup water
1 tsp oregano

¼ tsp black pepper
2 cups cottage cheese
3 tbsp arrowroot starch
1½ cups grated mozzarella
   cheese
3 tbsp melted butter
3 tbsp sour cream

Bring water to a boil. Boil noodles for 12 to 15 minutes until tender. Drain and set aside.

In a small bowl, mix tomato paste, water, oregano, and black pepper.

In an electric blender or food processor, purée cottage cheese and arrowroot until smooth.

Preheat oven to 350°.

In a well-oiled square or rectangular baking dish, spread a thin layer of sauce, top with a layer of noodles, spread a layer of puréed cottage cheese, and sprinkle with a layer of grated cheese. Repeat layers until all ingredients are used, ending with a layer of noodles.

Mix melted butter and sour cream. Spread over noodles. Cover casserole and bake for 45 minutes. Remove cover and bake for a final 15 minutes before serving. Serves 4 to 6.

Tostadas

This easy, nutritious Mexican meal is a close cousin to the taco.

BEANS

2 cups cooked pinto beans
1 tsp cumin powder

½ tsp sea salt
1 garlic clove, crushed
2 tbsp oil

Combine beans, cumin, salt, and garlic in a bowl. Heat oil in a frying pan. Pour beans into pan and stir-fry until excess liquid is evaporated and beans are pink and creamy. Remove from heat and set aside.

SAUCE

1 cup tomato juice
3 tomatoes, finely chopped
1 onion, finely chopped

½ tsp chili powder
½ tsp sea salt
1 clove garlic, crushed
cayenne to taste

Combine all ingredients in a bowl.

ASSEMBLING TOSTADAS

6 to 8 crisp flat tortillas
1½ cups grated Monterey
    jack or Cheddar cheese

1 cup shredded lettuce
1 cup alfalfa sprouts
1 cup tomatoes, chopped
½ cup sour cream

Spread beans on tortillas and sprinkle with grated cheese. Place under a broiler for 2 minutes until cheese is melted. Remove and top with lettuce, sprouts, tomatoes, sour cream, and sauce. Makes 6 to 8 tostadas.

Enchilada Casserole

This casserole will satisfy the child who craves Mexican food.

1 cup tomato juice
3 tomatoes, finely chopped
½ tsp chili powder
1 onion, finely chopped

cayenne to taste (optional)
2 cups cooked pinto beans
1½ cups grated Monterey
    jack cheese
6 soft corn tortillas

Preheat oven to 375°.

In a bowl, combine tomato juice, tomatoes, chili powder, onion, and cayenne (if desired).

Pour a thin layer of sauce into a round oiled casserole dish. Top with pinto beans, cheese, and a tortilla. Repeat layers, ending with a layer of cheese. Cover and bake for 30 minutes, until cheese is thoroughly melted. Serves 4 to 6.

Simple Cheese Fondue

Unlike the fondue found in gourmet restaurants, this version contains no alcohol. Your child will have fun dipping bread into a common pot of cheese sauce.

2 cups milk
4 tbsp whole wheat or rice
flour
2 cups grated Cheddar or
Swiss cheese

1 loaf sour dough whole
grain bread, cut into
1-inch cubes

In an electric frying pan or fondue pot, combine milk and flour. Cook over medium heat until mixture thickens lightly. Stir in cheese and cook until melted.

Set frying pan in the center of the table on lowest possible heat, or set fondue pot over a flame. Distribute cubes of bread and dip into cheese sauce to eat.

PROTEIN MAIN DISHES WITH EGGS

Noodle Soufflé

This light, fluffy dish will be a hit with any child who enjoys the texture of meringue.

1 quart water
8 ounces whole grain
noodles
4 eggs, separated
1 tsp nutritional yeast

¾ cup grated Cheddar
cheese
⅓ cup cottage cheese
⅓ cup milk

Bring water to a boil and cook noodles for 10 to 12 minutes until tender. Remove from heat, drain, and set aside.

Preheat oven to 350°.

In a bowl, mix egg yolks, yeast, and ½ cup Cheddar

cheese. In a blender or food processor, purée cottage cheese and milk. Mix into yolk mixture. Stir in noodles.

Beat egg whites until stiff but not dry. Fold into noodle mixture. Pour into a 2-quart soufflé dish. Sprinkle top with remaining cheese. Set in a pan of hot water. Bake for 20 minutes until set. Serves 4 to 6.

Lentil Loaf with Gravy

This loaf can be sliced and served like meat loaf. Leftovers can be sent to school topped with ketchup in a whole grain sandwich.

LOAF

2 cups cooked lentils	½ tsp sage
1 cup whole grain bread crumbs	½ tsp oregano
	½ tsp thyme
2 eggs	2 tsp tamari soy sauce
¼ cup coarsely chopped walnuts	1 tbsp nutritional yeast
	½ tsp kelp powder

Preheat oven to 350°.

Combine all ingredients to form a stiff dough. If mixture is too moist, add additional bread crumbs. Pour into a well-oiled loaf pan and bake for 1 hour until firm.

GRAVY

2 cups water	1 tbsp nutritional yeast
¼ cup whole wheat pastry flour	½ tsp kelp powder
	¼ tsp black pepper
¼ cup soy flour	1 tsp cumin powder
2 tbsp tamari soy sauce	

Combine all ingredients in a saucepan. Cook over medium heat, stirring occasionally, until sauce thickens to become a light brown gravy. Serve with lentil loaf. Serves 6 to 8.

Carrot Loaf with Tomato Sauce

This simple, nutritious main dish has added appeal if made in a springform pan like a cake and served in slices with a generous topping of sauce.

LOAF

2 cups grated carrots	½ tsp kelp powder
1 cup whole grain bread crumbs	½ tsp sea salt
	½ tsp rosemary
3 eggs	½ tsp tarragon
⅓ cup soy flour	1 tbsp chopped parsley
¼ cup soy grits soaked in ¼ cup water	½ cup coarsely chopped almonds
2 tbsp nutritional yeast	3 tbsp tahini

Preheat oven to 350°.

Combine all ingredients to form a stiff dough. If too sticky, add more bread crumbs; if too dry, add water. Pour into a well-oiled spring-form pan and bake for 30 minutes until golden brown and firm.

TOMATO SAUCE

1 tsp oil	2 tomatoes, chopped
2 onions, chopped	1 tsp nutritional yeast
2 cups tomato juice or vegetable juice	½ tsp rosemary
	½ tsp allspice
	¼ cup brown rice flour

Heat oil in a frying pan. Sauté onions until transparent. Add remaining ingredients and cook over medium heat without boiling until sauce thickens, about 10 minutes, being certain to stir occasionally.

Remove rim from spring-form pan and cut loaf into cake-size pieces. Top with sauce. Serves 4 to 6.

Denver Sandwiches

These sandwiches are stuffed with small vegetable omelets. For interest as well as extra nutritional values we suggest adding cheese slices, sprouts, and sliced tomatoes.

OMELETS

8 eggs, separated	1 red pepper, chopped
2 onions, chopped	¼ tsp sea salt
2 green peppers, chopped	⅛ tsp black pepper
	½ tsp nutritional yeast

In a bowl, mix egg yolks, onions, green peppers, red pepper, salt, pepper, and yeast. In a separate bowl, beat whites until frothy with a wire whisk. Fold whites into yolk mixture.

Heat a lightly oiled frying pan over medium heat. Pour in egg mixture and allow to brown lightly on one side. Cut omelet into quarters and turn to brown lightly on the second side.

ASSEMBLING SANDWICHES

8 slices whole grain toast	2 tomatoes, sliced
2 tbsp natural mayonnaise	1 cup alfalfa sprouts
	cheese slices (optional)

Spread mayonnaise on all slices of bread and fill with omelets, tomatoes, sprouts, and cheese. Makes 4 sandwiches.

Fancy Filled Omelets

Even children who hate eggs will occasionally admit they enjoy an omelet if the filling is appealing enough. Start with a basic cheese omelet for high protein, and fold it over any of the suggested fillings.

BASIC CHEESE OMELET FOR TWO

6 eggs, separated	¼ tsp black pepper
1 tsp nutritional yeast	(optional)
½ tsp sea salt	1 cup grated Cheddar cheese

In a bowl, mix egg yolks, yeast, salt, and pepper. In a separate bowl, beat egg whites until white but not stiff. Fold whites into yolk mixture.

Heat a lightly oiled frying pan over medium heat. Pour omelet mixture into frying pan. When eggs begin to set slightly, sprinkle grated cheese over the top. Have filling ready to place on half of omelet at this point. Fold omelet over filling and remove from pan. Cut in half to serve.

TOMATO AND SOUR CREAM FILLING

1 tsp oil　　　　　　　　　*¾ cup sour cream*
1 onion, chopped　　　　*¼ tsp salt*
3 tomatoes, chopped　　*¼ tsp black pepper*

Heat oil in a heavy frying pan. Sauté onion until transparent. Stir in tomatoes, sour cream, salt, and pepper. Cook until warmed.

AVOCADO AND TOMATO FILLING

1 ripe avocado, pitted,　　*2 tomatoes, sliced*
　peeled, and cut into　　*salt and pepper to taste*
　wedges

Place avocado and tomatoes on one half of omelet and sprinkle with salt and pepper before folding over.

ZUCCHINI-TAHINI FILLING

1 tsp oil　　　　　　　　*2 tbsp tahini*
1 zucchini, cut matchstick　*1 tsp tamari soy sauce*
　style　　　　　　　　　　*1 tsp dill weed*

Heat oil in a frying pan. Add zucchini and sauté until tender. Stir in tahini, tamari, and dill to form a sauce.

Egg Foo Yung

These Chinese-style eggs will add protein to any Oriental vegetable meal.

1 tbsp oil	*1 cup mung bean sprouts*
½ cup finely chopped celery	*8 eggs*
3 scallions, chopped	*1 tbsp nutritional yeast*
	1 tsp tamari soy sauce

Heat oil in a heavy frying pan. Sauté celery, scallions, and sprouts for 2 minutes. Remove from pan and set aside.

Return pan to low heat. Beat together eggs, yeast, and soy sauce. Pour into heated pan. Allow to cook one minute. Sprinkle sautéed vegetables over eggs. Continue to cook until firm. Turn and cook on other side until lightly browned. Serves 4 to 6.

Ravioli

Ravioli is a very special treat for anyone, young or old, who enjoys Italian food. If you have never made your own pasta, making this dish will be an exciting cooking adventure for you and your child to share.

PASTA

3½ cups whole wheat pastry flour	*½ tsp salt*
	4 eggs
	4 to 5 tsp cold water

Mix flour and salt in a bowl. Make a well in the flour and drop in eggs. Add water one teaspoon at a time. Mix with hands to form a dough. Turn onto a well-floured board and knead for 5 minutes until smooth and elastic. Cover and allow to stand for 30 minutes.

FILLING

1 cup ricotta cheese	*1 egg*
1 cup grated Parmesan cheese	*⅛ tsp black pepper*
	1 tbsp nutritional yeast
1 cup grated mozzarella cheese	*1 tbsp arrowroot starch*

Mix all ingredients until well combined.

ASSEMBLING RAVIOLI

Form dough into teaspoon-size balls. On a well-floured board, roll each ball into a circle as thin as possible. Place 2 teaspoons filling on one half of each circle. Fold dough over filling to form a half circle. Press edges together with a fork. Allow assembled ravioli to stand 40 minutes.

SAUCE

2 tbsp olive oil	2 bay leaves
2 onions, chopped	1 12-ounce can tomato paste
3 garlic cloves, minced	1½ cups water
1 tsp oregano	4 tomatoes, chopped

Heat oil in a heavy frying pan. Sauté onions and garlic until onions are transparent. Add oregano and bay leaves.

In an electric blender or food processor, purée tomato paste, water, and tomatoes until smooth. Pour into cooking onions and continue to cook for 30 minutes.

COOKING RAVIOLI

Bring 2 quarts water to a boil. Place 8 ravioli at a time into boiling water. Boil for 10 minutes and remove with a slotted spoon. Place cooked ravioli in a pan in a 200° oven to keep warm while cooking remaining ravioli. Before serving, pour sauce over ravioli. Serves 6 to 8.

Chilies Rellenos

These cheese-stuffed and egg-coated chilies are only for children who enjoy a spicy treat, but other children can enjoy the same dish using bell peppers.

8 large Mexican or Italian green peppers or bell peppers	4 cups grated Monterey jack or Cheddar cheese
4 tomatoes, chopped	8 eggs, separated
1 cup tomato juice	2 tbsp water
1 tsp tamari soy sauce	¼ cup whole wheat pastry flour
pinch cinnamon	¼ tsp sea salt
pinch black pepper	¼ cup butter or ghee
pinch cayenne pepper	(see page 78)

Place whole peppers 2 inches from broiler. Set oven to highest possible temperature and brown peppers 5 minutes on each side until blistered. Remove and place in a paper bag for 10 minutes until cool enough to handle.

While peppers cool, make a sauce by blending tomatoes, tomato juice, soy sauce, cinnamon, black pepper, and cayenne in an electric blender or food processor until smooth. Set aside.

Remove stems and seeds from peppers and peel blistered skin. Stuff each with ½ cup grated cheese.

In a bowl, beat egg yolks and water until lemon-colored. Stir in flour and sea salt. In a separate bowl, beat whites until stiff. Fold whites into yolk mixture.

Melt butter in a frying pan. Pour four circles of ¼ cup egg batter each into hot butter. Place a stuffed pepper in the center of each circle of batter. As batter begins to set, pour more over each pepper. After 3 minutes, turn and brown lightly on the second side. Place finished peppers in a casserole dish and keep warm in a 300° oven while cooking second batch of peppers. Serve with sauce. Serves 4 to 6.

Yorkshire Pudding with Gravy

The English usually eat Yorkshire pudding with roast beef, but in our house we find this light mixture of eggs and milk with a soy gravy a fine and tasty protein dish all by itself.

YORKSHIRE PUDDING

2 eggs	1 cup whole wheat pastry
1 tsp nutritional yeast	flour
½ tsp sea salt	1 cup milk
	4 tbsp ghee (see page 78)

Preheat oven to 400°.

In a blender or electric food processor, blend eggs, nutritional yeast, salt, flour, and milk.

Put ghee in a 9- by 9-inch shallow baking dish and place in oven for 10 minutes. Remove and swirl oil so that it evenly coats pan. Pour batter into pan. Bake for 15 minutes, then reduce heat to 375° and bake a final 15 minutes until crisp and brown.

GRAVY

2 cups water	*¼ tsp kelp powder*
½ cup soy flour	*½ tsp cumin powder*
¼ tsp black pepper	*½ tsp coriander powder*
1 tbsp nutritional yeast	*1 tbsp tamari soy sauce*

While pudding bakes, prepare gravy. Mix all ingredients in a saucepan. Cook over medium heat, stirring occasionally, until thickened into a gravy.

Remove pudding from oven. Cut into squares and serve with gravy. Serves 4 to 6.

16.

VEGETABLE DISHES

Sautéed Eggplant, Zucchini, and Tomato Combination

These vegetables complement each other beautifully to make a simple but delicious vegetable dish.

1 tbsp oil
1 cup chopped, peel
* eggplant*
1 cup diced zucchini

1 cup chopped tomatoes
¼ tsp salt
¼ tsp pepper

Heat oil in a heavy frying pan. Add eggplant. Cover and cook for 15 minutes until darkened in color. If eggplant sticks to pan, add 1 tablespoon water. Stir in zucchini and tomatoes. Season with salt and pepper and continue to cook until zucchini is tender. Serves 4.

Broiled Eggplant Slices

This simplest way of all to serve eggplant brings out its chewy, almost meatlike flavor.

| 1 eggplant, sliced into rounds | 2 tbsp oil salt and pepper to taste |

Brush eggplant slices with oil on both sides. Sprinkle with salt and pepper. Place under a broiler for 5 minutes until brown. Turn and brown on other side. Serves 4.

Baked Zucchini

This dish has a Greek flavor.

4 small tender zucchini squash	½ tsp cumin powder
2 tbsp olive oil	¼ tsp sea salt
1 garlic clove, crushed	⅛ tsp black pepper (optional)

Remove stem and tip of zucchini. Cut in half and slice in half lengthwise, to form four quarters.

In a small bowl, beat oil, garlic, cumin, salt, and pepper. Rub mixture over zucchini quarters. Place in an oiled casserole dish, cover, and bake at 350° for 20 minutes, until zucchini is tender but not soft. Serves 4 to 6.

Baked Winter Squash

Any winter squash retains its full flavor when baked.

| 1 or 2 (depending on size) Hubbard, butternut, pumpkin, acorn, or other winter squash | 2 tbsp corn oil 1 tbsp tamari soy sauce |

Cut squash in half or in quarters and remove seeds. In a small bowl, beat oil and tamari. Rub mixture over squash. Bake at 350° for 1 hour until tender.

Carrots and Raisins

This is a sweet dish for children who like vegetables to be a treat.

½ cup raisins
1 cup water

1 tsp arrowroot starch
    dissolved in 1 tsp water
2 cups steamed sliced
    carrots

In a saucepan, cook raisins in water for 15 minutes over medium heat. Stir in arrowroot and water mixture. Continue stirring for 3 minutes until sauce thickens. Pour sauce over carrots before serving. Serves 4.

Baked Carrots

Carrots are not only a versatile and healthful vegetable, but are cheap all year round. Baking any vegetable is a wonderful way to capture its full flavor and sweetness. Carrots are especially sweet prepared in this simple way.

8 carrots
1 tbsp corn oil

1 tbsp tamari soy sauce
¼ cup water

Scrub each carrot with a vegetable brush. Combine the soy sauce and oil, stirring with a fork until the mixture looks milky. Rub the tamari-oil mixture on the carrots. Place the carrots in a casserole dish. Pour the water in the bottom of the dish and bake at 350° for 20 minutes until tender. Serves 4 to 6.

Carrots in Nondairy Cream Sauce

Many children enjoy cream sauce. This recipe is especially good for the child who cannot tolerate dairy products. The sauce can be used with other vegetables—green beans, peas, corn, or celery—just as successfully as with carrots.

4 tbsp brown rice flour or
   whole wheat pastry flour
1 tbsp tahini

½ tsp sea salt
2 cups water
1 tsp sesame oil
2 cups steamed sliced carrots

Beat all ingredients except carrots until thoroughly combined. Pour into a saucepan and cook over medium heat, stirring occasionally, until sauce thickens, about 10 minutes. Stir in carrots. Serves 4.

Sweet and Sour Beets

1 cup water
1 tbsp lemon juice mixed
   with 2 tsp arrowroot
   starch

½ tsp grated lemon rind
1 tbsp liquid barley malt
2 cups steamed beets, cut
   julienne style

In a saucepan, bring water to a gentle boil. Stir in lemon juice and starch, lemon rind, and malt. Continue stirring for 3 minutes until thickened. Stir in beets. Serves 4.

Nondairy Baked Stuffed Potatoes

4 large baked potatoes
½ pound tofu
1 tbsp tahini
1 tsp lemon juice

3 tbsp finely chopped chives
1 tsp fresh dill weed
¼ tsp sea salt
1 tsp olive oil
4 sprigs parsley

Preheat oven to 400°.

Slice baked potatoes down the center. Carefully remove potato, leaving shells intact. Place potato in bowl and set aside.

In a blender or food processor, purée tofu, tahini, and lemon juice until smooth. Stir into potato. Add chives, dill weed, sea salt, and olive oil. Mix until thoroughly combined.

Spoon mixture into potato shells. Bake for 15 minutes until thoroughly heated. Garnish with parsley. Serves 4.

Nondairy Scalloped Potatoes

For children who do not eat dairy products, this dish can provide an extra boost of protein with the goodness of potatoes.

1 quart water	*2 tbsp corn oil*
5 potatoes, thinly sliced	*1 tbsp nutritional yeast*
2 onions, sliced into rings	*½ tsp salt*
2 tbsp whole wheat pastry	*¼ tsp black pepper*
flour or brown rice flour	*1½ cups soy milk*

Bring water to a boil. Cook potato slices in boiling water until translucent, about 5 minutes. Drain and rinse with cold water.

Preheat oven to 375°.

Spread a thin layer of potatoes over the bottom of a lightly oiled casserole dish. Top with a layer of onions. Sprinkle with flour, oil, yeast, salt, and pepper. Repeat layers until all ingredients are used. Pour soy milk over casserole. Bake for 45 minutes until potatoes are soft. Serves 4.

Pan-Fried Potatoes

With a heavy cast-iron skillet, potatoes can be fried brown and crusty without oil or butter.

6 boiled potatoes, cooled	*4 to 6 tbsp water*
and diced	

Heat skillet over a medium flame. Add potato cubes and 1 tablespoon water. Allow potatoes to stick to pan and brown. Scrape them free with a spatula. Add 1 tablespoon water and repeat. Continue in this manner until potatoes are well browned and crisp. Serves 4 to 6.

Creamed Spinach with Tofu

This dish is good for the child who enjoys a creamy dish with the flavors of garlic and ginger.

1 carrot, sliced	*1 garlic clove, crushed*
1 pound spinach, stemmed	*4 slices fresh ginger root*
1 tbsp oil	*½ tsp salt or kelp powder*
1 pound tofu, cut into	*1 tsp nutritional yeast*
half-inch cubes	

Steam carrot until tender. Add spinach and steam until wilted but still bright green in color. Remove from heat and purée in an electric blender or food processor until smooth, adding ½ cup water if necessary. Set aside.

Heat oil in a heavy frying pan. Add tofu and sauté until lightly browned. Stir in garlic, ginger, salt or kelp, and nutritional yeast. Add puréed carrot and spinach. Cook over low heat for 10 minutes until flavors are well absorbed. Serves 4.

Baked Cauliflower

Baking is one of the best ways to retain the full flavor of cauliflower.

1 head cauliflower	*1 tsp tamari soy sauce*
1 tbsp oil	*¼ cup water*

Preheat oven to 350°.

Remove leaves from cauliflower and wash head. In a small bowl, beat oil and soy sauce until thoroughly combined. Rub mixture over cauliflower. Pour water into a covered casserole dish. Place cauliflower in dish and bake covered for 30 minutes until it can be easily pierced with a fork. Serves 4.

Breaded Cauliflower

This simple dish is one Michael remembers as a childhood favorite.

*1 head cauliflower, broken
  into florets*

*2 tbsp sesame oil
½ cup bread crumbs
2 tsp nutritional yeast*

Steam cauliflower until it can be easily pierced with a fork.

Heat oil in a heavy frying pan. Sauté bread crumbs until lightly browned and crisp. Stir in cauliflower and nutritional yeast. Serves 4.

Tamari-Glazed "Trees" (Broccoli)

Our daughter's favorite vegetable is broccoli, which she has always called "trees." Don't throw away the "trunks" of the trees. These stalks can be used if they are peeled and sliced in the shape of bamboo shoots.

*1 head broccoli
½ cup water*

*1 tsp tamari soy sauce
  mixed with 1 tsp
  arrowroot starch*

Steam broccoli florets and sliced stems until darkened in color and still crisp.

Bring water to a boil. Stir in soy sauce and starch. Pour over steamed broccoli and toss. Serves 4.

Steamed Cabbage

Most children turn up their noses in disdain at boiled cabbage, which often feels, looks, and tastes lifeless. Cabbage lightly steamed and served with butter or a homemade butter substitute can have a surprisingly enthusiastic response.

Cut one head cabbage in quarters and cut out core. Place in a steamer. Steam for 10 minutes until cabbage can be pierced with a fork but still retains its light green color. Serves 4 to 6.

VEGETABLE DISHES WITH DAIRY PRODUCTS

Creamed Corn

When we were tempted to buy a sugar-packed can of creamed corn one day so that we could enjoy that favorite childhood taste, we decided that it was time to create a healthful substitute. This delicious recipe is dedicated to children who love creamed corn as much as we do.

2 cups corn kernels	1 tbsp arrowroot starch
¼ cup milk	dissolved in ¼ cup milk
	1 tsp liquid malt

Heat corn in ¼ cup milk. When hot, add the arrowroot-milk mixture and the barley malt.

Cook over medium heat until the milk sauce has thickened. Makes about 2 cups.

Glazed Baked Yams

This simple dish makes the skins of yams desirable even to the fussiest of children.

4 to 6 unpeeled yams, sliced	⅓ cup liquid barley malt
into 2-inch rounds	2 tbsp butter

Preheat oven to 325°.

Place yam slices in a tight layer in an ovenproof dish. In a saucepan, heat malt and butter until butter is melted. Beat with a fork until well combined. Drizzle over yams. Bake for 40 minutes until yams are soft.

Puréed Yam Bake

This simple casserole is a naturally sweet dinner treat with a crunchy nut topping.

4 to 6 yams, steamed	1 cup whole grain bread
2 tbsp butter	crumbs
	½ cup chopped almonds

Preheat oven to 375°.

Purée or mash yams until smooth. Spoon into a well-oiled casserole dish and smooth top.

Melt butter in a frying pan. Stir in bread crumbs and almonds to coat thoroughly. Sprinkle over mashed yams. Bake for 30 minutes until top is lightly browned and crisp. Serves 4 to 6.

Creamed Green Beans with Almonds

If your child likes a cream sauce, here is a perfect way to serve green beans.

1 cup milk	½ tsp sea salt
2 tbsp soy flour	1 tsp nutritional yeast
1 tbsp brown rice flour	2 cups steamed green beans
¼ tsp black pepper	½ cup chopped almonds

In a saucepan, mix milk, soy and rice flours, pepper, salt, and nutritional yeast. Cook over medium heat, stirring occasionally, until sauce thickens. Stir in green beans. Pour into a serving bowl and top with almonds.

Lemon Buttered Beans

Most children love butter, and a lemon-butter sauce will make them more likely to eat their vegetables. This recipe can also be made with carrots, cauliflower, broccoli, or peas.

2 cups sliced green beans   2 tsp lemon juice
2 tbsp melted butter   1 tsp nutritional yeast

Steam green beans until tender. In a small bowl, mix melted butter, lemon juice, and nutritional yeast. Toss beans with mixture just before serving. Serves 4.

Artichokes with Garlic Butter Sauce

Children enjoy taking apart the artichoke flower and uncovering the heart as they eat.

4 artichokes   1 cup water
¼ cup butter   1 tsp arrowroot starch
1 garlic clove, crushed   dissolved in 1 tsp water
⅛ tsp sea salt

Steam artichokes in one inch of water for 1 hour until any leaf is easily pulled off.

In a saucepan, heat butter, garlic, salt, and water to a gentle boil. Stir in arrowroot paste. Continue stirring for 3 minutes until sauce thickens.

Serve artichokes with individual servings of sauce for dipping leaves and heart.

Scalloped Potatoes

An all-American favorite, scalloped potatoes is not only a delicious vegetable dish but also a good source of protein.

1 quart water   ¼ tsp black pepper
5 potatoes, thinly sliced   1½ cups milk
1 cup grated Cheddar cheese   2 tbsp whole wheat pastry
½ tsp salt   flour or brown rice flour

Bring water to a boil. Add potato slices and boil until transparent, about 5 minutes. Drain and rinse with cold water.

Preheat oven to 375°.

Arrange a thin layer of potatoes in a casserole dish.

Sprinkle with grated cheese, salt, and pepper. Repeat layers until all ingredients are used. Mix milk with flour and pour over casserole. Bake for 35 minutes until potatoes are soft. Serves 4 to 6.

VEGETABLE DISHES WITH EGGS

Corn Custard

If your child enjoys corn and custard, he will thoroughly delight in this combination.

1½ cups corn kernels
3 eggs, beaten
3 tbsp noninstant milk
  powder
1 tsp nutritional yeast

½ tsp sea salt
1 tsp dill weed
2 cups milk, scalded and
  cooled to lukewarm

Preheat oven to 350°.
Mix all ingredients and pour into a well-oiled casserole dish. Place dish in a pan of hot water and bake for 45 minutes until firm. Serves 4 to 6.

Yam or Sweet Potato Custard

Although this dish is as sweet as a dessert, it is a wholesome energy- and protein-packed addition to any child's meal. For a variation, grated carrot can easily be substituted for yams or sweet potatoes.

2 cups grated sweet potato
  or yam
2 eggs, beaten
2 cups milk or soy milk
¼ cup noninstant milk
  powder

1 tbsp nutritional yeast
2 tbsp blackstrap molasses
½ tsp cinnamon
¼ tsp salt
¼ tsp nutmeg

Preheat oven to 325°.

Combine sweet potato or yam with eggs. Gradually stir in milk or soy milk. Mix in remaining ingredients excluding nutmeg. Pour into an oiled casserole dish. Sprinkle with nutmeg. Set in a pan of hot water and bake for 1 hour until firm. Serves 4.

Light and Fluffy Squash Cakes

These little cupcakes are wonderful for the child who "can't stand" eggs or vegetables.

2 cups mashed cooked winter squash	¼ tsp sea salt
	⅛ tsp cinnamon
2 tbsp blackstrap molasses	⅛ tsp powdered ginger
2 tbsp whole wheat pastry flour or brown rice flour	3 eggs, separated
	⅓ cup chopped pecans or walnuts

Preheat oven to 350°.

Combine squash, molasses, flour, salt, cinnamon, ginger, and egg yolk in a bowl. In a separate bowl, beat egg whites until stiff. Fold into squash mixture.

Spoon batter into oiled muffin tins. Sprinkle with nuts and bake for 45 minutes until lightly browned and crisp. Makes 12 cupcakes.

SALADS

Israeli Salad

Friends who had spent a year in Israel found that when they returned home, their daughter missed this food more than any other Israeli dish.

3 ripe tomatoes, cut into
  thin wedges
1 onion, thinly sliced
2 green peppers, sliced
1 large cucumber, thinly
  sliced

¼ tsp sea salt
⅛ tsp black pepper
1 tsp cider vinegar or lemon
  juice
2 tbsp olive oil

Place all vegetables in a bowl. Sprinkle with salt and
pepper and toss. Add vinegar or lemon juice and olive oil.
Toss once more. Serves 4.

Cucumber "Licorice" Salad

Anise has the unmistakable flavor of licorice. Children
enjoy the idea of eating "candy" in their salad.

2 cucumbers, peeled and
  grated
2 tsp anise seed

1 tsp lemon juice
2 tbsp safflower oil
1 tbsp liquid barley malt

Toss cucumbers and anise seed. In a small bowl, mix lemon
juice, oil, and malt until thoroughly combined. Pour over
cucumber and anise seed and toss. Serves 4.

Marinated Carrots

These are like an extra-special pickle, but can be prepared
fresh without the bother and mess of canning.

3 carrots, cut in matchstick
  style
2 cups water
1 tbsp cider vinegar
1 tsp dill weed

1 tsp peppercorns
1 garlic clove, chopped
1 bay leaf
½ tsp sea salt

Place carrots in a covered jar. Add remaining ingredients.
Shake and place in refrigerator to marinate for two days
or longer.

Sweet Ginger Beets

This is a quick pickle that children love as a snack or a colorful addition to a meal, especially at picnics.

2 cups beets, cut matchstick style	*2 tsp maple syrup*
1½ cups water	*½ tsp finely grated orange peel*
½ tsp finely grated fresh ginger	*2 tbsp orange juice*
	½ tsp sea salt

Place beets in a jar. Mix other ingredients and pour over beets. Cover and refrigerate for at least two days.

Corn Salad

2 cups corn kernels, steamed	*¼ tsp sea salt*
1 green pepper, chopped	*½ cup water*
1 sweet red pepper, chopped	*1 tsp liquid barley malt*
1 tsp lemon juice or cider vinegar	*1 tsp arrowroot starch dissolved in 1 tsp water*

In a bowl, toss corn and peppers. In a saucepan, heat lemon juice, salt, water, and malt. When hot, stir in arrowroot paste. Continue stirring for 3 minutes until sauce thickens. Pour over corn and peppers and toss well. Allow to marinate 30 minutes before serving. Serves 4 to 6.

Shoestring Turnips

Kids hate turnips, right? Wrong. These shoestring turnips have the look of store-bought potato sticks. You will be surprised to hear your child ask for more of this mystery food.

2 cups raw turnips, cut matchstick style	*1 tsp olive oil or safflower oil*
	½ tsp tamari soy sauce

Toss turnips with oil and soy sauce. Allow to marinate 1 hour and toss again before serving. Serves 4.

Carrot and Raisin Salad

This sweet salad is a regular at our house.

2 cups grated carrot
½ cup raisins
2 tbsp oil
¼ tsp blackstrap molasses

1 tsp lemon juice or
  cider vinegar
1 tsp liquid barley malt
½ tsp nutritional yeast
⅛ tsp sea salt

In a bowl, toss carrot and raisins. In a small bowl, mix remaining ingredients until well combined. Pour over carrots and raisins and toss. Serves 4 to 6.

Chinese Radish Pickle

These are quick, easy pickles with a spicy flavor and an extra crunchy texture.

1 6-inch daikon radish,
  sliced thin
2 tbsp tamari soy sauce

2 tbsp water
½ tsp finely grated ginger
  (optional)

Toss daikon with tamari, water, and, if desired, ginger. Allow to marinate at least 3 hours and toss again before serving. Serves 6 to 8.

Nondairy Cole Slaw

Tofu mayonnaise is an easy-to-make substitute to use in cole slaw if your child does not eat dairy products.

1½ cups grated cabbage
½ cup grated carrot
¼ cup crumbled tofu
1 tsp lemon juice

1 tbsp tahini
1 tsp liquid barley malt
¼ tsp sea salt
¼ cup water

In a bowl, toss cabbage and carrot. In an electric blender or food processor, purée remaining ingredients. Pour over cabbage and carrot and toss before serving.

Caraway Cole Slaw

2 cups grated cabbage
1 tbsp caraway seeds

¼ tsp salt
1 tsp lemon juice
2 tbsp olive oil

In a bowl, toss cabbage, caraway, and salt. Add lemon juice and olive oil and toss once again. Serves 4.

Eggplant Salad

If your child likes humus, he will also enjoy this Greek salad as a dip for bread.

1 large, light eggplant
  (heavy eggplants are
  bitter)
1 onion, finely chopped
3 tbsp tahini

1 garlic clove, crushed
¼ tsp black pepper or
  ⅛ tsp cayenne
¼ tsp sea salt
⅛ tsp kelp powder

Cook the eggplant until soft in its own skin. One of three methods can be used: (1) Bake at 400° for 30 minutes until soft. (2) Place directly on the burner of a gas stove. Cook over medium heat, turning carefully, until the entire surface is charred and the eggplant is soft. This method gives the flavor of outdoor cooking. (3) Place over hot coals on a barbecue grill, turning until entire surface is charred and inside is soft.

After cooking eggplant, remove outer skin and discard. Mash or purée eggplant with remaining ingredients. Serve alone or as a dip for bread or vegetables.

VEGGIES AND DIPS

Children who would never consider eating cooked broccoli or cauliflower and green beans will happily devour them if they are left raw, cut into finger-food size, arranged beautifully on a plate, and served with a small bowl of dip next to the child's plate.

Vegetables that are great for dipping include:

Broccoli florets
Cauliflower
  florets
Carrot sticks
Celery sticks
Tomato wedges

Green beans
Yellow wax beans
Red radishes
Daikon radish
  sticks
Green pepper
  slices

Cucumber sticks
Asparagus
Turnip sticks
Red pepper slices
Mushrooms

VEGAN DIPS

Avocado Tofu Dip

1 ripe avocado
¼ cup crumbled tofu
½ tsp lemon juice
¼ cup water

½ garlic clove, crushed
⅛ tsp sea salt or kelp
* powder*
½ tsp nutritional yeast

Purée all ingredients until smooth in an electric blender or food processor.

Tahini Dip

½ cup tahini
1 tbsp tamari soy sauce

½ tsp dill weed
¼ cup water

Mix all ingredients until smooth.

Cucumber Tofu Dip

1 cucumber, peeled and
    chopped
¼ cup tofu, crumbled
1 tbsp tahini

1 tsp olive oil
2 tbsp parsley
½ tsp nutritional yeast
¼ tsp sea salt

In an electric blender or food processor, blend all ingredients until smooth. If cucumber is dry, it may be necessary to add 1 or 2 tablespoons water to blend.

Tomato Dip

2 tomatoes, chopped
1 tbsp tahini

1 tsp tamari soy sauce
1 tbsp olive oil
¼ tsp mustard powder

In an electric blender or food processor, blend all ingredients until smooth.

Peanut Butter Dip

¼ cup peanut butter

¼ cup water
2 tbsp lemon juice

Blend all ingredients until smooth.

Tartar Dip

⅔ cup eggless or cashew
   mayonnaise (see recipes
   below)

2 tbsp finely chopped dill
   pickle

Mix mayonnaise and pickle.

Thousand Island Dip

⅔ cup eggless or cashew
   mayonnaise (see recipes
   below)

2 tbsp finely chopped dill
   pickle
2 tbsp tomato juice

Mix all ingredients.

Eggless Mayonnaise

1 cup soy milk
1 tbsp arrowroot starch
   dissolved in 1 tbsp water
½ cup water
½ cup soy milk powder

⅛ tsp crushed garlic
1 tsp chopped onion
2 tbsp lemon juice
½ tsp sea salt
½ cup safflower oil

Bring soy milk to a gentle boil in a saucepan. Stir in arrowroot paste. Continue stirring for 3 to 5 minutes until thickened. Remove from heat and allow to cool.

In an electric blender, blend thickened soy milk, water, soy milk powder, garlic, onion, lemon juice, and salt until well combined. Slowly pour in oil while blending.

Cashew Mayonnaise

¾ cup raw cashews
½ tsp sea salt
⅛ tsp minced garlic

1 cup water
1 cup safflower or
   sunflower oil
2 tbsp lemon juice

In an electric blender or food processor, blend cashews, salt, garlic, and water until smooth. While blending, gradually pour in oil. When mixture is thick, add lemon juice.

DAIRY DIPS

Tomato Sour Cream Dip

1 cup sour cream	*pinch oregano*
¼ cup tomato juice	*pinch dry mustard*
	3 tbsp olive oil

In an electric blender or food processor, blend sour cream, tomato juice, oregano, and mustard. Gradually pour in oil to thicken while blending.

Sour Cream Dip

½ cup sour cream	*⅛ tsp salt*
⅛ tsp crushed garlic	*1 tsp dill weed*
	2 tbsp water

Mix all ingredients and allow to sit for 15 minutes before serving.

Avocado Dairy Dip

1 ripe avocado	*⅛ tsp crushed or minced*
¼ cup sour cream	*garlic*
	pinch cayenne

Blend all ingredients until smooth.

Two-Cheese Dip

½ cup cottage cheese
¼ cup grated Cheddar
  cheese
1 tbsp olive oil

⅛ tsp minced garlic
pinch black pepper
3 tbsp water

In an electric blender or food processor, blend all ingredients until smooth.

Cottage Cheese Tomato Dip

½ cup cottage cheese
2 tomatoes, chopped
½ tsp rosemary

1 tbsp chopped chives
⅛ tsp sea salt
½ tsp nutritional yeast
2 tbsp water

In a blender or electric food processor, blend all ingredients until smooth.

Yogurt Dip

1 cup yogurt
½ tsp cumin powder

¼ tsp crushed garlic
⅛ tsp salt
pinch cayenne (optional)

Mix all ingredients and allow to stand for 1 hour before serving.

Yellow Yogurt Dip

1 tsp butter
1 garlic clove, thinly sliced
¼ tsp turmeric

⅛ tsp salt
⅛ tsp coriander powder
1 cup yogurt

Melt butter in a heavy frying pan. Sauté garlic and add turmeric, salt, and coriander. Stir in yogurt and cook for 5 minutes. Remove from heat and cool before serving.

EGG DIPS

Old-Fashioned Mayonnaise

2 eggs
½ tsp dry mustard
¼ tsp sea salt

¼ tsp kelp powder
1¼ cups safflower or
* sunflower oil*
3 tbsp lemon juice

In an electric blender or food processor, blend eggs, mustard, salt, kelp powder, and ½ cup oil. While blending, gradually add remaining oil. When thickened, stir in lemon juice.

Avocado Mayonnaise Dip

1 ripe avocado
¼ cup mayonnaise
1 tbsp lemon juice

⅛ tsp sea salt or kelp
* powder*
pinch cayenne

Purée ingredients in an electric blender or food processor until smooth.

Tomato and Cheese Mayonnaise Dip

1 cup cottage cheese
¼ cup mayonnaise
1 tomato, chopped

1 tsp tamari soy sauce
½ tsp kelp powder
1 garlic clove, finely
* chopped*

In an electric blender or food processor, purée all ingredients until smooth.

Simple Hollandaise Dip

¾ cup mayonnaise
2 tbsp milk

1 tbsp lemon juice
¼ tsp salt
2 tbsp chopped fresh parsley

Mix all ingredients until thoroughly combined.

Mayonnaise Supreme Dip

¾ cup mayonnaise
2 tbsp finely chopped fresh
  parsley

1 tbsp finely chopped chives
pinch cayenne (optional)
¼ cup heavy cream,
  whipped

In a bowl, beat mayonnaise, parsley, chives, and cayenne (if desired). Fold in whipped cream.

Peanut Mayonnaise

⅓ cup crunchy peanut
  butter
1 cup mayonnaise

1 tsp lemon juice
½ garlic clove, crushed
pinch cayenne

Beat all ingredients until smooth.

Tossed Salad

Raw vegetable salads are an ingenious invention since they encourage your children to eat a large variety of vegetables in one meal, thereby receiving and abundant variety of vitamins and minerals. Tossed salads do not have to be a dull repetition of lettuce, tomatoes, and cucumbers; they can incorporate a large number of vegetables. For further interest, the vegetables can be chopped coarsely or finely. Among the large number of possible combinations you can use in your children's salads are the following suggestions:

Romaine, torn or chopped
Salad bowl lettuce, torn or chopped
Boston lettuce, torn or chopped
Red leaf lettuce, torn or chopped
Spinach, torn or chopped
Beat greens, finely chopped
Chard, finely chopped
Cabbage, chopped or grated
Cucumbers, chopped, grated, or sliced
Zucchini, sliced, chopped, or grated
Yellow summer squash, sliced, chopped, or grated
Carrots, grated
Red radishes, sliced or grated
Daikon radish, sliced or grated
Mustard greens, torn or chopped
Chinese cabbage, sliced or chopped
Collard, chopped
Broccoli, chopped or broken into florets
Cauliflower, chopped or broken into florets
Avocado, chopped or sliced
Green peppers, chopped or sliced
Red peppers, chopped or sliced
Celery, chopped
Tomatoes, sliced, chopped, or cut into wedges
Onions, sliced or chopped
Alfalfa sprouts
Fenugreek sprouts
Mung bean sprouts
Lentil sprouts
Sunflower sprouts
Buckwheat sprouts
Wheat sprouts
Peas
Steamed corn kernels

In addition to vegetables, tossed salad can include a number of other highly nutritious ingredients:

Nutritional yeast, lightly sprinkled over salad
Raw wheat germ, lightly sprinkled over salad
Dulse, soaked in water, drained, and added to salad

Nori seaweed, toasted over gas flame or in oven and
   crumbled
Sunflower seeds
Almonds, chopped
Cashews, whole or chopped
Pumpkin seeds
Brazil nuts, chopped
Filberts, chopped
Roasted peanuts

Your child will enjoy your unusual combinations of vegetables, nuts, seeds, and supplemental foods more if they
are served with a tempting and tasty salad dressing. In fact,
many children (and adults) regard the salad as merely a
vehicle for a mouth-watering dressing.

NONDAIRY DRESSINGS

Orange Tahini Dressing

¼ cup water   *⅓ cup fresh orange juice*
½ cup tahini   *1 tbsp tamari soy sauce*

Mix all ingredients until smooth.

Tahini Dill Dressing

¼ cup tahini   *3 tbsp sesame oil*
¼ cup water   *1 tbsp dill weed*
                                 1 tbsp tamari soy sauce

Combine all ingredients and mix until smooth.

Simple Tamari Dressing

2 tbsp tamari soy sauce   *½ cup sesame or*
1 tbsp lemon juice   *safflower oil*

Place all ingredients in a covered jar and shake until light brown and milky.

French Dressing

¾ cup olive oil
3 tbsp cider vinegar
2 tbsp tomato juice

2 tsp liquid barley malt
¼ tsp dry mustard
⅛ tsp black pepper
½ tsp sea salt

Place all ingredients in a jar. Cover and shake until well combined.

Green Goddess Dressing

2 scallions, chopped
3 tbsp chopped watercress
1 tbsp chopped parsley
2 tbsp tahini

¼ cup water
½ cup safflower or
   sunflower oil
3 tbsp lemon juice
½ tsp sea salt

In an electric blender or food processor, purée all ingredients until smooth.

Tofu Dressing

1 cup water
1 cup crumbled tofu
1 garlic clove, chopped

2 tsp tamari soy sauce
3 tbsp lemon juice
2 tbsp tahini
½ tsp sea salt

In an electric blender or food processor, purée all ingredients until smooth.

Avocado Grapefruit Dressing

1 ripe avocado *½ cup grapefruit juice*
1 tomato, chopped

In an electric blender or food processor, purée all ingredients until smooth.

DAIRY DRESSINGS

Creamy Dill Dressing

¾ cup sour cream or *3 tbsp water*
puréed cottage cheese *1 tbsp olive or sesame oil*
1 tbsp dill weed

Beat all ingredients until thoroughly combined.

Creamy French Dressing

¼ cup sour cream or *2 tsp liquid barley malt or*
puréed cottage cheese *1 tsp honey*
2 tbsp tomato juice *¼ tsp paprika*
1 tbsp cider vinegar *⅛ tsp black pepper*
¾ cup olive oil *¼ tsp dry mustard*

Beat all ingredients until well combined.

Avocado Sour Cream Dressing

1 ripe avocado *¾ cup olive oil*
½ cup sour cream *1 garlic clove, crushed*
2 tbsp cider vinegar *½ tsp sea salt*

Blend all ingredients in an electric blender or food processor.

Caesar Salad Dressing

2 tbsp lemon juice
2 tbsp cider vinegar
2 tbsp water
⅔ cup olive oil

¼ tsp sea salt
1 garlic clove, crushed
¼ tsp black pepper
¼ cup grated Romano
   cheese

Place all ingredients in a covered jar and shake until well combined.

Yogurt Herb Dressing

1 cup yogurt
2 tbsp olive oil
1 tbsp tamari soy sauce
1 garlic clove, crushed

1 tsp dill seed, crushed
2 tsp finely chopped fresh
   parsley
2 tsp finely chopped chives

Mix all ingredients until well combined.

DRESSINGS WITH EGGS

Yogurt Mayonnaise Dressing

1 cup yogurt
½ cup mayonnaise
½ tsp salt
1 tsp paprika
1 garlic clove, crushed

2 tsp dill weed
1 tbsp finely chopped fresh
   parsley
2 tbsp finely chopped chives

Beat all ingredients until well combined.

Russian Dressing

1 cup sour cream or
  puréed cottage cheese
1 tbsp lemon juice
¼ cup tomato juice

1 garlic clove, crushed
¼ tsp paprika
1 hard-boiled egg, finely
  chopped

Mix all ingredients well.

17.

SWEETS WITHOUT SUGAR

FROZEN NONDAIRY TREATS

Frozen desserts and snacks are everyone's summertime favorites, and children are no exception. Some children, however, cannot have ice cream, even homemade ice cream, because they are allergic to dairy products. For them especially we offer these recipes, ranging from simple juice popsicles to fancy frozen nut creams.

Fruit Sherbet

2 ripe bananas
3 cups fruit juice

1 papaya or avocado,
    seeded and peeled
2 tbsp sunflower oil

In an electric blender or food processor, blend ingredients until smooth. Pour into freezer trays. Allow to freeze until edges are just frozen. Beat with a fork or rotary beater. Return to freezer. Allow to freeze and beat once again. Return to freezer and serve when desired. Makes 1 quart.

Juice Popsicles

Pour fruit juice—grape, apple, orange, cherry, or pineapple—or any punch or sweetened tea into plastic popsicle maker and freeze.

Grape Snow

1 cup ice cubes or   *1 cup grape juice*
   crushed ice

In an electric food processor or blender, blend at high speed to create grape snow. Makes 2 cups.

Orange Snow

1 orange, peeled and   *1½ cups orange juice*
   chopped with membrane   *1½ cups ice cubes*

In an electric blender or food processor, blend orange juice and orange into a smooth purée. Blend in ice cubes to produce a "snow" consistency. Makes 3 cups.

Berry Ice

2 cups berries: strawberries,   *2 cups apple juice*
   blueberries, cranberries,
   raspberries, or seedless
   grapes

In an electric blender or food processor, blend until smooth. Pour into freezer trays. Freeze until mushy, beat, and freeze until fully frozen. Makes 1 quart.

Banana Sherbet

3 ripe bananas   *2 cups pineapple juice*

In an electric blender or food processor, blend until smooth. Turn into freezer trays. Allow to become mushy, beat, and freeze fully before serving. Makes 1½ pints.

Vanilla Nut Cream

1 tbsp agar agar flakes   *1½ cups water*
1 cup boiling water   *¼ cup sunflower oil*
1 cup raw cashews or   *1 tbsp vanilla extract*
* blanched almonds*

Sprinkle agar agar flakes over boiling water in a saucepan. Continue to boil for 3 minutes until agar agar is totally dissolved. Allow to cool for 5 minutes.

Stir in nuts and water. In an electric blender or food processor, blend until smooth. If desired, strain through a double layer of cheesecloth. Return to blender or processor and slowly add oil and vanilla while blending. Turn into freezer trays. Freeze until mushy, beat, and freeze once again. Makes nearly 1 quart.

Variations: To flavor this basic nut cream, simply add fruit, carob, or other flavoring before adding oil.

Coconut Sesame Cream

3 cups hot water   *1 tbsp slippery elm powder*
1 cup diced fresh coconut   *3 tbsp honey*
½ cup tahini   *1 tbsp vanilla*
                                    ⅓ cup sunflower oil

In an electric blender, blend water, coconut, tahini, and slippery elm. Strain through a double layer of cheesecloth.

Return to blender and add honey and vanilla. Continue to blend and slowly add oil. Turn into freezer trays. Allow to freeze partially, beat, and return to freezer until ready to serve. Makes 1 quart.

Variations: Add berries, fruit, or carob before adding oil.

Fancy Frozen Bananas

¼ cup liquid barley malt
½ cup carob powder
4 bananas

½ cup chopped nuts or
  unsweetened shredded
  coconut

Mix malt and carob powder. Spread on a plate. Place sticks in bananas. Roll bananas in carob-malt mixture. Spread chopped nuts or coconut on a plate. Roll bananas in nuts or coconut, and freeze on a piece of waxed paper.

Frozen Bananas

The simplest frozen treat is a banana with a stick inserted and frozen.

NONDAIRY PUDDINGS AND GELATINS

Aduki Pudding

Bean pudding? Surprisingly enough, this high-protein dish may well become one of your child's favorite snacks.

½ cup aduki beans, soaked
  in water overnight
2 cups apple juice
¼ cup brown or sweet
  rice flour
1 cup apple juice mixed
  with 1 cup water

1 cup water
½ tsp agar agar flakes
2 tsp vanilla
1 tsp instant grain
  coffee substitute
¼ cup almond or cashew
  butter

In pressure cooker or saucepan, cook beans in apple juice until soft: 45 minutes in a pressure cooker, 1½ hours in a pan.

In a separate saucepan, combine rice flour with apple juice and water mixture. Cook over medium heat until thickened, about 15 minutes.

In a third pot, combine water, agar agar, vanilla, and grain coffee. Boil for 3 minutes until agar agar is totally dissolved.

Purée cooked aduki beans, rice flour mixture, agar agar mixture, and nut butter until smooth. Chill for 2 hours before serving. Serves 4 to 6.

Apple Pudding

⅓ cup brown or sweet rice flour	3 cups apple juice ¼ cup cashew or almond butter or tahini

In a saucepan, combine flour and apple juice. Cook over medium heat for 10 minutes until thickened, stirring occasionally to prevent lumps. Add nut butter and purée in an electric food processor or blender until creamy.

Nondairy Carob Pudding

¼ cup brown or sweet rice flour ¼ cup carob powder 3 cups apple juice	3 tbsp cashew, almond, or peanut butter or tahini 1 tbsp vanilla

In a saucepan, combine flour, carob powder and apple juice. Cook over medium heat, stirring occasionally, for 20 minutes until thickened. Add nut butter and vanilla, and purée in an electric blender or food processor until smooth.

Fruit Gel Dessert

2½ cups fruit juice, grape,   1 tbsp agar agar powder or
    apple, pineapple, apricot,   1½ tsp agar agar flakes
    or peach

Place juice in a saucepan and sprinkle with agar agar. Bring
to a boil. Continue to boil for 5 minutes until thoroughly
dissolved. Pour into a gelatin mold and allow to set for 3
hours at room temperature or 2 hours in the refrigerator
until firm. Serves 4.

Variation: Before pouring mixture into gelatin mold, add
whole fresh berries or diced fruit.

NONDAIRY EGGLESS COOKIES AND SQUARES

Eggless Peanut Butter Cookies

½ cup peanut butter   ¾ cup whole wheat pastry
½ cup liquid barley malt   flour
¼ cup date sugar   ½ cup raw wheat germ
¼ cup safflower or   1 tsp aluminum-free
    sunflower oil   baking powder

Preheat oven to 350°.

Cream together peanut butter, malt, date sugar and oil.
Combine flour, wheat germ, and baking powder in a
separate bowl. Mix into peanut butter mixture to form
cookie dough. Place by spoonfuls onto a well-oiled baking
sheet. Flatten with a fork. Bake for 15 minutes until brown
and crisp. Makes 1½ dozen.

Eggless Oatmeal Cookies

1½ cups rolled oats   ½ cup whole wheat pastry
2 cups boiling apple juice   flour
¼ cup brown rice flour   1 tsp cinnamon
2 tbsp sesame oil   1 tsp vanilla
                              ½ cup raisins or carob chips

Preheat oven to 375°.

In a dry heated skillet, toast oats until lightly browned. Stir into boiling apple juice and allow to sit for 5 minutes. Stir in remaining ingredients. Drop by spoonfuls onto a well-oiled baking sheet and bake for 15 minutes until golden brown.

Bean Brownies

High-protein aduki beans give these brownies a chewy texture.

1 cup aduki beans, soaked in water overnight	*¾ cup applesauce*
3 cups apple juice	*1 tsp cardamom powder*
1 tbsp vanilla extract	*¼ cup sesame or safflower oil*
1 cup roasted carob powder	*3 tbsp liquid barley malt*
	1 cup walnuts

Cook beans in apple juice for 45 minutes in a pressure cooker or for 2 hours in a saucepan.

Preheat oven to 350°.

Purée beans with juice in an electric blender or food processor until smooth. Stir in remaining ingredients.

Pour batter into a well-oiled 9- by 15-inch baking pan. Bake for 1 hour and 15 minutes until firm. Cut into squares before serving. Makes 2 dozen squares.

Holiday Spice Cookies

At Christmas you can cut these cookies into Santa Claus shapes; at Valentine's Day into hearts; at Easter into bunnies. They taste better if aged for a week, but they seldom last that long around our house.

½ cup blackstrap molasses	*¼ tsp powdered cloves*
½ cup liquid barley malt	*¼ tsp powdered allspice*
½ cup safflower oil	*5½ cups whole wheat pastry flour*
¾ tsp powdered ginger	
¾ tsp cinnamon	*3 tbsp nutritional yeast*

Cream molasses, malt, and oil until well combined. In a separate bowl, mix remaining ingredients. Stir dry mixture into creamed mixture to form a stiff dough. Chill for 30 minutes.

Preheat oven to 375°.

Roll dough as thin as possible and cut into desired shapes. Bake on a well-oiled baking sheet for 8 minutes until lightly browned. Makes 4 to 5 dozen.

NONDAIRY EGGLESS CAKES

Eggless Carob Cake

½ cup safflower or
  sunflower oil
¾ cup liquid barley malt
1 cup water or apple juice
1 cup whole wheat pastry
  flour
¾ cup brown rice flour

¾ cup roasted carob
  powder
1 tbsp aluminum-free
  baking powder
1 tsp grain coffee substitute
1 tsp vanilla

Preheat oven to 350°.

In a large bowl, mix oil and malt until well combined. Measure apple juice into a small bowl. In a third bowl, mix whole wheat pastry flour, brown rice flour, carob powder, baking powder, and grain coffee with a wire whisk.

Alternately add apple juice and flour mixture to malt and oil, stirring with each addition. Stir in vanilla. Pour batter into a well-oiled 10-inch spring-form pan and bake for 35 minutes until center springs back to the touch. Frost with Carob Nut Butter Frosting.

Carob Nut Butter Frosting

¼ cup cashew, peanut, or
  almond butter

⅔ cup roasted carob
  powder
½ cup water

In an electric blender, blend ingredients until smooth. This frosting will drip over the sides of your carob cake. If you want a thicker frosting, add less water.

Strawberry Shortcake

Children love strawberry shortcake, and it can easily be enjoyed by those unable to eat dairy products if topped with a little Banana Nut Cream.

SHORTCAKE BISCUITS

2 cups whole wheat pastry flour

4 tsp aluminum-free baking powder

¼ cup sunflower or safflower oil

¾ cup apple juice

Preheat oven to 450°.

In a bowl, mix flour and baking powder. Rub in oil to form a mixture the texture of coarse corn meal. Stir in apple juice to form a dough. Roll on a lightly floured board and cut into circles with a 3-inch cookie cutter or drinking glass. Place on a lightly oiled baking sheet and bake for 20 minutes until lightly browned.

Remove from oven and allow to cool. Makes 18 biscuits.

STRAWBERRY TOPPING

1 quart fresh strawberries   *1 tbsp honey or maple syrup*

Slice strawberries. Add sweetener and mash with a potato masher until juicy.

BANANA NUT CREAM

2 ripe bananas   *1 cup water*

1 cup raw cashews   *½ tsp vanilla extract*

Place all ingredients in an electric blender or food processor and purée until thick and smooth. (If you will not be using it immediately, stir in 2 teaspoons pineapple juice to prevent bananas from darkening.)

ASSEMBLING SHORTCAKE

Slice biscuits. Top a slice with strawberry topping, cover with another slice, and add another serving of topping. Spoon a serving of Banana Nut Cream over the top. Serves 4 to 6.

NONDAIRY PIES

Children who are unable to eat dairy products can snack on a large variety of fruit pies and nut cream pies as well as pies filled with nondairy puddings mentioned earlier in this chapter.

Basic Oil Crust

This recipe makes a double crust for fruit pies.

¾ cup whole wheat pastry
    flour
¾ cup whole wheat flour

⅓ cup sunflower or
    safflower oil
3 tbsp ice water

Combine flours, and stir in oil to form a mixture the texture of coarse corn meal. Stir in ice water one tablespoon at a time until dough forms a ball. If necessary, add one more tablespoon of ice water.

Divde dough into two balls and chill for 30 minutes. Roll into 12-inch circles between pieces of waxed paper. To line a lightly oiled pie plate, remove the top layer of waxed paper. Fill pie and follow the same procedure for the top pastry. Trim edges, tuck under, and pinch decoratively.

Berry Pie

3 cups fresh strawberries   2 tbsp maple syrup
   blueberries, or raspberries   2 tbsp arrowroot starch

Place berries in a bowl. Stir in maple syrup. Sprinkle with
arrowroot starch and stir to coat berries evenly. Use to fill
pie crust. Bake at 375° for 45 minutes until lightly
browned.
   Variations: Use sliced peaches or apricots instead of
berries.

Apple or Pear Pie

3 cups sliced apples or pears   1 tbsp arrowroot starch
¼ cup liquid barley malt

Place apple or pears in a bowl. Drizzle with malt and stir
until well coated. Sprinkle with starch and toss to coat
evenly. Pour into a lined pastry shell and cover. Bake for
45 minutes at 375°.

Basic Crumble Crust

The malt in this recipe makes the crust crunchy and fresh
even after a day or two in the refrigerator. It is an excellent
crust for any cream or pudding pie.

½ cup raw wheat germ   ⅓ cup coarsely chopped
½ cup unsweetened   walnuts or pecans
   shredded coconut   ⅓ cup sunflower or
½ cup rolled oats   safflower oil
¼ cup whole wheat flour   3 tbsp liquid barley malt

   Preheat oven to 400°.
   In a bowl, combine wheat germ, coconuts, oats, flour,
and nuts. Stir in oil until well distributed. Stir in malt

until ingredients are evenly coated. Press into a lightly oiled 9-inch pie plate and bake for 10 to 15 minutes until lightly browned. Allow to cool, and then fill with desired filling.

Banana Nut Cream Pie

*3 ripe bananas, sliced and
    sprinkled with lemon
    juice*
one baked pie shell
1 cup raw cashews

2 cups water
1 tbsp sunflower oil
1 tsp vanilla
*4 tbsp arrowroot starch
    dissolved in 2 tbsp water*

Arrange banana slices in cooked Crumble Crust shell. In an electric blender or food processor, blend cashews, water, and oil. Pour into a saucepan and bring to a gentle boil. Stir in vanilla and arrowroot paste. Continue stirring for 5 minutes until thickened. Pour over bananas and allow to cool before serving.

Pear or Apple Sesame Cream Pie

1 tsp safflower oil
*2½ cups sliced apples or
    pears*
¼ cup tahini
1 tbsp maple syrup

1 cup water
*2 tbsp arrowroot starch
    dissolved in 1 tbsp water*
½ tsp vanilla extract
one baked pie shell

Heat oil in a heavy frying pan. Sauté apples or pears until soft.

Beat tahini, maple syrup, and water until thoroughly combined. Heat in a saucepan until nearly boiling. Stir in arrowroot. Contintue stirring for 3 minutes until thickened.

Add vanilla and apples or pears. Pour into Crumble Crust pie shell and allow to cool before serving.

Raw Fruit Pies

3½ cups raw berries,   *2 tbsp arrowroot starch*
    peaches, apricots, or   *dissolved in 2 tbsp water*
    melon   *one baked pie shell*
1 cup water

In an electric blender or food processor, blend ½ cup fruit with 1 cup water. Heat in a saucepan nearly to boiling. Stir in arrowroot paste and continue stirring until thickened. Pour over remaining 3 cups of fruit and stir in until well coated. Pour into baked Crumble Crust pie shell and allow to cool before serving.

NONDAIRY CANDIES

Occasionally every child wants a candy, and yours will feel deprived if one is never granted. The candies we have created for this book are made with malt and resemble to a remarkable degree the candies bought in stores.

Carob Toffee or Lollipops

¾ cup liquid barley malt   *1 cup roasted carob powder*

In a saucepan mix malt and carob until well combined. Cook over medium heat until mixture bubbles. Continue cooking, stirring constantly, for 1 minute. Remove from heat. Allow to cool only until mixture can be handled.

With moistened hands, form into balls for candies. For lollipops press a stick into balls. Candy will resemble a stiff toffee when thoroughly cooled. Makes 2 dozen candies.

Lemon, Orange, or Strawberry Lollipops

½ tsp oil
¾ cup rice syrup

1 tsp lemon, orange, or
    strawberry extract

Lightly oil a heavy-bottomed pan and heat over medium heat. Pour in flavoring and rice syrup. Cook, stirring constantly, until mixture begins to bubble. Reduce heat and continue stirring for 5 minutes until a drop becomes hard when dropped into cold water. Remove from heat and cool only until you are able to handle the mixture.

With moistened hands, form into balls and insert lollipop sticks. Candy will harden when cool. Makes 1 dozen candies.

Peppermint Suckers

¾ cup liquid barley malt

½ tsp peppermint extract
½ tsp oil

Stir peppermint extract and malt until well combined. Oil a heavy-bottomed pan. Pour malt and peppermint into pan. Cook over medium heat until mixture begins to bubble. Reduce heat to low and continue to cook, stirring constantly for 5 minutes, until a drop of the mixture becomes hard when dropped into cold water. Remove from heat and allow to cool only until mixture can be handled.

With moistened hands, shape into balls and insert lollipop sticks. Candy will become very hard when thoroughly cooled. Makes 1 dozen candies.

Popcorn Balls

Popcorn balls were one of those treats that our mothers always said were too much work to make. Then one day we discovered that with malt, popcorn balls can be much easier than apple pie. With a little help from a hungry child, this recipe takes only a few minutes to throw together.

2 tbsp oil   ¼ cup butter
½ cup popping corn   ½ cup liquid malt

Pop corn in 2 tablespoons of oil. Heat butter in a pan. When hot, stir in malt. Then add popped corn. Stir ingredients until popcorn is uniformly coated. Remove from heat. Wet hands. When popcorn is cool enough to handle, shape it into balls by squeezing it between both hands.

FROZEN DAIRY TREATS

Frozen dairy treats not only are a summertime delight for active children, but also provide protein and calcium. If the following recipes are not to be served within a day or two after preparation, they should be processed in an ice-cream maker.

Carob Carob-Chip Ice Cream

3 cups milk   1 tbsp arrowroot starch
¼ cup roasted carob   dissolved in 1 tbsp milk
   powder   1 cup carob chips
                              1 cup heavy cream, whipped

In a saucepan, bring milk to a gentle boil. Stir in carob powder and arrowroot paste. Continue stirring for 3 minutes until thickened. Remove from heat and allow to cool.

Stir in carob chips and turn into a freezer tray. Place in freezer until edges freeze. Remove, fold in cream, and return to freezer. When partially frozen, beat until smooth. Return to freezer to harden before serving. Makes 4 to 5 cups.

Fruit Ice Cream

1½ cups milk
2 tbsp arrowroot starch
    dissolved in 2 tbsp milk
1 tbsp honey
3 cups fresh fruit: peeled
    sliced peaches, papayas,

or apricots, or straw-
    berries, pitted cherries,
    blueberries, or raspberries
1 cup heavy cream, whipped

Bring milk to a gentle boil in a saucepan. Stir in arrowroot paste. Continue stirring for 3 minutes until mixture thickens and there is no taste of starch. Remove from heat and set aside.

In an electric blender or food processor, blend honey with 1½ cups of fruit. Stir into thickened milk. Add remaining whole fruit and turn into a freezer tray.

When mixture begins to thicken, fold in whipped cream and beat until smooth. Return to freezer. Allow to freeze partially once again and beat. Return to freezer until hard and ready to serve. Makes 5 to 5½ cups.

Milk Ice

4 cups milk
3 tbsp honey

1 tsp vanilla, almond,
    lemon, or orange extract

Heat milk. Remove from heat and stir in honey and flavoring. Turn into a freezer tray and freeze until edges are crystallized. Remove and beat. Return to freezer. Allow to freeze partially once again and beat. Return to freezer until hard and ready to serve. Makes 1 quart.

DAIRY PUDDINGS AND GELATINS

Maple Nut Pudding

2 cups milk
1 tbsp arrowroot starch and
    2 tbsp brown rice flour
    dissolved in 3 tbsp milk

1 tbsp maple syrup
⅔ cup walnut pieces

Heat milk nearly to boiling. Stir in arrowroot, flour, and milk paste. Continue stirring for 7 minutes until mixture has thickened and there is no taste of raw flour. Stir in maple syrup and nuts. Serves 4.

Carob Milk Pudding

2 cups milk
3 tbsp roasted carob powder

2 tbsp arrowroot starch
dissolved in 2 tbsp milk

In a saucepan, heat milk nearly to boiling. Stir in carob powder and arrowroot paste. Continue stirring for 5 minutes until thickened. Serves 4.

Creamy Fruit and Nut Gel

2½ cups fruit juice: grape, apple, pineapple, apricot, or peach
1 tbsp agar agar powder or 1½ tsp agar agar flakes
2 tsp arrowroot starch dissolved in 1 tbsp water

⅔ cup cream cheese
1¼ cups sliced or chopped fruit: grapes, pineapple, peaches, apricots, blueberries, or strawberries
¾ cup chopped walnuts

Pour juice into a saucepan and sprinkle with agar agar. Bring to a gentle boil. Continue to boil for 5 to 10 minutes until agar agar is thoroughly dissolved. Stir arrowroot paste and continue stirring for 3 minutes until slightly thickened. Remove from heat.

In an electric blender or food processor, blend hot juice mixture with cream cheese until smooth. Stir in nuts and fruit. Pour into a gelatin mold or bowl and allow to set until firm. Serves 6 to 8.

Butterscotch Pudding

2 cups milk
2 tbsp butter
⅓ cup liquid barley malt

2 tbsp arrowroot starch
dissolved in 2 tbsp milk

In a saucepan, heat milk, butter, and malt nearly to boiling. Stir in arrowroot starch and continue stirring for 3 minutes until thickened. Remove from heat. Serves 4.

Coconut Pudding

2 cups milk
¾ cup unsweetened
    shredded coconut

2 tbsp arrowroot starch
    dissolved in 2 tbsp milk
1 tbsp honey
½ tsp vanilla or almond
    extract

In a saucepan, bring milk nearly to boiling. Stir in coconut and arrowroot paste. Continue stirring for 3 to 5 minutes until thickened. Remove from heat and stir in honey and flavoring. Serves 4.

Fruit Yogurt Gel

2½ cups fruit juice: grape,
    apple, or pineapple
1 tbsp agar agar powder or
    1½ tsp agar agar flakes

2 tsp arrowroot starch
    dissolved in 1 tbsp water
1 cup yogurt

Measure juice into a saucepan and sprinkle with agar agar. Boil gently for 5 to 10 minutes until dissolved. Stir in arrowroot paste. Continue stirring for 3 minutes until slightly thickened. Remove from heat. Allow to cool and stir in yogurt. Pour into a bowl or gelatin mold. Serves 6 to 8.

EGGLESS DAIRY COOKIES AND SQUARES

Carrot Cookies

¼ cup blackstrap molasses
¼ cup liquid barley malt
4 tbsp sunflower oil
½ cup mashed cooked
  carrots
¾ cup whole wheat pastry
  flour
¾ cup raw wheat germ

½ cup noninstant powdered
  milk
½ tsp cinnamon
½ tsp nutmeg
1 tsp aluminum-free baking
  powder
1 cup coarsely chopped nuts
1 cup raisins
water

Preheat oven to 350°.

In a bowl, beat molasses, malt, and oil until well combined. Stir in carrots.

In a separate bowl, combine all dry ingredients and mix thoroughly. Add dry ingredients to liquid mixture to form a batter. If mixture is too dry, stir in water one tablespoon at a time until batter can be dropped by spoonfuls onto a lightly oiled baking sheet. Bake for 12 to 15 minutes until edges are browned. Makes 3 dozen.

Coconut Carob-Chip Cookies

½ cup sunflower or
  safflower oil
½ cup liquid barley malt
½ cup milk
1 cup unsweetened
  shredded coconut
¾ cup carob chips
½ cup whole wheat pastry
  flour

½ cup raw wheat germ
½ cup noninstant
  powdered milk
1 cup rolled oats
1 tsp aluminum-free baking
  powder
1 tbsp vanilla extract

Preheat oven to 350°.

In a bowl, beat oil, malt, and milk until well combined. In a separate bowl, mix coconut, carob chips, flour, wheat germ, milk powder, oats, and baking powder. Mix dry ingredients into liquid mixture. Stir in vanilla. Drop batter by spoonfuls onto a well-oiled baking sheet. Bake for 10 minutes. Makes 2½ dozen.

Cream Cheese Cookies

¼ cup liquid barley malt	1 cup whole wheat pastry
⅓ cup sunflower oil	flour
½ cup cream cheese	3 tbsp finely chopped nuts

In a blender or electric food processor, blend malt, oil, and cream cheese until smooth. Stir in flour and nuts to form a stiff dough. Shape dough into two long rolls.

Wrap in waxed paper and chill until firm.

Preheat oven to 400°.

Cut cookie rolls into thin slices and bake on a lightly oiled baking sheet for 5 minutes until lightly browned. Makes 2 dozen.

Scotch Shortcake

3½ cups rolled oats	⅔ cup liquid barley malt
½ cup oat flour	1 cup soft butter
	1 tsp vanilla

Preheat oven to 325°.

In a bowl, mix oats and oat flour. In a separate bowl, cream malt and butter. Combine the two mixtures and mix well. Stir in vanilla. Press into a well-oiled 9- by 13-inch baking pan. Bake for 30 minutes until lightly browned. Cool for 10 minutes before cutting into squares. Makes 2 dozen squares.

EGGLESS DAIRY CAKES

Sour Cream Carob Cake

½ cup safflower or
   sunflower oil
½ cup liquid barley malt
1½ cups sour cream
½ cup brown rice flour

1 cup whole wheat pastry
   flour
1 cup roasted carob powder
1 tbsp aluminum-free
   baking powder

Preheat oven to 350°.

In a bowl, beat oil, malt, and sour cream until well combined. In a separate bowl, mix dry ingredients. Stir dry ingredients into liquid mixture a few tablespoons at a time. Pour batter into a well-oiled spring-form pan and bake for 40 minutes until done. Frost with Sour Cream Carob Frosting.

Sour Cream Carob Frosting

¼ cup butter

⅔ cup roasted carob powder
½ cup sour cream

In an electric blender or food processor, blend all ingredients until smooth. Spoon frosting over top of cake, allowing it to drip over the sides.

Eggless Coconut Cake

½ cup safflower or
   sunflower oil
½ cup liquid barley malt
1¼ cups whole wheat
   pastry flour
1¼ cups brown rice flour

1 cup unsweetened
   shredded coconut
1 tbsp aluminum-free
   baking powder
1 tbsp vanilla
1½ cups milk

Preheat oven to 350°.

In a bowl, beat oil and malt. In a separate bowl, mix whole wheat pastry flour, rice flour, coconut, and baking powder. In a third bowl, mix vanilla and milk. Alternately stir dry mixture and milk with vanilla into oil and melt mixture to form a cake batter. Pour into a well-oiled 10-inch spring-form pan or into lined cupcake tins. Bake cake for 40 minutes or cupcakes for 25 minutes. Makes one cake or 24 cupcakes. Frost with Pat's Fluffy Coconut Frosting.

Pat's Fluffy Coconut Frosting

4 tbsp brown rice flour
1 cup milk
½ cup soft butter
¼ cup honey

1 tsp vanilla
1 cup unsweetened
shredded coconut

Combine rice flour and milk in a saucepan. Cook over medium heat, stirring occasionally, until thick. Remove from heat and cool.

Add butter, honey, and vanilla. Beat until fluffy. Frost cupcakes or cake and sprinkle with coconut.

DAIRY CANDIES

By adding milk powder to malt and cooking, a number of candies that are incredibly similar to toffee can be easily and quickly made. If you use rice syrup rather than malt, the candy becomes a nougat-like treat.

Simple Vanilla Toffee

¾ cup liquid barley malt
1 tsp vanilla extract

1 cup noninstant powdered
milk

In a saucepan, heat malt until thin. Stir in vanilla and milk powder. Cook, stirring constantly, until mixture bubbles at edges of pan. Remove from heat and cool only until mixture can be handled. With moistened hands, shape into balls or any desired shape. Makes 1½ dozen candies.

Coconut Toffee

1 cup liquid barley malt
1¼ cups noninstant
  powdered milk

1 cup unsweetened
  shredded coconut

In a saucepan, heat malt until thin. Stir in milk powder and coconut. Cook until mixture is well combined and bubbles at edges of pan. Remove from heat and cool only until mixture can be handled.

With moistened hands, shape mixture into desired shapes. Makes 2 dozen candies.

Soft Peanut Butter Toffee

½ cup liquid barley malt
⅓ cup peanut butter

1 cup noninstant powdered
  milk

In a saucepan, heat malt until thin. Stir in peanut butter until well combined. Stir in milk powder to form a dough. Remove from heat and cool until mixture can be handled.

With moistened hands, shape into balls. Makes 1½ dozen candies.

Vanilla Nougat

¾ cup rice syrup
1 tsp vanilla extract

1 cup noninstant
  powdered milk

In a saucepan, heat rice syrup until thin. Stir in vanilla and powdered milk powder. Continue cooking until well combined. Remove from heat and cool until mixture can be handled.

With moistened hands, shape into candies. Makes 1 dozen candies.

SWEETS AND TREATS WITH EGGS

Eggs are the ideal protein food because of their excellent balance of amino acids. Yet many children hate eggs even when their parents have no objection to eating them. If you feel your child could use a little more high-quality protein, sweets are a wonderful place to hide eggs. They not only lose their taste in ice creams, puddings, custards, cakes, and pies, but also make all these wonderful foods lighter, smoother, and generally more suitable to your child's taste.

FROZEN TREATS WITH EGGS

Ice creams are richer and sherbets are lighter when eggs are used. If ice creams are not to be eaten within a day or two, they should be processed in an ice cream maker.

Banana Ice Cream

2 cups milk	*1 cup heavy cream*
2 eggs, well beaten	*1 tsp lemon juice*
	1 cup puréed bananas

Heat milk to boiling. Beat ¼ cup hot milk gradually into eggs. Pour eggs and milk into remaining hot milk and cook for 1 minute over medium heat. Remove from heat and stir in heavy cream and lemon juice. Cool. Stir in banana purée. Pour into a freezer tray and freeze until edges are firm. Beat with a fork or rotary beater and return to freezer. Freeze partially and beat once again. Freeze until firm before serving. Makes 1 quart.

Carob Ripple Ice Cream

one recipe Maple Ice Cream Custard (see page 322)
½ cup water   *½ cup roasted carob powder*

Place Maple Ice Cream Custard in a bowl. In a separate bowl, mix water and carob until well combined. Stir into ice cream a little at a time with a wooden spoon to achieve a marble effect. Return to freezer tray and refreeze until ready to serve. Makes 4 to 5 cups.

Orange Milk Sherbet

2 cups orange sections with   *1 quart milk*
   membrane removed   *3 egg whites, stiffly beaten*

In an electric blender or food processor, blend orange sections and milk. Place in a freezer tray and freeze until edges are firm. Beat with a fork until smooth. Return to freezer until partially frozen. Beat once again and fold in beaten egg whites. Return to freezer until completely frozen. Makes 1½ quarts.

Strawberry Milk Sherbet

2 cups fresh strawberries   *1 quart milk*
                         2 egg whites, stiffly beaten

In an electric blender or food processor, blend berries and milk until smooth. Pour into a freezer tray and freeze until edges are firm. Beat with a fork or rotary beater. Return to freezer until partially frozen. Beat once again. Fold in beaten egg whites, and freeze until ready to serve. Makes 1½ quarts.

Maple Ice Cream Custard

3 cups milk
4 eggs, separated
3 tbsp maple syrup

1 tsp arrowroot starch
1 cup heavy cream
2 tsp vanilla extract

Scald milk in a heavy-bottomed saucepan. Remove from heat. In a bowl, beat egg yolks, maple syrup, and arrowroot. Stir milk into egg mixture. Pour back into saucepan and cook over medium heat, stirring occasionally, until thick. Stir in heavy cream and vanilla. Cool and refrigerate for 2 hours.

Remove from refrigerator and beat egg whites until peaked. Fold into custard. Pour into a freezer tray and freeze until edges are firm. Remove and beat with a fork or rotary beater until smooth. Return to freezer until partially frozen. Beat once again and return to freezer until firm and ready to serve. Makes 4 to 5 cups.

EGG PUDDINGS AND CUSTARDS

Fresh Strawberry Pudding

¾ cup apple cider or juice
1 tbsp arrowroot starch
1 tbsp brown rice flour

3 egg yolks
2 cups fresh strawberries,
   sliced and mashed

In a saucepan, combine cider or juice, arrowroot, and flour. Cook over medium heat for 10 minutes, stirring occasionally, until thickened. Reduce heat to low and stir in egg yolks. Cook for 3 minutes, until extremely thick, smooth, and pastelike. Remove from heat and stir in mashed strawberries. Serve warm or cool. This pudding makes an excellent filling for a baked pie shell. Serves 4.

Baked Custard

¼ cup malt or 1 tbsp
   maple syrup
3 eggs, beaten

2 tsp soy flour
2 cups milk, scalded and
   cooled to lukewarm
¼ tsp nutmeg

Preheat oven to 350°.

Beat all ingredients except nutmeg until well combined. Pour into oiled custard cups or a casserole dish. Sprinkle with nutmeg. Place in a pan of hot water and bake for 45 minutes to 1 hour until firm. Serves 4 to 6.

Maple Nut Custard

2 tbsp maple syrup
3 eggs, beaten
2 tsp soy flour

2 cups milk, scalded and
   cooled to lukewarm
1 tsp vanilla extract
1 cup coarsely chopped
   walnuts

Preheat oven to 350°.

Beat all ingredients until well combined. Pour into lightly oiled custard cups or a casserole. Place in a pan of hot water and bake for 45 minutes to 1 hour until firm. Serves 4 to 6.

Rich and Creamy Carob Pudding

2 cups milk
3 tbsp noninstant
   powdered milk
½ cup carob powder

1 tsp vanilla extract
2 tbsp lecithin granules
3 eggs, beaten
1 tbsp brown rice flour

Beat all ingredients until well combined. Place in the top of a double boiler. Cook, stirring occasionally, until pudding thickens. Serves 4 to 6.

Coconut Custard Pudding

2 cups milk
2 tbsp brown rice flour
2 tbsp liquid barley malt
3 eggs, beaten

⅔ cup unsweetened
  shredded coconut
1 tsp vanilla extract or
  ½ tsp almond extract

In a saucepan, combine milk, rice flour, and malt. Cook over medium heat, stirring occasionally, until mixture thickens. Reduce heat and stir in coconut and eggs. Continue cooking, stirring constantly, for 5 minutes until smooth and thick. Remove from heat and stir in vanilla or almond extract. Serves 4 to 6.

COOKIES AND SQUARES WITH EGGS

When eggs are used, cookies and squares have a more conventional taste and texture. Most of these goodies can be sent to school for a class party, and the children will never guess that white flour and sugar are absent. Wheat germ and malt are the secret of their light and often chewy texture.

Carob Brownies

½ cup oil
¾ cup liquid barley malt
2 eggs
½ cup roasted carob powder
1 tbsp vanilla extract

2 tsp aluminum-free baking
  powder
¾ cup raw wheat germ
¾ cup whole wheat pastry
  flour

Preheat oven to 350°.

Beat oil, malt, eggs, carob powder, and vanilla until well combined. In a bowl, mix baking powder, wheat germ, and pastry flour. Gradually mix dry mixture into malt mixture. Spread into a 9- by 13-inch baking pan and bake for 20

minutes until edges are crisp. Cool slightly before cutting.
Makes 18 brownies.

Coconut Blond Brownies

½ cup sunflower or
    safflower oil
¾ cup liquid barley malt
2 eggs
½ cup noninstant
    powdered milk
1 tbsp vanilla extract

2 tsp aluminum-free baking
    powder
¾ cup raw wheat germ
¾ cup whole wheat pastry
    flour
⅔ cup unsweetened
    shredded coconut

Preheat oven to 350°.

In a bowl, beat oil, malt, eggs, milk powder, and vanilla
until well combined. In a separate bowl, mix dry ingredients. Gradually stir dry ingredients into liquid mixture.
Spread batter in a well-oiled 9- by 13-inch baking pan.
Bake for 20 minutes until edges are lightly browned. Cool
slightly before cutting into bars. Makes 18 brownies.

Miriam's Carob-Chip Cookies

½ cup safflower or
    sunflower oil
¾ cup liquid barley malt
2 eggs
½ cup noninstant
    powdered milk
1 tbsp vanilla extract

2 tsp aluminum-free baking
    powder
¾ cup raw wheat germ
¾ cup whole wheat pastry
    flour
1 cup carob chips

Preheat oven to 350°.

In a bowl, beat oil, malt, eggs, milk powder, and vanilla
extract until well combined. In another bowl, mix baking
powder, wheat germ, and pastry flour. Gradually add dry
ingredients to liquid mixture to form a batter. Fold in
carob chips. Drop by spoonfuls onto a well-oiled baking
sheet. Bake for 10 minutes until edges are lightly browned.
Makes 3 dozen.

Soft and Chewy Peanut Butter Cookies

¼ cup safflower or
  sunflower oil
½ cup peanut butter
2 eggs
⅔ cup liquid barley malt

½ cup noninstant
  powdered milk
2 tsp aluminum-free
  baking powder
1 cup raw wheat germ
⅔ cup whole wheat pastry
  flour

Preheat oven to 350°.

In a bowl, beat oil, peanut butter, eggs, malt, and milk powder until well combined. In a separate bowl, mix baking powder, wheat germ, and pastry flour. Gradually mix dry ingredients into peanut butter mixture to form a cookie batter. Drop by spoonfuls onto a well-oiled baking sheet and bake for 10 to 15 minutes until edges are just hardly browned. Makes 2 dozen.

Macaroons

3 egg whites
3 tbsp liquid barley malt
1 cup rolled oats

¾ cup unsweetened
  shredded coconut

Preheat oven to 350°.

Beat egg whites until stiff. In a separate bowl, combine malt, oats, and coconut. Fold in egg whites. Drop by spoonfuls onto a lightly oiled baking sheet. Bake for 12 minutes until lightly browned. Makes 2 dozen.

CAKES AND CUPCAKES WITH EGGS

Eggs are indispensable for really light, airy cakes that resemble the kind made with white flour and sugar. Even with eggs this special moistness and lightness are difficult if not impossible to achieve without the addition of brown rice flour to cake and cupcake recipes. The rice flour lightens the batter in both color and texture and will make your cakes "authentic" in your child's eyes.

Light and Moist Two-Layer Carob Cake

⅓ cup soft butter
⅓ cup sunflower or
  safflower oil
½ cup liquid barley malt
5 eggs, separated
2 cups sour cream or milk

1⅓ cups roasted carob
  powder
1⅓ cups whole wheat
  pastry flour
1⅓ cups brown rice flour
2 tsp aluminum-free baking
  powder

Preheat oven to 350°.

Cream butter, oil, malt, and egg yolks until smooth. Stir in sour cream or milk. In a separate bowl, combine carob powder, flours, and baking powder. Gradually add dry mixture to liquid ingredients to form a smooth batter.

Beat egg whites until stiff and fold into batter. Pour batter into two 9-inch cake pans and bake for 25 to 30 minutes until a toothpick can be inserted and come out clean. Remove from pan and allow to cool on racks before frosting with Carob Frosting.

Carob Frosting for Two-Layer Cake

½ cup butter
1¼ cups roasted carob
  powder

1 tbsp instant grain coffee
  substitute
1 cup water

In an electric blender or food processor, blend ingredients until thick and smooth. Frosts a double layer cake.

Blueberry Cupcakes

¼ cup sunflower or
    safflower oil
⅓ cup liquid barley malt
4 eggs, separated
1 tbsp vanilla extract
1½ cups whole wheat
    pastry flour

1½ cups brown rice flour
⅓ cup noninstant
    powdered milk
2 tsp aluminum-free baking
    powder
1½ cups milk or pineapple
    juice
1⅓ cups fresh blueberries

Preheat oven to 350°.

Beat together oil, malt, egg yolks, and vanilla. In a separate bowl, mix flours, milk powder, and baking powder. Alternately add dry mixture and milk or juice to oil and malt mixture to form a smooth batter. Beat egg whites until stiff. Fold into batter. Fold in blueberries. Spoon batter into well-oiled or lined cupcake tins and bake for 20 minutes until a toothpick inserted comes out clean. Makes 2 dozen cupcakes.

Apple Spice Frosting

¼ cup soft butter
1½ cups noninstant
    powdered milk

½ cup apple juice
2 tbsp apple butter or
    cider jelly
½ tsp cinnamon

In an electric blender or food processor, blend all ingredients until smooth and thick.

Spice Cupcakes

½ cup safflower oil
⅓ cup liquid barley malt
4 eggs, separated
1 cup milk
½ cup apple juice
1½ cups whole wheat
    pastry flour

1½ cups brown rice flour
2 tsp aluminum-free
    baking powder
1 tsp cinnamon
½ tsp powdered ginger
½ tsp powdered cloves
½ tsp powdered allspice

Preheat oven to 350°.

Beat oil, malt, and egg yolks until smooth. In a separate bowl, combine milk and apple juice. In a third bowl combine dry ingredients and mix well. Alternately stir milk mixture and dry ingredients into oil, malt, and egg yolk combination to form a smooth batter. Beat whites until stiff and fold into batter. Pour batter into lined or well-oiled cupcake tins and bake for 20 to 25 minutes until a toothpick comes out clean when inserted. Frost with Apple Spice Frosting (page 328). Makes 2 dozen cupcakes.

Natural Boston Cream Pie

One day our daughter came home from kindergarten and announced that Boston cream pie had been voted the favorite cake in the class. She followed her announcement with the question, "What is Boston cream pie?" We decided it was time to take out the flours and the bowls and get to work. After a failure or two, we came up with this dessert. If you have only recently converted to natural food cookery and are a former sugar addict, you may feel that this recipe doesn't match the "real" Boston cream pie —but try it anyway. You'll learn to love it as much as we do!

THE CAKE

⅓ cup liquid barley malt
¼ cup sunflower or
*   safflower oil*
4 eggs, separated
1 tsp vanilla extract

¾ cup whole wheat pastry
*   flour*
¾ cup brown rice flour
1 tsp aluminum-free baking
*   powder*
½ cup milk or apple juice

Preheat oven to 350°.

In a bowl, beat malt, oil, egg yolks, and vanilla. In a separate bowl, mix flours and baking powder until well combined. Alternately add flour mixture and milk or juice to malt mixture to form a smooth batter. Beat egg whites until stiff. Fold into batter. Pour into a well-oiled 9-inch cake pan and bake for 30 minutes until done. Cool for 10 minutes, remove from pan, and cool completely on a wire rack.

CUSTARD FILLING

1½ cups milk
2 tbsp liquid barley malt
2 tbsp arrowroot starch

2 tbsp brown rice flour
2 eggs (or egg yolks),
  well beaten
1 tsp vanilla extract

In a saucepan, mix milk, malt, arrowroot, and rice flour. Cook over medium heat, stirring occasionally, until thickened. Reduce heat to low and stir in vanilla and eggs. When custard is uniformly yellow and thick, remove from heat.

FILLING CAKE

Slice cake into two layers. Separate layers and spread custard on one layer. Cover with the other layer.

FROSTING

¼ cup soft butter
½ cup roasted carob
  powder

1 tsp instant grain coffee
  substitute
½ cup water

In an electric blender or food processor, blend ingredients until smooth. Spread over cake, allowing some frosting to drip over sides.

MERINGUE AND CHIFFON PIES

Whenever we whip egg whites at our house, our older daughter, who normally hates eggs, takes a fingerful and announces that it tastes like whipped cream, which she always loves. Meringue and chiffon pies are special treats that add the good protein of eggs to the joy of a child's favorite goodie.

Lemon Meringue Pie

one Basic Oil Crust shell
  (see page 306)
1½ cups apple juice
¼ cup arrowroot starch and
  ¼ cup brown or sweet
  rice flour dissolved in
  ⅓ cup apple juice

4 eggs, separated
1 tsp lemon juice
2 tsp liquid barley malt

Preheat oven to 350°.

Bake pie shell for 15 minutes and remove from oven.

In a saucepan, bring apple juice to a gentle boil. Stir in arrowroot, flour, and juice paste. Continue stirring for 5 minutes until mixture thickens. Reduce heat to low and stir in egg yolks and lemon juice. Cook for 3 minutes, stirring constantly. Remove from heat and pour into pie shell.

Beat egg whites and malt until they peak. Spread decoratively over lemon filling. Return to oven and bake for 10 minutes until lightly browned. Cool before serving.

Strawberry Chiffon Pie

one Basic Oil Crust shell
  (see page 306)
¾ cup apple cider or juice

1 tbsp brown rice flour
1 tbsp arrowroot starch
3 eggs, separated
2 cups mashed strawberries

Bake pie shell at 350° for 15 minutes and let cool.

In a saucepan, combine cider or juice, flour, and arrowroot. (You can first make the arrowroot into a smooth paste with a little of the juice.) Cook over medium heat, stirring occasionally, until thickened. Reduce heat and stir in egg yolks and strawberries. Cook, stirring constantly, for 3 minutes. Remove from heat and cool.

Beat egg whites until stiff. Fold into cooled strawberry mixture. Pour into pie shell. Bake at 350° for 5 to 10 minutes until chiffon is set. Remove and cool before serving.

Rhubarb Meringue Pie

one Basic Oil Crust shell
  (see page 306)
2 cups chopped rhubarb
1 cup apple cider or juice
2 tbsp maple syrup
3 tbsp brown rice flour and
  3 tbsp arrowroot starch
  dissolved in 3 tbsp
  apple juice

3 eggs, separated
2 tsp orange rind
juice of one orange
½ tsp vanilla

Bake pie shell at 350° for 10 to 15 minutes until firm but not browned. Remove from oven.

In a saucepan, combine rhubarb and apple juice. Cook until rhubarb is soft and slightly thickened. Stir in maple syrup and arrowroot, flour, and juice paste. Continue stirring for 5 minutes until mixture is thickened and there is no taste of raw flour. Reduce heat and stir in egg yolk, orange rind, and orange juice. Continue stirring until thick and smooth. Pour into baked pie shell.

Combine egg whites and vanilla. Beat until stiff and spread decoratively over pie. Bake at 350° for 10 minutes until delicately browned. Cool before serving.

Carob Chiffon Pie

one Basic Oil Crust shell
  (see page 306)
1 cup milk
½ cup roasted carob
  powder

3 tbsp arrowroot starch
  dissolved in 2 tbsp milk
3 eggs, separated
½ cup heavy cream,
  whipped

Bake pie shell at 350° for 15 minutes. Remove from oven.

In a saucepan, combine milk and carob powder. Cook over medium heat nearly to boiling. Stir in arrowroot paste and continue stirring until thickened. Reduce heat to low and stir in egg yolks. Continue stirring for 3 minutes until further thickened. Remove from heat and cool.

Beat egg whites until stiff. Fold whites and whipped cream into carob mixture. Pour into baked pie shell before serving.

18.

SHAKES, PUNCHES, AND JUICES

NONDAIRY DRINKS

Apricot Punch

This drink is a wonder disguise for nutritional yeast.

2 cups unpasteurized
  apricot juice

1 tbsp nutritional yeast
pinch allspice powder
drop of mint extract

Beat or blend all ingredients until well combined.

Apple Mint Drink

Combining juice and tea is an economical way to serve juice without losing any flavor.

2 cups mint tea   2 cups apple juice

Combine tea and apple juice.

Apple Zinger Drink

Apple juice and Red Zinger tea are a delicious and thirst-quenching combination.

2 cup Red Zinger tea   *2 cups apple juice or cider*

Combine tea and juice. Serve hot or cold.

HOMEMADE SODAS

Soda pop is as American as apple pie and as common as hamburger. It's no wonder your child will occasionally ask for a soda, especially if friends are coming to visit. Our solutions are simple and healthful. They combine juices or teas with sparkling mineral water. The neighbor children will never guess the difference.

Grape Soda

1 cup grape juice   *1 cup sparkling mineral
                              water*

Combine juice and mineral water.

Orange Soda

2 cups fresh orange juice   *1 cup sparkling mineral
                                      water*

Combine juice and mineral water.

Root Beer

*1 tsp ground or chopped
   licorice root*
1 tsp star anise

3 cups water
*2 cups sparkling mineral
   water*

Simmer licorice root and anise in water until sweet and darkened in color. Allow to cool. Stir in mineral water.

Cherry Soda

2 cups cherry juice   1 cup sparkling mineral
                                                  water

Combine juice and mineral water.

Mystery Soda

1 tsp ground or chopped   2 cups water
   licorice root   1 cup sparkling mineral
                                                  water

Simmer licorice root in water until sweet. Allow to cool. Stir in mineral water.

Sparkling Punch

1 cup fresh orange juice   1 cup pineapple juice
1 cup apple juice   2 cups sparkling mineral
1 cup mint tea   water

Combine all ingredients.

PARTY PUNCHES

These punches are mild and healthful. If any seem a little dull for your child's friends, just add mineral water to perk them up.

Pineapple Punch

1 quart sweet cider
3 cups pineapple juice
2 cups water

1 6-ounce can unsweetened
pineapple rings and
juice from can mixed
with 3 cups water

Combine cider, pineapple juice, and water. Pour canned pineapple with its juice and water into a cake pan or gelatin mold, arranging pineapple decoratively in the container. Freeze and use as a float for punch.

Sweet Cider Punch

2 quarts sweet apple cider
2 cups currants or raisins
2 oranges, sliced

2 lemons, sliced
1 stick cinnamon
2 cups water

Combine all ingredients in a large pot. Cook over low heat for 45 minutes until flavors are well combined. Serve hot or cold. Makes 2½ quarts.

Fall Punch

4 cups sweet cider
2 cups fresh cranberries

2 bananas
2 cups water

In an electric blender or food processor, purée ingredients in batches until smooth. Makes 2 quarts.

Summer Strawberry Punch

1 quart apple juice

1 quart strawberries

In an electric blender or food processor, blend strawberries and apple juice in batches until smooth.

FRESH FRUIT DRINKS

Fresh fruit drinks are the special delight of summer, when nearly every child would prefer a big bowl of cherries to a chocolate bar.

Strawberry Banana Shake

2 cups apple juice

1 cup fresh strawberries
1 ripe banana

In an electric blender or food processor, blend ingredients until smooth.

Papaya Orange Shake

2 cups fresh orange juice   1 papaya, peeled and seeded

In an electric blender or food processor, blend until smooth.

Blueberry Banana Shake

2 cups apple juice

1 cup fresh blueberries
1 ripe banana

In an electric blender or food processor, blend ingredients until smooth.

Melon Shake

1 cantaloupe or honeydew
  melon, peeled and seeded

3 cups apple juice
1 tsp lemon juice

In an electric blender or food processor, blend ingredients until smooth.

NUT AND SOY MILKS

For the many children who cannot tolerate dairy milk, these milks can be nutritional "lifesavers" and thoroughly enjoyable snack foods. Any of these milks can be substituted for dairy milk in recipes for smoothies given later in this chapter.

Fortified Soy Milk

*2 cups soybeans, soaked
    24 to 48 hours in
    refrigerator
2 quarts water
1 tbsp sunflower oil*

*1 tbsp nutritional yeast or
    1 tsp B$_{12}$ powder
1 tbsp blackstrap molasses
1 tsp vanilla extract*

Drain soybeans and discard soaking water. In an electric blender or food processor, liquify soybeans in 2 quarts water. Strain through cheesecloth. Heat over a double boiler for 30 minutes, stirring constantly. Allow to cool. Pour through a wire strainer and blend in batches until smooth. To the last batch, add oil, yeast or B$_{12}$, molasses, and vanilla. Stir the fortified and flavored batch into the rest of the soy milk. Refrigerate. Makes slightly over 2 quarts.

Carob Soy Milk

*1 cup commercial soy milk
    or Fortified Soy Milk (see
    recipe above)*

*1 tsp roasted carob powder
    dissolved in 2 tsp water*

Combine soy milk with carob and water mixture. Serve hot or cold.

Spiced Soy Milk

pinch each of ginger,　　　　1 cup soy milk
　cinnamon, and cardamom

Combine ingredients. Serve hot or cold.

Almond Milk

1 cup blanched almonds　　　1 quart water
　　　　　　　　　　　　　1 tbsp sunflower oil

In a blender or electric food processor, blend ingredients
in batches until smooth.

Cashew Milk

1 cup raw cashews　　　　　1 quart water
　　　　　　　　　　　　　1 tbsp sunflower oil

In a blender or electric food processor, blend ingredients
in batches until smooth.

Coconut Milk

1½ cups fresh shredded or　　1 quart water
　grated coconut　　　　　　1 tbsp sunflower oil

In an electric blender or electric food processor, blend
ingredients in batches until smooth.

Tahini Milk

½ cup tahini　　　　　　　1 tbsp honey, maple syrup,
2 cups water　　　　　　　　or malt
　　　　　　　　　　　　　1 tsp vanilla extract

In an electric blender or food processor, blend ingredients until smooth.

VEGETABLE DRINKS

Many children like to drink juice with their meals. Nutritional yeast, kelp powder, and spirulina, three important supplemental foods for children, are easily combined with the flavors of vegetables. Many children who hate nutritional yeast in fruit or milk smoothies will love it in a vegetable drink. In addition, vegetable drinks are naturally high in mineral content.

Tomato Vegetable Cocktail

1 cup chopped cucumbers
1 cup chopped tomatoes
1 green pepper, chopped
¼ cup alfalfa sprouts

⅛ cup mung bean sprouts
½ tsp spirulina
½ tsp kelp powder
1 tsp nutritional yeast
2 cups water

In an electric blender or food processor, blend ingredients until smooth. If necessary, blend in batches. If desired, strain through a double layer of cheesecloth.

Creamy Tahini Vegetable Drink

½ cup chopped cucumber
½ cup chopped tomatoes
½ cup alfalfa sprouts
¼ cup lentil or mung bean
  sprouts

¼ cup tahini
½ tsp spirulina
½ tsp kelp powder
2 tsp nutritional yeast
2 cups water

In an electric blender or food processor, blend ingredients until smooth. If necessary, blend in batches. If desired, strain through a double layer of cheesecloth.

Green Drink

½ cup cucumber, chopped
½ cup alfalfa sprouts
¼ cup lentil or mung bean
   sprouts
¼ cup chopped mustard
   greens, collard, or chard

½ tsp spirulina
½ tsp kelp powder
1 tsp nutritional yeast
1 tsp tamari soy sauce
   (optional)
1 tsp lemon juice
2½ cups water

In an electric blender or food processor, blend all ingredients until smooth. If necessary, blend in batches. If desired, strain through a double layer of cheesecloth.

DAIRY SMOOTHIES

Smoothies are dairy drinks with the good taste of milkshakes. They can be made with added noninstant powdered milk for an extra protein boost. Some smoothies can hide the taste of vitamin-rich nutritional yeast, and others are excellent vehicles for the calcium, phosphorus, and iron found in blackstrap molasses.

Carob Coconut Smoothie

1 cup milk
¼ cup noninstant
   powdered milk
1 tsp roasted carob powder

1 tsp nutritional yeast
1 tsp blackstrap molasses
2 tbsp unsweetened
   shredded coconut

In an electric blender or food processor, blend all ingredients until smooth.

Banana Smoothie

1 cup milk
¼ cup noninstant
   powdered milk

1 ripe banana
¼ tsp vanilla
½ tsp blackstrap molasses

In a blender or electric food processor, blend all ingredients until smooth and thick.

Date Smoothie

1 cup milk
¼ cup noninstant
powdered milk

⅓ cup chopped pitted dates
1 tsp nutritional yeast
(optional)

In an electric blender or food processor, blend ingredients until smooth.

Orange Smoothie

1 cup milk
¼ cup noninstant
powdered milk

juice of 2 oranges

In an electric blender or food processor, blend milk and milk powder until frothy. Pour into a glass and stir in orange juice. Serve immediately. Makes 1.

Melon Smoothie

1 cup chopped cantaloupe
or honeydew melon

¼ cup noninstant
powdered milk
1 cup milk

In an electric blender or food processor, blend until thick and smooth. Makes 1 large serving.

Strawberry Smoothie

1 cup milk
½ cup strawberries

¼ cup noninstant
powdered milk

In an electric blender or food processor, blend until smooth.

Banana Peanut Smoothie

1 cup milk
1 tsp peanut butter

¼ cup noninstant
  powdered milk
1 ripe banana

In an electric blender or food processor, blend until thick and smooth.

Molasses Smoothie

1 cup milk
¼ tsp vanilla extract

1 tsp blackstrap molasses
¼ cup noninstant
  powdered milk

In an electric blender or food processor, blend until frothy.

Coconut Smoothie

1 cup milk
½ cup fresh grated coconut

2 tbsp noninstant
  powdered milk
drop of almond extract

In an electric blender or food processor, blend until thick and smooth.

EGG DRINKS

The most usable types of protein are eggs and milk. Egg-nogs are quick and easy ways to give your child the protein of an entire meal as a midday treat. In some, the eggs can be hidden, giving the drink the taste of a soda-fountain milkshake. In others, egg whites are beaten separately to give the drink a special bubbliness that most children love.

Old-Fashioned Eggnog

1 cup milk
3 tbsp noninstant
  powdered milk
¼ tsp vanilla extract

1 egg
¼ tsp anise, almond, or
  rum extract
sprinkle of nutmeg

In an electric blender or food processor, blend all ingredients except nutmeg until thick and frothy. Sprinkle with nutmeg.

Bubbly Eggnog

1 cup milk
1 egg, separated
½ tsp vanilla

2 tbsp noninstant
  powdered milk
sprinkle of nutmeg

In an electric blender or food processor, blend milk, egg yolk, vanilla, and milk powder until smooth. In a separate bowl, beat white until stiff. Fold into eggnog and sprinkle with nutmeg.

Lemon Eggnog

1 tbsp lemon juice
1 egg, separated

½ tsp maple syrup
¼ cup milk powder
1 cup milk

In a bowl, beat lemon juice, egg yolk, and maple syrup. Beat in milk powder and milk. In a separate bowl, beat egg white until stiff. Fold into eggnog just before serving.

Apricot or Peach Eggnog

1 cup milk	2 tbsp noninstant
½ cup chopped fresh	powdered milk
apricots or peaches	1 egg

In an electric blender or food processor, blend all ingredients until smooth and thick.

Banana Eggnog

1 cup milk	2 tbsp noninstant
1 ripe banana	powdered milk
	½ tsp blackstrap molasses
	1 egg

In an electric blender or food processor, blend all ingredients until smooth.

Strawberry Froth

1 cup milk	¼ cup noninstant
⅓ cup strawberries	powdered milk
	1 egg, separated

In an electric blender or food processor, blend milk, strawberries, milk powder, and egg yolk. Beat white until stiff. Fold into eggnog just before serving.

Almond Eggnog

1 cup milk	¼ cup noninstant
¼ cup blanched almonds	powdered milk
¼ tsp almond extract	1 egg

In an electric blender or food processor, blend until smooth.

Pineapple Coconut Eggnog

1 cup milk   ¼ cup fresh grated coconut
¼ cup crushed pineapple   1 egg

In an electric blender or food processor, blend until smooth. Serve immediately.

19.

SANDWICHES AND OTHER LUNCH-BOX SUGGESTIONS

A box lunch should be a balanced meal including a good complementary-protein food, vegetables or fruit, an exciting drink, and, whenever possible, a healthful treat. All should be appealing to your child and—just as important —acceptable in appearance to his peers, so that your child will not be the object of ridicule at school.

Sandwiches are the basic lunchtime protein dish. They are easy to prepare and store well. Therefore, the recipes in this chapter are mainly for sandwich fillers. For younger children, cutting sandwiches into unusual shapes—houses, circles, or stars—will make them especially attractive. The excess bread can be saved and used as bread crumbs in casseroles and loafs. Older children will enjoy an occasional deviation from the sandwich theme. They will find a portion of leftover quiche, loaf, or casserole quite acceptable as a cold lunch.

Vegetables are best supplied raw in pieces, accompanied by a container of dips. Fruits, if they combine well with the rest of the lunch, are nearly always welcomed by children. For desserts or snacks, there are a large number of possibilities in chapter 17, "Sweets Without Sugar." Drinks can be made with the help of chapter 18, "Shakes, Punches, and Juices."

NONDAIRY SANDWICH FILLERS

Soy Sandwich "Meat"

This protein-rich filler looks so much like meat that your child's lunch will not seem different from those of the other kids in his class. Preparing Soy Sandwich "Meat" is time-consuming, but because of the many different meal possibilities that it offers and because of its high protein content, we recommend it enthusiastically. This "meat" has the texture of soft clay. It can be shaped like hot dogs, meat balls, or sausages and pan-fried to replace these in any recipe. Here we simply suggest slicing it thin and using it as you would any other sandwich meat. Alone or in combination with cheese, lettuce, tomatoes, cucumbers, green peppers, or onions, it makes a tasty and nutritious lunch.

2 cups soybeans	1 tsp black pepper
3 to 6 cups water	¼ cup tamari soy sauce
1 cup whole wheat flour	2 tbsp oregano
2 eggs or ¼ cup oil	2 tbsp liquid barley malt
¼ cup nutritional yeast	1 tsp garlic powder
2 tsp fennel seed	2 tsp dry mustard
	2 tsp allspice

Pressure-cook soybeans in 3 cups water for 3 hours, or cook in a covered pan with 6 cups water for 6 hours.

When beans are soft, drain them, reserving liquid for use in soups or gravies. Mash beans with a potato masher or purée in an electric blender or food processor.

In a bowl, mix soybean purée and all remaining ingredients until well combined.

Fill two empty vegetable tins or 16-ounce soup cans with soybean mixture. Cover both cans with foil wrap.

Pour 5 cups of water into a pressure cooker, place cans in the pressure cooker (foil end out of water), and pressure-cook at 15 pounds pressure for 45 minutes. Or place cans on a rack in a covered steamer and steam for 3 hours.

Allow cans to cool. Remove soy "meat" from cans as you would a bread from a loaf pan. Cool, slice, and use in a variety of sandwiches.

Dried-Fruit Butter

1¾ cups water   *1 cup pitted raisins*
1 cup pitted dates   *1 tbsp finely grated*
1 cup pitted prunes   *orange rind*

In a saucepan, combine water and dried fruits. Cook over medium heat, stirring occasionally, until thickened. Remove from heat and stir in orange rind. For a smooth spread, blend in an electric blender or food processor. Makes 3 cups spread that can be combined with nut butters, Tofu Sandwich Spread, or dairy cheese in sandwiches.

Tofu Sandwich Spread

This spread combines well with lettuce and tomatoes for a wholesome sandwich.

1 pound tofu   *½ garlic clove, crushed*
2 tbsp nutritional yeast   *½ tsp kelp powder*
2 tbsp tahini   *½ tsp powdered cumin*
        ½ tsp lemon juice

Mash all ingredients together and stir until well combined. Makes 2 cups.

Peanut Butter and Celery Spread

3 tbsp peanut butter   *2 tbsp mashed tofu*
        4 tbsp finely chopped celery

Cream peanut butter and tofu until smooth. Stir in chopped celery. Makes ½ cup.

Nondairy Butter

For children who do not eat dairy products, sandwiches can be dry and uninviting. This homemade substitute is an excellent alternative to commercial processed margarines. It can be flavored with lemon, onion seasoning, or garlic powder if desired.

¼ cup soy flour
⅓ cup water
¼ tsp sea salt

½ cup sunflower, safflower,
 or sesame oil
⅛ tsp turmeric

In a saucepan, combine flour and water. Cook over medium heat, stirring occasionally, for 10 minutes until thickened. Remove and refrigerate until cool.

Blend in an electric blender or food processor with salt. Gradually add oil while blending until mixture thickens to consistency of butter. Add turmeric for yellow color. Refrigerate. Makes 1 cup.

DAIRY SANDWICH FILLERS

Milky Peanut Spread

½ cup peanut butter
¼ tsp cinnamon

¼ cup noninstant
 powdered milk
2 tbsp water or apple juice

Cream ingredients until well combined. Use on sandwiches in combination with sliced bananas or raisins.

Cheesie Tomato Spread

2 tbsp tomato paste
2 tsp nutritional yeast

½ cup grated Cheddar
  cheese
3 tbsp cottage cheese

In an electric blender or food processor, blend until smooth.
Makes ⅔ cup.

Two-Cheese Spread

½ cup cottage cheese

½ cup grated Cheddar
  cheese

In an electric blender or food processor, blend cheese
until smooth. Makes 1 cup.

Date Cheese Spread

½ cup cottage cheese,
  creamed in blender

⅓ cup finely chopped dates
⅓ cup chopped nuts
¼ tsp lemon juice

Mix all ingredients until thoroughly combined. Makes
1 cup.

EGG SANDWICH SPREADS

Egg Salad Spread

2 hard-boiled eggs, chopped
2 tsp mayonnaise

1 tbsp finely chopped celery
½ tsp nutritional yeast
⅛ tsp sea salt

Mix all ingredients until thoroughly combined. Makes 2
sandwiches.

Green Bean and Egg Spread

1 cup steamed green beans　　*¼ cup chopped walnuts*
2 tbsp oil　　　　　　　　　　*3 hard-boiled eggs, chopped*
1 tsp chopped onion　　　　　*1 tsp nutritional yeast*
2 tbsp chopped celery　　　　*1 tsp tamari soy sauce*

Mix all ingredients and grind through a meat grinder or in an electric food processor to form a smooth, thick spread. Makes 2 cups.

Egg and Lentil Spread

3 hard-boiled eggs　　　　　*1 tbsp nutritional yeast*
1 cup cooked lentils　　　　　*2 tbsp tahini*
2 tbsp cottage cheese　　　　*1 tsp tamari soy sauce*

In an electric blender or food processor, blend all ingredients until smooth. Makes 1½ cups.

BIBLIOGRAPHY

Abrahamson, E. M., and Pezet, A. W. *Body, Mind and Sugar*. New York: Avon Books, 1977.

Airola, Paavo. *Are You Confused?* Phoenix, Ariz.: Health Plus, 1978.

————. *Everywoman's Book*. Phoenix, Ariz.: Health Plus, 1979.

————. *How to Get Well*. Phoenix, Ariz.: Health Plus, 1978.

————. *Hypoglycemia: A Better Approach*. Phoenix, Ariz.: Health Plus, 1977.

Amherst (Mass.) Food Co-op Publication. "I Think I'm Allergic to Cupcakes," May 1980.

Bairacli-Levy, Juliette de. *Nature's Children*. New York: Schocken Books, 1971.

Ballentine, Rudolph. *Diet and Nutrition*. Honesdale, Pa.: Himalayan International Institute, 1978.

Bauch, Dorothy. *How to Live with Your Teenager*. New York: McGraw-Hill, 1953.

Bickel, Barbara. "Through the Body." *Let's Live*, August 1979.

Bieler, H. *Food Is Your Best Medicine*. New York: Vintage Books, 1973.

Brentlinger, W. W. "Our Kids' Killer Diets." *Let's Live*, February 1980.

Brenton, Myron. *How to Survive Your Child's Rebellious Teens: New Solutions for Troubled Parents*. Philadelphia: Lippincott, 1979.

Brewer, Gail Sforza. *What Every Pregnant Woman Should Know*. New York: Random House, 1977.

————. *The Pregnancy Workbook Over Thirty*. Emmaus, Pa.: Rodale Press, 1978.

Brody, Jane E. "How to Get Children to Eat What's Good for Them." *New York Times*, October 17, 1979.

————. "Feeding the Unborn: Some Dietary Wisdom for Mothers to Be." *New York Times*, November 28, 1979.

Committee on Nutrition and Human Needs, U.S. Senate. *Dietary Goals for the United States*. Washington, D.C.: U.S. Government Printing Office, 1977.

Craft, Kathy. "Claremont School: Where Nutrition Is a Way of Life." *Let's Live*, August 1979.

Christopher, John R. *Childhood Diseases*. Springville, Utah: Christopher Publications, 1979.

Davis, Adelle. *Let's Have Healthy Children*. New York: Harcourt Brace Jovanovich, 1951.

Doyle, Roger. *The Vegetarian Handbook*. New York: Crown Publishers, 1979.

Dufty, William. *Sugar Blues*. New York: Warner Books, 1975.

Feingold, B. *Why Your Child Is Hyperactive*. New York: Random House, 1974.

Ginott, Haim. *Between Parent and Teenager*. New York: Macmillan, 1969.

Hunter, Beatrice T. *Consumer Beware*. New York: Bantam Books, 1972.

Kelly, Marguerite, and Parsons, Elia. *The Mother's Almanac*. Garden City, N.Y.: Doubleday, 1975.

Kinderlehrer, Jane. *Confessions of a Sneaky Organic Cook*. Emmaus, Pa.: Rodale Press, 1971.

Kohl, Herbert. *Growing with Your Children*. Boston: Little, Brown, 1978.

Lappé, Frances Moore. *Diet for a Small Planet*. New York: Ballantine Books, 1971.

Larson, Gena. *Better Food for Better Babies and Their Families*. New Canaan, Conn.: Keats Publishing, 1972.

Leach, Penelope. *Your Baby and Child from Birth to Age Five*. New York: Alfred A. Knopf, 1978.

Lerza, C., and Jacobson, M. *Food for People, Not for Profit*. New York: Ballantine Books, 1975.

Lloyd, Douglas S. *Child Development Chart*. Hartford, Conn.: Connecticut State Department of Health, 1973.

McCoy, Kathy, and Wibbelsman, Charles, M.D. *The Teenage Body Book*. New York: A Wallaby Book (Simon & Schuster), 1978.

Null, Gary. *Protein for Vegetarians*. New York: Jove (Harcourt Brace Jovanovich), 1978.

————. *The New Vegetarian*. New York: William Morrow and Co., 1978.

Nutrition Research, Inc. *Nutrition Almanac*. New York: McGraw-Hill, 1979.

Pauling, L. *Vitamin C and the Common Cold*. San Francisco: W. H. Freeman, 1970.

Pfeiffer, C. *Mental and Elemental Nutrients*. New Canaan, Conn.: Keats Publishing, 1975.

"A Plague on Our Children." *Nova*, WGBH-TV transcripts, Boston, Mass., 1979.

Price, W. *Nutrition and Physical Degeneration*. La Mesa, Calif.: Price-Pottenger Foundation, 1972.

Pryor, Karen Wylie. *Nursing Your Baby*. New York: Harper & Row, 1973.

Register, V., and Sonnenberg, L. "The Vegetarian Diet." *Journal of the American Diet Association*, 62 (1973).

Riepma, S. *The Story of Margarine*. Washington, D.C.: Public Affairs Press, 1970.

Robertson, L.; Falinders, C.; and Godfrey, B. *Laurel's Kitchen*. New York: Bantam Books, 1978.

Schowalter, John. *The Family Handbook of Adolescence*. New York: Alfred A. Knopf, 1979.

Shandler, Nina and Michael. *How to Make All the Meat You Eat Out of Wheat*. New York: Rawson, Wade, 1980.

Sherman, Mikie. *Feeding the Sick Child*. Washington, D.C.: Department of Health, Education and Welfare, 1978.

Sloan, Sara. *Guide for Nutra Lunches and Natural Foods*. Atlanta, Ga.: Food Service Program, Fulton County Schools, 1979.

————. *From Classroom to Cafeteria* (for teachers and managers).

Smith, Lendon. *Feed Your Kids Right*. New York: McGraw-Hill, 1979.

Stone, Randolph. *Health Building*. Orange, Calif.: Pierre Pametier, 1978.

Sussman, Vic. *The Vegetarian Alternative*. Emmaus, Pa.: Rodale Press, 1978.

Thakkur, Chandrashehar G. *Ayurveda: The Indian Art and Science of Medicine*. New York: ASI Publishers, 1974.

Tiger, Lionel. "The Fat of the Land." *Newsweek*, July 2, 1979.

U.S. Department of Health, Education and Welfare. *Health Status of Children: a Review of Surveys 1963–1972*. Rockville, Md.: Bureau of Community Health Services, 1978.

"Vegetarian Nutrition for Pregnant and Breast Feeding Women." *Vegetarian Times*, December 1979.

Vyhmeister, Irma B., and Sonnenberg, Lydia M. "Safe Vegetarian Diets for Children." *Pediatric Clinics of North America*, 24, no. 1 (February 1977).

Watt, B., and Merrill, A. *Composition of Foods*. USDA Agricultural Handbook, no. 8, New York, 1975.

Wigmore, Ann. *Health Children*. Boston, Mass.: Health Institute, 1970.

Williams, Phyllis, R.N. *Nourishing Your Unborn Child*. New York: Avon Books, 1975.

Williams, R. J. *Nutrition Against Disease*. New York: Bantam Books, 1975.

Yates, John. "The Ties That Bind Also Heal." *Prevention*, October 1979.

Yntema, Sharon. *Vegetarian Baby*. Ithaca, N.Y.: McBooks Press, 1980.

INDEX

Recipe titles are set in *italic type.*

Acidosis, 35
Acne, 186
Activities about food, 151–156
Adolescence, 180–201; and dietary needs, 181–182
Aduki pudding, 300–301
Airola, Dr. Paavo, 20, 113
Alfalfa, 68
All-American complementary protein main dishes, 238–267
Allergies, 24, 105–106, 186
Almond(s): *creamed green beans with, 276; eggnog, 346;* milk, *340;* mineral-rich water, 112, 122, 205–206, 208, 210, 211
Alphabet soup, 229
Alternatives to sugar, offering, 147–148
American diet, 19–21; since W.W.II, 34, 44
Amino acids, 21–22
Anemia, 60, 89–91, 96
"Antiminerals," 66
"Antivitamins," 46, 66, 102, 177
Apple(s): baked stuffed, 217–218; banana lunch, 211; mint drink, 334; or pear

pie, 307; or pear sesame cream pie, 308–309; pudding, 301; spice frosting, 328; wedges as finger foods, 214; zinger drink, 335
Apricot: or peach eggnog, 346; punch, 334
Arteriosclerosis, 33, 72, 73–74
Arthritis, 20, 186
Artichokes with garlic butter sauce, 277
Asparagus on toast with cheese sauce, 255
Atherosclerosis, 20
Autotoxemia, 20
Avocado: banana lunch, 210; dairy dip, 287; grapefruit dressing, 295; mayonnaise dip, 289; soup, summer, 236; sour cream dressing, 295; tofu dip, 284; and tomato filling, 263; wedges as finger foods, 214
Ayurvedic medicine, 34, 77

Babies, vegetarian food for, 205–215
Baked carrots, 270
Baked cauliflower, 273
Baked custard, 323
Baked snacks, 39
Baked stuffed pears or apples, 217–218